Exploring Neural Networks with C#

Exploring Neural Networks with C#

Ryszard Tadeusiewicz
Rituparna Chaki
Nabendu Chaki

Programs by Tomasz Gąciarz, Barbara Borowik & Bartosz Leper

CRC Press
Taylor & Francis Group
Boca Raton London New York

CRC Press is an imprint of the
Taylor & Francis Group, an **informa** business

CRC Press
Taylor & Francis Group
6000 Broken Sound Parkway NW, Suite 300
Boca Raton, FL 33487-2742

First issued in hardback 2017

© 2014 by Taylor & Francis Group, LLC
CRC Press is an imprint of Taylor & Francis Group, an Informa business

No claim to original U.S. Government works

Version Date: 20140618

ISBN-13: 978-1-4822-3339-1 (Pbk)
ISBN-13: 978-1-138-44017-3 (Hbk)

Visit the Taylor & Francis Web site at
http://www.taylorandfrancis.com

and the CRC Press Web site at
http://www.crcpress.com

Contents

Foreword ix

Preface xi

Acknowledgments xv

1 Introduction to Natural and Artificial Neural Networks............................1
    1.1   Why Learn about Neural Networks? 1
    1.2   From Brain Research to Artificial Neural Networks.................................. 1
    1.3   Construction of First Neural Networks 5
    1.4   Layered Construction of Neural Network 10
    1.5   From Biological Brain to First Artificial Neural Network...................... 12
    1.6   Current Brain Research Methods 13
    1.7   Using Neural Networks to Study the Human Mind 19
    1.8   Simplification of Neural Networks: Comparison with Biological Networks.......... 20
    1.9   Main Advantages of Neural Networks 21
    1.10 Neural Networks as Replacements for Traditional Computers 23
    1.11 Working with Neural Networks 24
    References..25

2 Neural Net Structure...27
    2.1   Building Neural Nets 27
    2.2   Constructing Artificial Neurons 28
    2.3   Attempts to Model Biological Neurons..33
    2.4   How Artificial Neural Networks Work.. 34
    2.5   Impact of Neural Network Structure on Capabilities 39
    2.6   Choosing Neural Network Structures Wisely...41
    2.7   "Feeding" Neural Networks: Input Layers.. 44
    2.8   Nature of Data: The Home of the Cow 45
    2.9   Interpreting Answers Generated by Networks: Output Layers............................ 46
    2.10 Preferred Result: Number or Decision?.. 48
    2.11 Network Choices: One Network with Multiple Outputs versus Multiple Networks with Single Outputs 50
    2.12 Hidden Layers 52
    2.13 Determining Numbers of Neurons... 54

References..57
Questions and Self-Study Tasks... 58

3 **Teaching Networks**..**59**
   3.1   Network Tutoring...59
   3.2   Self-Learning..61
   3.3   Methods of Gathering Information.. 62
   3.4   Organizing Network Learning.. 64
   3.5   Learning Failures..67
   3.6   Use of Momentum... 69
   3.8   Duration of Learning Process.. 71
   3.9   Teaching Hidden Layers... 72
   3.10 Learning without Teachers.. 72
   3.11 Cautions Surrounding Self-Learning....................................... 73
   Questions and Self-Study Tasks..74

4 **Functioning of Simplest Networks**...**75**
   4.1   From Theory to Practice: Using Neural Networks................... 75
   4.2   Capacity of Single Neuron.. 77
   4.3   Experimental Observations..81
   4.4   Managing More Inputs..85
   4.5   Network Functioning... 87
   4.6   Construction of Simple Linear Neural Network...................... 87
   4.7   Use of Network... 88
   4.8   Rivalry in Neural Networks... 92
   4.9   Additional Applications.. 92
   Questions and Self-Study Tasks... 93

5 **Teaching Simple Linear One-Layer Neural Networks**.......................**95**
   5.1   Building Teaching File 95
   5.2   Teaching One Neuron... 97
   5.3   "Inborn" Abilities of Neurons... 100
   5.4   Cautions..101
   5.5   Teaching Simple Networks...101
   5.6   Potential Uses for Simple Neural Networks...........................105
   5.7   Teaching Networks to Filter Signals......................................106
   Questions and Self-Study Tasks.. 111

6 **Nonlinear Networks**...**115**
   6.1   Advantages of Nonlinearity... 115
   6.2   Functioning of Nonlinear Neurons.. 116
   6.3   Teaching Nonlinear Networks 118
   6.4   Demonstrating Actions of Nonlinear Neurons...................... 120
   6.5   Capabilities of Multilayer Networks of Nonlinear Neurons 124
   6.6   Nonlinear Neuron Learning Sequence 126
   6.7   Experimentation during Learning Phase................................129
   Questions and Self-Study Tasks.. 130

7 Backpropagation 133
7.1 Definition..133
7.2 Changing Thresholds of Nonlinear Characteristics 134
7.3 Shapes of Nonlinear Characteristics 135
7.4 Functioning of Multilayer Network Constructed of Nonlinear Elements.............137
7.5 Teaching Multilayer Networks 140
7.6 Observations during Teaching...141
7.7 Reviewing Teaching Results 144
Questions and Self-Study Tasks..148

8 Forms of Neural Network Learning 151
8.1 Using Multilayer Neural Networks for Recognition 151
8.2 Implementing a Simple Neural Network for Recognition...................152
8.3 Selecting Network Structure for Experiments....................................155
8.4 Preparing Recognition Tasks 156
8.5 Observation of Learning...159
8.6 Additional Observations 168
Questions and Self-Study Tasks..171

9 Self-Learning Neural Networks 173
9.1 Basic Concepts 173
9.2 Observation of Learning Processes 180
9.3 Evaluating Progress of Self-Teaching..186
9.4 Neuron Responses to Self-Teaching..188
9.5 Imagination and Improvisation 190
9.6 Remembering and Forgetting..195
9.7 Self-Learning Triggers 196
9.8 Benefits from Competition 199
9.9 Results of Self-Learning with Competition..203
Questions and Self-Study Tasks..206

10 Self-Organizing Neural Networks..209
10.1 Structure of Neural Network to Create Mappings Resulting
from Self-Organizing..209
10.2 Uses of Self-Organization 212
10.3 Implementing Neighborhood in Networks..215
10.4 Neighbor Neurons..217
10.5 Uses of Kohonen Networks 222
10.6 Kohonen Network Handling of Difficult Data..................................225
10.7 Networks with Excessively Wide Ranges of Initial Weights................228
10.8 Changing Self-Organization via Self-Learning..................................228
10.9 Practical Uses of Kohonen Networks..230
10.10 Tool for Transformation of Input Space Dimensions.........................234
Questions and Self-Study Tasks..238

11 Recurrent Networks **241**

11.1 Description of Recurrent Neural Network 241

11.2 Features of Networks with Feedback 245

11.3 Benefits of Associative Memory 247

11.4 Construction of Hopfield Network..248

11.5 Functioning of Neural Network as Associative Memory 251

11.6 Program for Examining Hopfield Network Operations.........................256

11.7 Interesting Examples 261

11.8 Automatic Pattern Generation for Hopfield Network...........................265

11.9 Studies of Associative Memory 269

11.10 Other Observations of Associative Memory 274

Questions and Self-Study Tasks...274

Index **277**

Foreword

I am very pleased to write the Foreword to this unique volume since I believe it is a very special publication that stands out among many others. It is about neural networks as *practical* tools capable of building trainable computing models. After training is completed, the models can provide solutions to difficult problems easily by capturing and interpreting knowledge from data. These neurocomputing models—as we call them—mimic nature and their biological prototypes such as brain and sense in their essential *learning and adaptation abilities.*

These naturally inspired models derive their power from the collective processing of neurons whose main advantage is the ability to learn and adapt to changing environments. As such techniques typically return encapsulated knowledge, the old adage that "knowledge is power" can be thus applied to all the neurocomputing models described in this book.

The study of any subject including neural networks can be made much easier and more pleasant if we acquire hands-on experience and simulate and visualize our experiments on a PC instead of reading theories. This book offers a real-life experimentation environment to readers. Moreover, it permits direct and personal exploration of neural learning and modeling.

The companion software to this book is a collection of online programs that facilitate such exploratory methods and systematic self-discovery of neural networks. The programs are available in two forms—as executable applications ready for immediate use as described in the book or as source codes in C#. The source code format allows users' modifications. Its parts can also be embedded into users' programs designed for various educational, research, or practical data analysis tasks. All programs are fully functional and their codes are usable for object-oriented design. This feature makes them easy to use without going into the details of the algorithms used.

The planned experiments are interesting and attractive, and running them can be regarded as playing a computer game. However, the unique insights of computational learning gained this way are both entertaining and educational at the same time. Guided self-activity has again trumped the passive study of theorems and axioms.

The book is written in a very convincing narrative, and can be easily followed by people outside the science–technology–engineering–mathematics (STEM) areas. To take advantage of neural networks as tools, such readers need only introductory experience in handling and editing computer files—knowledge that most of us have. In addition, the book can be read by high school students and hobbyists who have no formal computer training. Readers may be surprised, but throughout the book they will not find even a single mathematical formula! At the same time the source codes allow interested persons to become familiar with fine details of simulations and algorithms. Such details can be simply reverse-engineered from the codes of the program.

To make the reader completely relaxed and motivated, the authors go beyond the essential know-how. Lots of interesting observations and comments by the authors make the book a must-have and must-read-and-know. For serious students, each chapter concludes with questions and problems in varying degrees of difficulty, thus making controlled self-study complete and rewarding.

This book was also released in the Russian language in Russia. It can now be said to be used by neural network students spread over one sixth of the globe—in ten time zones from Central Europe to Far East Asia. The website with software posting continues recording hundreds of visits from the domains of Russia and the former Soviet republics.

As past president of IEEE's Computational Intelligence Society with over 6,000 members and the editor-in-chief of *IEEE Transactions on Neural Networks*, I am very interested in the success of neural network technology. I, therefore, highly recommend this book to all who want to learn neurocomputing techniques for their unique and practical educational value. I have taught this subject to senior undergraduate and graduate engineering and computer science students for a number of years. In addition to offering short courses for industry and business, I've taught this subject at the University of Louisville in the United States, at the National University of Singapore, and at the University of Catania in Italy. If I had access to this book earlier, I would have opened laboratory sessions to non-engineering students.

I sincerely hope that the readers of this volume find useful information relevant to their own interests in computational intelligence and will enjoy applying these techniques in their professional and personal pursuits.

Dr. Jacek M. Zurada

Professor, Department of Electrical and Computer Engineering, University of Louisville, Louisville, Kentucky; Life Fellow of IEEE; Foreign Member of Polish Academy of Sciences; National Professor of Poland; Honorary Professor at Hebei University, University of Electronic Science and Technology, Sichuan University, and University of Petroleum (all in China)

Preface

Neural networks are interesting and useful tools for researchers working on a wide range of problems from various disciplines and the networks continue to attract new users. Figure P.1 shows increasing profits from sales of neural network software.

As the figure indicates, the first commercially available software tools using neural networks emerged in the early 1990s. The dynamic growth of this portion of the market took place in or around 2000, and throughout the past decade interest in neural networks has increased steadily although not as fast as in the early years of development. In addition to the practical value of information tools based on neural networks, it is interesting that these networks are mapped into parts of the brains of humans and animals (Figure P.2).

The work of these neural network researchers initiated by the Russian scholar Pavlov led to a whole series of discoveries honored with the most valuable trophy a scholar can earn: the Nobel Prize. Table P.1 lists the Nobel Prize winners who contributed to our understanding of the principles according to which the biological brain functions and thus created the base on which we can build technical neural networks.

As you can see from the table, biologists in the early 1990s knew very much about brain function. The bio-cybernetics experts built cyber models (mathematical and computer simulations) of all the brain mechanisms. It was proven beyond a reasonable doubt that the brain collects and processes information more efficiently and economically than computer systems although computers dominate in the areas of speed and storage capacity.

Let us now see where and how neural network concepts apply to IT problems and you will see why they are so interesting. Figure P.3 depicts how classification tasks are performed by different information systems. Clearly, some tasks are easy and some are very difficult. The horizontal axis of the chart illustrates the degree of task difficulty.

The difficulty of a task is not the only measure of trouble faced by the person who wants to complete it. A second dimension of a problem is the availability of knowledge on which the solver can depend while reaching the solution. The rules for some tasks are specified although the number of rules or their complexity can continue to make a task more difficult. For example, a software developer for a large bank has a lot of work in a situation where tolerance of ignorance of the rules is zero. This is because the rules are consistent and known and can be used to construct tools required to solve the task.

We know how to use computers to solve tasks characterized by complete knowledge of the rules. On the basis of the rules, we can build an algorithm; on the basis of the algorithm, we can write a suitable program. In practice, the situation may be more complicated. We are often called upon to solve problems for which no rules are known. If we want to solve a task, we may have to make

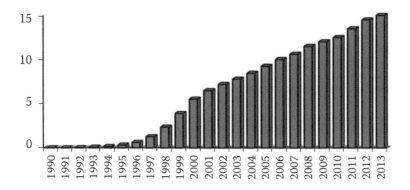

Figure P.1 Profits ($ million) from sales of software for creating and using neural networks in US market and estimated data for 2013.

decisions based observations of related phenomena or processes—we must deal with a situation symbolically (see center section of Figure P.3). Knowledge of the rules is insufficient in this case and the rules may not be known until the task is complete. Despite these shortcomings, we can use a convenient technique for deduction. By trying to develop a general rule (or more often a set of general rules), we can start to solve any problem.

However, we may face an even more complex situation that bears little resemblance to known rules. We may have to work with a number of examples of tasks that have been resolved correctly. The correct solution may come from observing the behavior of a system whose properties we want to model, although we do not know the internal structure of the system or why it works.

At first you might think that such situations do not exist. You are wrong! The human brain regularly solves such tasks, for example, tasks involving perception. A simple example might be recognizing people based on appearance—a fairly easy task for a human and a very difficult one for a computer.

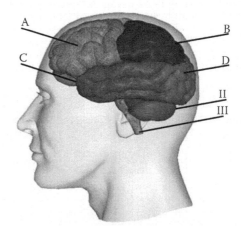

Figure P.2 Neural networks are computer imitations of some properties discovered through studies of the brains of humans and animals. A) Frontal lobe, B) Parietal lobe, C) Temporal lobe, D) Occipital lobe, II) Cerebellum, III) Brain stem.

Table P.1 Nobel Prizes Associated with Studies of the Nervous System, Results of Which Were Used Directly or Indirectly in Neural Networks

Year	Recipient	Study or Discovery
1904	I. P. Pavlov	Theory of conditioned reflexes
1906	C. Golgi	Structure of nervous system
1906	S. Ramón y Cajal	Brain structure consisting of networks of individual neurons
1920	S.A. Krogh	Descriptions of regulatory functions of body
1932	C.S. Sherrington	Muscle nervous control
1936	H. Dale and L.O. Hallett	Chemical transmission of nerve impulses
1944	J. Erlanger and H.S. Gasser	Single nerve processes
1949	W.R. Hess	Interbrain function
1963	J.C. Eccles, A.L. Hodgkin, and A.F. Huxley	Mechanisms of neuron electrical activities
1967	R. Granit, H.K. Hartline, and G. Wald	Primary physiological and chemical visual processes in eyes
1970	B. Katz B., U. Von Euler, and J. Axelrod.	Humoral transmitters in nerve terminals
1974	A. Claude, C. de Duve, and G.E. Palade	Structural and functional organization of cells
1977	R. Guillemin, A Schally, and R. Yalow	Brain production of peptide hormone
1981	R. Sperry	Specializations of cerebral hemispheres
1981	D.H. Hubel and T. Wiesel	Information processing in visual systems
1991	E. Neher and B. Sakmann	Functions of single ion channels in cells

The required approach to problem solving in this case is called induction and we know of no general rules that apply to this specific detailed problem. Instead, however, we have a handful of examples of specific tasks that are known to have correct solutions. The human mind is capable of analyzing generalized examples and drawing conclusions from them. Consider the example of a rat in a maze. Its brain is capable of learning the rules for finding the right way around the maze. The rat manages to learn how to navigate the maze by analyzing the degrees of similarity in the situations it encounters. In essence, the rat is using a neural network.

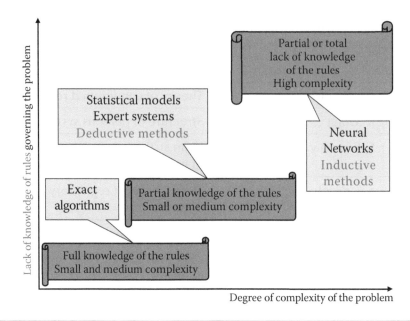

Figure P.3 Characteristics of IT tasks of varying difficulty and tasks for which neural networks are particularly well suited.

This book will give you the skills to explore the properties of neural networks. A series of highly specific programs form integral parts of this book. Following the procedures and using the programs will allow you to learn how to work with neural networks and evaluate your progress. You can download the programs legally (and for free!) from http://home.agh.edu.pl/~tad//index.php?page=programy&lang=en

More information about how these programs work and how to download them and use them appear in Chapter 4. The aforementioned website also contains complete source codes for all the applications along with a set of tools that will you to view and analyze these codes. This book and the website can be used in three ways:

If you are interested only in neural network information and do not want to "play" with software, you can simply read the book.

If you are curious about the workings of neural networks, you can download a ready-to-use program that will allow you to build and test neural networks on your computer. This way you can connect theory from the book with practice by using our programs and learn how to apply the methods.

If you are in the learning states and are passionate about programming, you will be able to see exactly how our programs were built, change them, and even improve them. We have nothing to hide!

Acknowledgments

The authors would like to express their heartfelt thanks to Professor Khalid Saeed, AGH University of Science & Technology, for his valuable help throughout the writing of this book. He has been kind enough to spend his time in the sincere pursuit and patient follow-up that remain the key factors in its preparation. It would not be an exaggeration to say that without Professor Saeed's help, the English version of the book may not have seen the light of the day.

The authors also express their sincere thanks to M.Sc. Jakub Tutaj for his long-time coordination of readers and online program users. Professor Tadeusiewicz, the first author of this book, published several books and articles in the Polish language. Many of those materials were useful during the writing of this book. We thank all those who helped translate the original Polish text into English. The table below lists the translators and their participation in building various chapters.

No.	Translator	Book Sections Where Translated Materials Were Used
1	Agata Barabasz	2.1, 2.2, 2.3
2	Daniel Bohusz	1.10, 1.11, 1.12
3	Barbara Borowik	9.1
4	Łukasz Brodziak	2.5, 2.10, 2.11
5	Dorota Bujak	11.10
6	Piotr Ciskowski	8.1, 8.2, 8.3, 8.4, 8.5, 8.6, 8.7
7	Piotr Czech	5.1, 5.2, 5.3, 5.4, 5.5, 5.6, 5.7, 5.8, 7.1, 7.2, 7.3, 7.4, 7.5, 7.6, 7.7
8	Tomasz Gąciarz	6.7
9	Michał Głamowski	10.1
10	Artur Górski	11.1, 11.2, 11.3, 11.4,
11	Adrian Horzyk	9.4
12	Arkadiusz Janeczko	1.5
13	Joanna Jaworek-Korjakowska	6.4, 9.3

14	Krzysztof Kajdański	4.1, 4.2, 4.3, 4.4, 4.5, 4.6, 4.7, 4.8, 4.9, 4.10
15	Marcin Krasiński	2.9
16	Marta Kraszewska	2.12
17	Agata Krawcewicz	1.3, 3.1, 3.2, 3.3, 3.4, 3.5, 3.6, 3.7, 3.8, 3.9, 3.10, 3.11, 3.12
18	Krzysztof Królczyk	1.4, 1.6, 2.7,
19	Natalia Kubera	1.7
20	Weronika Łabaj	6.1, 9.6, 9.7, 9.8, 9.9, 9.10
21	Michał Majewicz	6.3
22	Joanna Masapust	6.2, 9.2
23	Zbigniew Nagórny	11.7
24	Paweł Olaszek	1.1
25	Rafał Opiał	2.6, 2.8, 10.3, 10.4, 10.5, 10.6, 10.7, 10.8, 10.9, 10.10, 10.11
26	Adam Piłat	6.6
27	Leszek Pstraś	2.4
28	Maciej Ptak	11.5
29	Beata Słomińska	11.9
30	Ryszard Tadeusiewicz	Preface, 1.8, 1.9, 2.14, 6.8, 9.5, 11.11
31	Mirosław Trzupek	6.5
32	Bartosz Wiczyński	10.2
33	Marek Zachara	11.6, 11.8
34	Anastasiya Zharkova	2.13

We are especially thankful to Tomasz Gąciarz, Barbara Borowik, and Bartosz Leper for their contributions by writing the programs used in the book.

This book would not have been possible without the untiring efforts, encouragement, and support of Rich O'Hanley of Taylor & Francis from the development of the proposal to its implementation. Stephanie Morkert and Iris Fahrer were instrumental in maintaining the production schedule in spite of delays and lapses from our end. Last, but not least, we thank our families and friends for being so understanding and for allowing us to spend our spare time writing this book.

Chapter 1

Introduction to Natural and Artificial Neural Networks

1.1 Why Learn about Neural Networks?

Here we will talk about the development of artificial neural networks that were derived from examinations of the human brain system. The examinations were carried out for years to allow researchers to learn the secrets of human intelligence. Their findings turned out to be useful in computer science. This chapter will explain how the ideas borrowed from biologists helped create artificial neural networks and continue to reveal the secrets of the human brain.

This chapter discusses the biological bases of artificial neural networks and their development based on examinations of human brains. The examinations were intended to find the basis of human intelligence and continued secretly for many years for reasons noted in the next section. Subsequent chapters will explain how to build and use neural networks.

As you already know, neural networks are easy to understand and use in computer software. However, their development was based on a surprisingly complex and interesting model of the nervous system in a biological model. We could say that neural networks are simplified models of some functions of the human brain (Figure 1.1).

1.2 From Brain Research to Artificial Neural Networks

The intricacies of the brain have always fascinated scientists. Despite many years of intensive research, we were unable until recently to understand the mysteries of the brain. We are now seeing remarkable progress in this area and discuss it in Section 1.3. In the 1990s, when artificial neural networks were developed, much less information about brain functioning was available. The only known facts about the brain's workings related to the locations of the structures responsible for vital motor, perception, and intellectual functions (Figure 1.2).

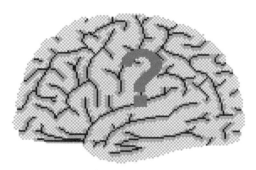

Figure 1.1 Human brain: a source of inspiration for neural network researchers.

Our knowledge about specific tasks performed by each brain element was limited. Medical research focusing on certain diseases and injuries led to some understanding of how brain parts responsible for controlling movements and essential sensations (somatosensory functions) work (Figure 1.3).

We learned which movement (paralysis) or sensation defects were associated with injuries of certain brain components. Our knowledge about the nature and localization of more advanced psychological activities was based on this primitive information. Basically, we could only conclude that the individual cerebral hemispheres functioned as well-defined and specialized systems (Figure 1.4).

One reason for the limited scientific knowledge of brain function was ethical. Regulations specified that experiments on human brains had to be restricted to observing and analyzing the

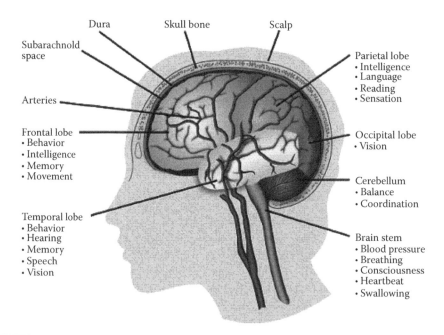

Figure 1.2 Localization of various functions within a brain. (Source: http://avm.ucsf.edu/ patient_info/WhatIsAnAVM/images/image015.gif)

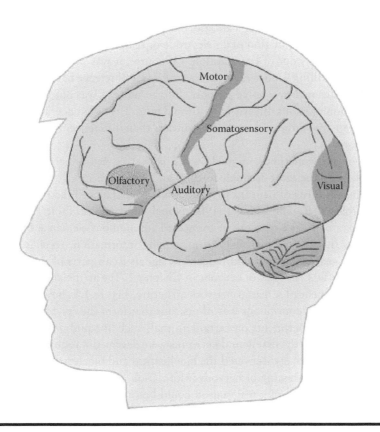

Figure 1.3 Main localizations of brain functions. (Source: http://www.neurevolution.net/wp-content/uploads/primarycortex1_big.jpg)

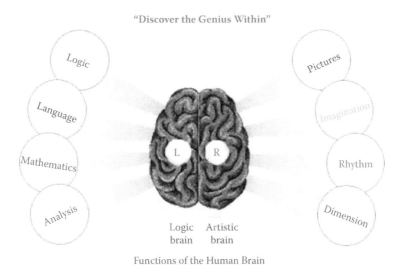

Figure 1.4 Generalized differences between main parts of the brain. (Source: http://www.ucmasnepal.com/uploaded/images/ucmas_brain.jpg)

relationships of functional, psychological, and morphological changes in patients with brain injuries. An intentional manipulation of an electrode or scalpel in a tissue of a healthy brain for real-life data collection was out of the question. Of course, it was possible to carry out experiments on animals, but killing innocent animals in the name of science has always been somewhat controversial even if dictated by a noble purpose. Furthermore, it was not possible to draw exact conclusions about human brains directly from animal tests. The differences in brain anatomy and physiology in humans and animals are more significant than differences in their musculoskeletal and circulatory systems.

Let us now look at the methods adopted by the pioneering neural network creators to equip their constructions with the most desirable features and properties modeled on the brain evolved by nature. The brain consists of neurons that function as separate cells acting as natural processors. Spanish histologist Ramón y Cajal (1906 Nobel laureate; see Table P.1 in Preface) first described the human brain as a network of connected autonomous elements. He introduced the concept of neurons that were responsible for processing information, receiving and analyzing sensations, and also generating and sending control signals to all parts of the human body. We will learn more about the structures of neurons in Chapter 2. The artificial equivalent of the neuron is the main component of a neural network structure. Figure 1.5 shows how an individual neuron was isolated from a continuous web of neurons that form the cerebral cortex.

As evident from the experiments on certain animals such as squid of the genus Loligo, our knowledge of neurons when the first neural networks were designed was quite extensive. Hodgkin and Huxley (1963 Nobel Prize) discovered the biochemical and bioelectrical changes that occur during distribution and processing of nervous information carrier signals. The most important result was that the description of a real neuron could be simplified significantly by a reduction of observed information processing rules to several simple relations described in Chapter 2. The extremely simplified neuron (Figure 1.6) still allows us to create networks that have interesting and useful properties and at the same time are economical to build. The elements shown in Figure 1.6 will be discussed in detail in subsequent chapters.

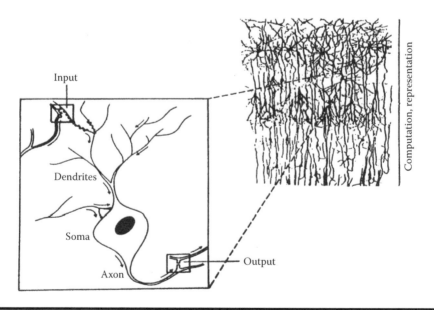

Figure 1.5 Part of the brain cortex treated as a neural network with selected neuron presentation.

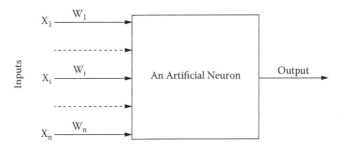

Figure 1.6 Simplified scheme of an artificial neuron.

A natural neuron has an extremely intricate and diverse construction (Figure 1.7). Its artificial equivalent as shown in Figure 1.6 has a substantially trimmed-down structure and is greatly simplified in the activity areas. Despite these differences, we can, with the help of artificial neural networks, duplicate a range of complex and interesting behaviors that will be described in detail in later chapters.

The neuron in Figure 1.7 is a product of a graphic fantasy. Figure 1.8 shows a real neural cell dissected from a rat brain—an exact match to a human neuron. It is possible to model simple artificial neurons easily and economically by means of an uncomplicated electronic system. It is also fairly easy to model them in a form of a computer algorithm that simulates their activities. The first neural networks were built as specialized electronic machines called perceptrons.

1.3 Construction of First Neural Networks

Let us see how biological information was used in the field of neurocybernetics to design economical and easy-to-use neural networks. The creators of the first neural networks understood the actions of biological neurons. Table P.1 in the Preface lists the number of Nobel prizes awarded throughout the twentieth century for discoveries related directly or indirectly to neural cells and their functions. The most astonishing discovery by biologists concerned the process by which one neuron passes a signal to another neuron (Figure 1.9).

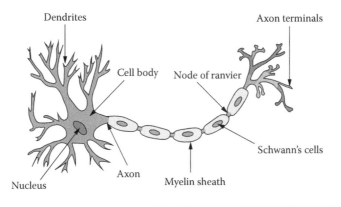

Figure 1.7 View of a biological neural cell. (Source: http://www.web-books.com/eLibrary/ Medicine/Physiology/Nervous/neuron.jpg)

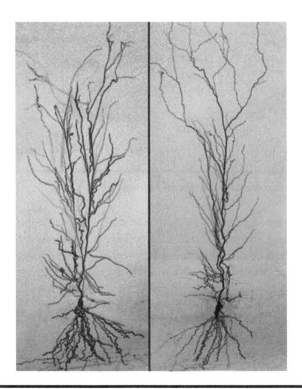

Figure 1.8 View of biological neurons in rat brain. (Source: http://flutuante.files.wordpress. com/2009/08/rat-neuron.png)

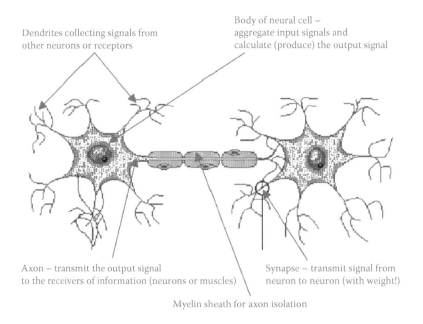

Figure 1.9 Smallest functional part of a neural system: two connected and cooperating neurons. The most important part of the structure is the synapse connecting the two neurons.

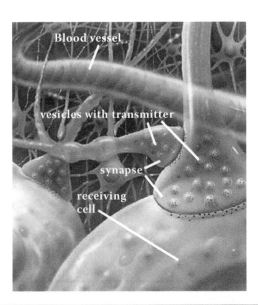

Figure 1.10 View of synapse reconstructed on the basis of hundreds of electron microscope observations. (Source: http://www.lionden.com/graphics/AP/synapse.jpg)

Researchers noted that the most important participants in information processing within the brain were the large and complicated cell bodies (axons and dendrites) used for communications between neurons. Synapses are also significant participants. They mediate the process of information passing between neurons. Synapses are so small that the resolving power of the optical microscopes typically used in biology was too low to find and describe them. They are barely visible in Figure 1.9. Their structural complexity could be understood only after the invention of the electron microscope (Figure 1.10).

John Eccles, a British neurophysiologist, proved that when a neural signal goes through a synapse, special chemical substances called neuromediators are engaged. They are released at the end of the axon from the neuron that transmits the information and travel to the postsynaptic membrane of the recipient neuron (Figure 1.11).

In essence, teaching a neuron depends on the ability of the same signal sent through an axon from a transmitting cell to release a greater or smaller quantity of the neuromediator to the synapse that receives the signal. If the brain finds a signal important during the learning process, the quantity of the neuromediator is increased or decreased. We should remember that the mechanism shown in the figure is an extremely simplified version of the complex biological processes that occur within a synapse in reality. The best way to understand the complexity is to discover how the synapses transmit information from neuron to neuron and the mechanism of the changes that take place in synapses as a brain learns and acquires new information.

The neural networks specialists readily used this information and the systems they built possessed one vital attribute: the ability to learn. Obviously, the complicated process of biological learning that requires very complex biochemical processes (Figure 1.12) was greatly simplified for the design of an efficient tool for resolving practical computer science problems. The type of learning utilized in neural networks is classified by psychologists as procedural memory. As we know, humans also have other types of memories. The memory and learning processes are illustrated in Figure 1.13.

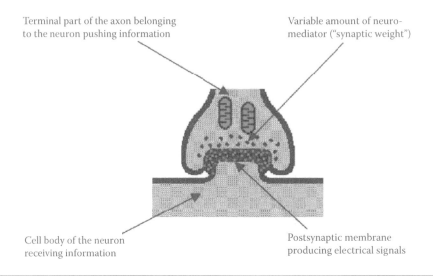

Terminal part of the axon belonging
to the neuron pushing information

Variable amount of neuro-
mediator ("synaptic weight")

Cell body of the neuron
receiving information

Postsynaptic membrane
producing electrical signals

Figure 1.11 Simplified scheme of a synapse structure and its main elements.

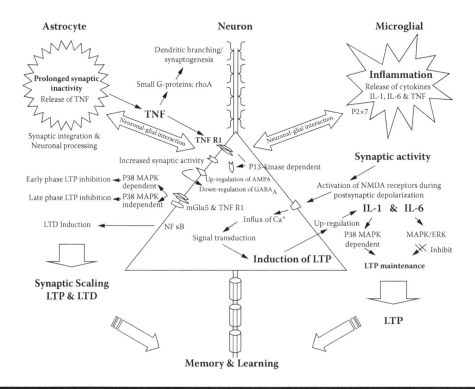

Figure 1.12 Biochemical mechanisms of learning and memory. (Source: http://ars.els-cdn.com/content/image/1-s2.0-S0149763408001838-gr3.jpg)

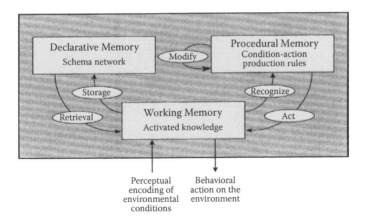

Figure 1.13   Different types of memories in human cognitive processes.

In the 1990s, the identification of the inner structures of the brain led to further development of neural networks. The hard work of many generations of histologists analyzing thousands of microscopic specimens and hundreds of less or more successful attempts to reconstruct the three-dimensional structures of the connections between neural elements produced useful results in the forms of schemas such as Figure 1.14.

Figure 1.14   Three-dimensional internal structure of connections within a brain. (Source: http://www.trbimg.com/img-504f806f/turbine/la-he-brainresearch18-154.jpg-20120910/600)

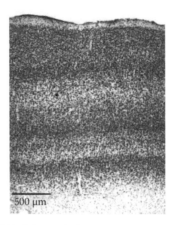

Figure 1.15 Layered structure of human brain cortex. (Source: http://hirnforschung.kyb.mpg. de/uploads/pics/EN_M2_clip_image002_01.jpg)

1.4 Layered Construction of Neural Network

Neural network designers focused mainly on implementing working models that were practical, tough, and extremely truncated. The space layouts of neurons and their connections based on neuroanatomic and cytological research had to be reduced to absolute minimum. The regular layer-like patterns created by neurons in several brain areas had to be followed. Figure 1.15 shows the layered structure of the cerebral cortex. Figure 1.16 illustrates the layered structure of the retina of the eye.

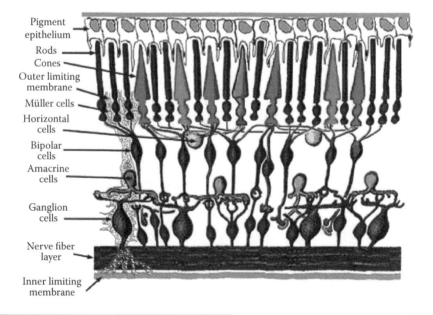

Figure 1.16 Layered structure of the retina component of the eye. (Source: http://www.theness. com/images/blogimages/retina.jpeg)

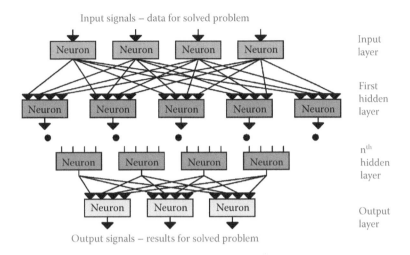

Input signals – data for solved problem

Output signals – results for solved problem

Figure 1.17 Typical neural network structure.

The technicalities involved in designing neural networks in layers are easy to handle. At best, neural networks are biologically "crippled" models of actual tissues. They are functional enough to produce results that are fairly correct—at least in context of neurophysiology.

According to the popular movie *Shrek*, "Ogres are like onions. They have layers." Like onions, neural networks also have layers. A typical neural network has the structure shown in Figure 1.17. The main problem for a designer is to set up and maintain the connections between the layers. The schematic of neural connections in a brain is very complicated and connection details differ according to the specific brain area. The first topological brain map was created in the nineteenth century and it divided the brain based on identical neural connection templates (Figure 1.18). The original map marked similar connections with the same color; different colors indicated differences. The map shows what are called Brodmann's areas.

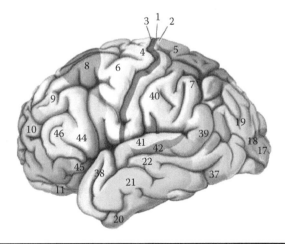

Figure 1.18 Brodmann's map of brain regions with different cell connections. (Source: http://thebrain.mcgill.ca/flash/capsules/images/outil_jaune05_img02.jpg)

Brodmann divided the cortex into 52 regions. Currently we treat brain structures more subtly, but Brodmann's scheme depicts the problem we face in analyzing neuron connections into a network. The answer varies according to the brain area involved.

If our sole task is to build an artificial neural network, it may be wise to adapt its connection structure with respect to the single problem the network is to solve. It is obvious that a well-chosen structure can greatly increase the speed of network learning. The problem in most cases is that we are unable to determine the best way to work out the problem. We cannot even guess which algorithms are suitable and which ones should be employed after learning. The *a priori* selection of network elements is not possible. Therefore, the decisions about connecting layers and single elements in networks are arbitrary. Usually each element is connected to every other element. Such a homogeneous and completely connected network reduces the effort required to define it. However, this design increases computing complexity. More memory or increased chip complexity may be needed to recreate all connections between elements.

It is worth mentioning that without such simplification, network definition would require thousands of parameters. The deployment of such a structure would be a programmer's worst nightmare. In contrast, using fully connected elements involves no special efforts of the designer and the use has become almost routine and harmless because the learning process eliminates unnecessary connections.

1.5 From Biological Brain to First Artificial Neural Network

In summary, the artificial neural networks invented in the 1990s had strong foundations in the anatomical, physiological, and biochemical activities of the human brain. The designers of neural networks did not attempt to make exact copies of brains. Instead, they treated the brain as an inspiration. Therefore, the construction and principles governing artificial neural networks applied in practice are not exact reflections of the activities of biological structures.

Basically, we can say that the foundations of modern neural networks consist of certain biological knowledge elements that are well known and serve as sources of inspiration. Neural networks do not duplicate the precise patterns of brains. The structure designed by a neurocybernetic scientist is totally the product of computer science because neural networks models are created and simulated using typical computers. A graphical metaphor of this process assembled by students of Akademia Górniczo-Hutnicza in Krakow shows the first author as an explorer of neural networks (Figure 1.19).

We must remember that during the evolution of neural networks, all biological knowledge must be considered thoroughly and simplified before it can serve as a basis for constructing artificial neurocybernetic systems. This fact fundamentally influences the properties of neural networks. Contrary to appearances, it also decides the properties and possibilities of neural networks considered tools that help us understand the biological processes of our own brains. We will address this issue in the next subsection.

While preparing this book, we could not ignore the remarkable progress of brain research in the past decade. Accordingly, the concepts determining when and for what purpose neural networks should be applied also have undergone an evolution. In the next subsection, we will talk about concurrent problems connected with human nervous system research and we try to demonstrate the role neural networks may play in future research.

Figure 1.19 Incorporating knowledge of biological neurons into structures of modern computers.

1.6 Current Brain Research Methods

The variety of tools available for researchers in the twenty-first century would have been incomprehensible to the pioneers who gave us the basic knowledge about the structure and functionality of the nervous system. Their work underlined creation of the first neural network in the 1990s. The skull—more precisely the cranium—was impenetrable by early observation techniques. The interior of the brain could only be viewed after the death of a patient and postmortem examination failed to yield any insight into its activities. Anatomists tried to analyze the core structures that processed information and their connectivities by dissecting brains into pieces. With modern technology, the internal brain structures of living humans can be observed and analyzed with extraordinary precision and without harm, as shown in Figure 1.20. Two techniques that led to the improved representation of the human brain and its internal structures are computerized tomography (CT) and nuclear magnetic resonance (NMR).

In early March 2013, two terabytes of unique data hit the web: the first batch of images from a massively ambitious brain-mapping effort called the Human Connectome Project (Van Essen 2013). Thousands of images showed the brains of 68 healthy volunteers, with different regions glowing in bright jewel tones. These data, freely available for download via the project's site, revealed the parts of the brain that act in concert to accomplish a task as simple as recognizing a face. The project leaders said their work was enabled by advances in brain-scanning hardware and image-processing software.

"It simply wouldn't have been feasible five or six years ago to provide this amount and quality of data, and the ability to work with the data," said David Van Essen, one of the project's principal investigators and head of the anatomy and neurobiology department at the Washington University School of Medicine in St. Louis. Based on a growing understanding that the mechanisms of perception and cognition involve networks of neurons that sprawl across multiple

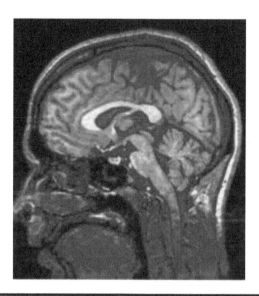

Figure 1.20 Internal brain structures of living humans can be analyzed with astounding precision. (Source: http://www.ucl.ac.uk/news/news-articles/1012/s4_cropped.jpg)

regions of the brain, researchers have begun mapping those neural circuits. While the Human Connectome Project looks at connections among brain regions, a $100 million project announced in April 2013 and called the BRAINInitiative will focus on the connectivity of small clusters of neurons.

As of this writing, only the 5-year Human Connectome Project has delivered data. The $40 million project funds two consortia; the larger, international group led by Van Essen and Kamil Ugurbil of the University of Minnesota will eventually scan the brains of 1200 twin adults and their siblings. The goal, says Van Essen, is "not just to infer what typical brain connectivity is like but also how it varies across participants, and how that relates to their different intellectual, cognitive, and emotional capabilities and attributes." To provide multiple perspectives on each brain, the researchers employ a number of cutting-edge imaging methods. They start with magnetic resonance imaging (MRI) scans to provide basic structural images of the brain using both a 3-tesla machine and a next-generation 7-T scanner. Both provide extremely high-resolution images of the convoluted folds of the cerebral cortex.

The next step will be a series of functional MRI (fMRI) scans to detect blood flow throughout the brain and show brain activities for subjects at rest and engaged in seven different tasks (including language, working memory, and gambling exercises). The fMRI is "souped up." Ugurbil pioneered a technique called multiband imaging that takes snapshots of eight slices of the brain at a time instead of just one. To complement the data, on basic structure and blood flow within the brain, each participant will be scanned using a technique called diffusion MRI that tracks the movements of water molecules within brain fibers. Because water diffuses more rapidly along the lengths of the fibers that connect neurons than across them, this technique allows researchers to directly trace connections of sections of the brain.

The Connectome team had Siemens customize its top-of-the-line MRI machine to let the team alter its magnetic field strength more rapidly and dramatically to produce clearer images.

Each imaging modality has its limitations, so combining them gives neuroscientists their best view yet of what goes on inside a human brain. First, however, all that neuroimaging data must be purged of noise and artifacts and organized into a useful database.

Dan Marcus, director of the Neuro-informatics Research Group at the Washington University School of Medicine, developed the image-processing software that automatically cleans up the images and precisely aligns the scans so that a single "brain ordinate" refers to the same point on both diffusion MRI and fMRI scans. That processing is computationally intensive, says Marcus: "For each subject, that code takes about 24 hours to run on our supercomputer."

Finally, the team adapted open-source image analysis tools to allow researchers to query the database in sophisticated ways. For example, a user can examine a brain simply through its diffusion images or overlay that data on a set of fMRI results. Some neuroscientists think that all this data will be of limited use. Karl Friston, scientific director of the Wellcome Trust Centre for Neuroimaging at University College London (2013), applauds the project's ambition, but criticizes it for providing a resource "without asking what questions these data and models speak to." Friston would prefer to see money spent on hypothesis-directed brain scans to investigate "how a particular connection changes with experimental intervention or disease."

The Connectome team thinks the open-ended nature of the data set is an asset, not a weakness. They hope to provoke research questions they never anticipated and in fields other than their own. "You don't have to be a neuroscientist to access the data," says Marcus. "If you're an engineer or a physicist and want to get into this, you can."

Diagnostics allow us to detect and locate certain brain areas that exhibit high levels of activities at certain moments (see Figure 1.21). Linking such sections with the type of activity a person is performing at a specific moment allows us to presume that certain brain structures are specialized to provide specific responses. This led to better understanding of functional aspects of neural compounds.

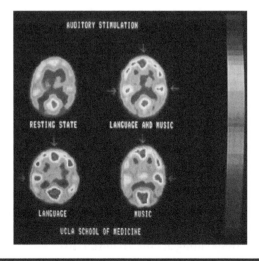

Figure 1.21 PET image showing brain activity during performance of certain tasks by research subject. (Source: http://faculty.vassar.edu/abbaird/resources/brain_science/images/ pet_image.jpg)

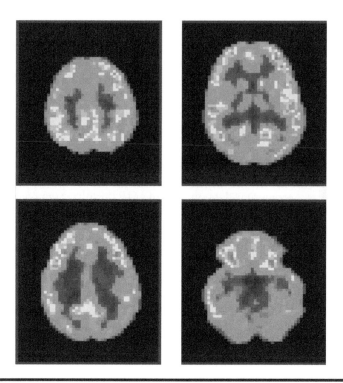

Figure 1.22 PET image of a human brain not focused on a specific task or object.

Figure 1.22 shows four profiles at different heights obtained by positron emission tomography (PET) imaging of a human brain viewed from inside. Its owner is awake, is not focused on anything specific, and has no task to accomplish. We can see that most of his brain is inactive (shown as blue or green areas in original scan; places where neurons work were shown as yellow and red areas). Why does the scan reveal activity? Although our test subject is relaxed, he continues to think; he moves even if his movements are not noticeable. He feels cold or heat. His activities are scattered and weak. If he focuses on solving a difficult mathematical problem, the brain areas responsible for abstract thinking immediately increase their activity, resulting in red areas as shown in Figure 1.23.

PET imaging can be used to study minimal activities and exhausting efforts. If a picture suddenly draws the attention of our research object, millions of neurons in the rear part of his brain will be activated to analyze the picture as shown in Figure 1.24. During listening and speech comprehension, triggers responsible for analysis and remembering sounds are activated in temporal lobes as shown in Figure 1.25.

The methods briefly described here allow us to record temporary brain states and explain how the brain is organized. In fact, combinations of various imaging techniques allow us to view internal structures during many types of activities and reveal correlations between certain brain areas and an individual's corresponding actions (Figure 1.26).

These changes can be recorded dynamically (creating something like a movie or computer animation) and provide an enormous advantage over static pictures. The process is similar to dividing the motions of a runner into sections or the serial snapshots used to produce animated

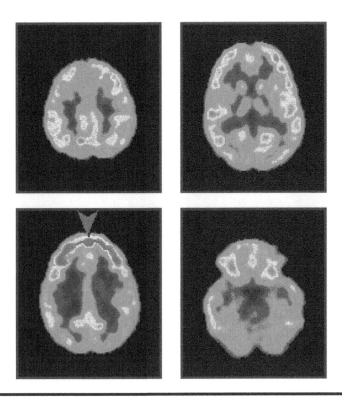

Figure 1.23   PET image of a human brain focused heavily on a mathematical equation. Intensive marks in the frontal lobe (shown in red on original scan) are activated by this exercise.

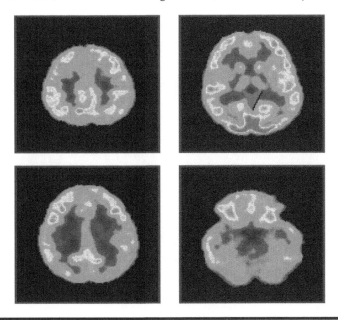

Figure 1.24   PET image of brain activity while a subject watches something interesting. We can see spots marking activity in rear lobes (arrow) responsible for acquisition and identification of visual signals.

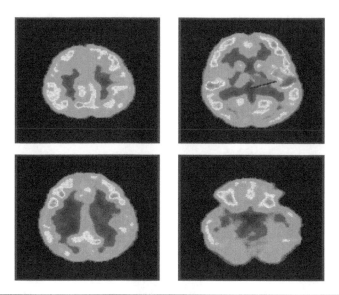

Figure 1.25   Listening to a conversation activates mostly temporal lobes because they are responsible for signal analysis. Note that speech comprehension areas are located only in one side of brain; listening to music changes the color on both sides of the image.

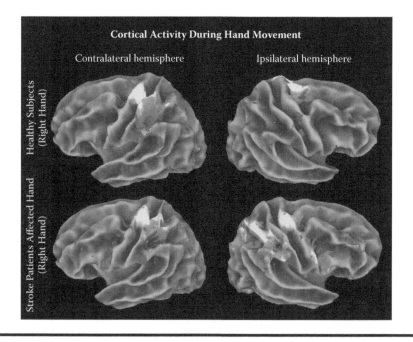

Figure 1.26   Tracking changes connected with performing specific tasks. (Source: http://www. martinos.org/neurorecovery/images/fMRI_labeled.png)

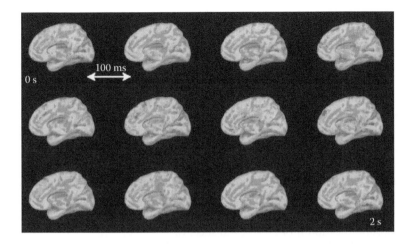

Figure 1.27   Dynamic processes occurring within a brain. (Source: http://www.bic.mni.mcgill. ca/uploads/ResearchLabsNeuroSPEED/restingstatedemo.gif)

movies. Figure 1.27 shows animation of brain structures. Presenting such still images of anatomical features in sequence gives an illusion of movement that allows us to track which structures activate and in what order to analyze a specific action.

1.7 Using Neural Networks to Study the Human Mind

The examples presented above were obtained by modern methods of brain examination. The 1990s, also known as "the decade of the brain," revealed so much information that the human brain no longer seemed mysterious. That statement is misleading. The brain structure has been explored thoroughly and we have some understanding of its functionality. However, a common problem for studies of highly complex objects appeared: the reconstruction of a whole that results in wastes of separate, distributed, and specific information.

One very efficient technique used in modern science is decomposition—the method of dividing an object into parts. Do you have a problem with description of a huge system? Divide it into several hundred pieces and investigate each piece! Are you at a loss to understand a complex process? Let us find several dozen simple subprocesses that constitute the complex system and investigate each one separately. This method is very effective. If separated subsystems or subprocesses remain resistant to your scientific methods, you can always divide them into smaller and simpler parts. However, decomposition creates other difficulties: who will compile the results of all these research fragments? How and when and in what form will the results be compiled?

In analyzing very complex systems, the synthesis of results is not easy, especially if the results were obtained by various scientific techniques. It is hard to compose a whole picture by integrating anatomic information derived from case descriptions based on physiological data and biochemical results generated by analytical devices. Computer modeling can work as a common denominator for processing information obtained from various sources. It was proven experimentally that a computer model describing anatomy can be joined with computer records of physiological processes and computer descriptions of biochemical reactions. The current approach attempts to build our entire body of knowledge from separate investigations of different biological systems by various scientists.

With reference to neural systems and in particular to the human brain, various computer models may be used to combine results of many different research projects in an effort to achieve an integrated explanation of the functionality of these extraordinarily complex systems. Some of those models will be explained later in the text. In this preliminary chapter, we would like to state that the easiest approach is to attempt to describe our knowledge of the brain in relation to artificial neural networks. Obviously, the human brain is far more complex than the simplified neural networks.

However, it is common in science that the use of simplified models leads to the discovery of rules that allow extrapolation on a larger scale. For example, if a chemist carries out a reaction in a small sample, we are entitled to presume that the same reaction takes place under similar conditions in a vast ocean or on a distant star and the extrapolation is usually valid. Moreover, it is much easier to handle a small laboratory sample than an ocean or a star. While looking for a scientific truth, simplification is often a key to success.

That is why, despite the simplicity of neural networks, researchers use them more and more frequently to model human brain processes to achieve better comprehension. To realize how much we rely on this tool, we will try to compare the complexities of artificial neural networks and animal and human neural systems.

1.8 Simplification of Neural Networks: Comparison with Biological Networks

Artificial neural networks are very simplified in comparison with the neural systems of most living creatures. The comparison can be observed in Figure 1.28. Typical neural networks (usually programs for general-purpose computers) are shown at bottom left at lowest levels of complexity and

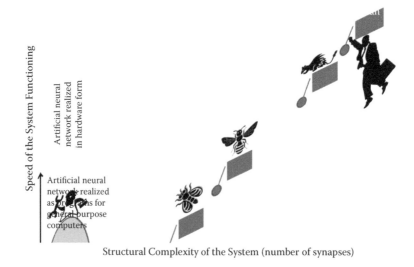

Figure 1.28 Localization of artificial neural networks and selected real neural systems showing relation between structural complexity of a system and speed of functioning.

functioning speed. Both dimensions on this plot are represented on a logarithmic scale to show the huge distance between smallest and largest presented values for various organisms.

The structural complexity measured by the number of synapses in neuroinformatic systems can vary from 10^2 for a typical artificial neural network used for technological purposes up to 10^{12} for the human brain. This dimension for artificial neural networks is limited by value around 10^5 or 10^6 because of computer memory limitations, where appropriate values for the fairly simple brains of flies and bees are characterized by 10^8 and 10^9 synapses, respectively. In comparison with these neural systems, mammal central nervous systems have huge numbers of synapses (10^{11} for rats and 10^{12} for humans).

Let us consider the almost linear relation between structural complexity of biological neural systems and their speed of functioning (Figure 1.28). In fact, it is a general rule caused by massively parallel biological neural system functioning. When a system consists of more elements (more neurons and more synapses) and all these elements work together simultaneously, the speed of data processing increases proportionally to the system structural dimensions.

For artificial neural networks, the speed of system functioning depends on the form of network realization. When a neural network is realized as a program-simulating neural activity (e.g., learning or problem solving) on a general-purpose computer, the functioning speed is limited by the performance limits of the processor. Clearly it is impossible to speed processing beyond the hardware limitations with any type of program. Therefore, artificial neural networks realized as programs on general-purpose computers are rather slow.

It is possible to achieve high speed functioning by an artificial neural network when it is realized in hardware form (see ellipse in Figure 1.28). In a bibliography or on the Internet, readers can find many examples of neural networks realized as specialized electronic chips such as field-programmable gate arrays (FPGAs). Other solutions involve optoelectronics—chips are fabricated using partial analog technologies; neurochips that combine electronic silicon and biological parts (living neural cells or neural tissues treated as device components).

All such methods of hardware realization of artificial neural networks may operate very fast (Figure 1.28) but the structural complexity of such systems is always very limited and elasticity of system application is not satisfactory for most users. Therefore, in practice, most users of artificial neural networks prefer software solutions and accept their limitations.

Figure 1.28 indicates that some biological neural systems can be located within artificial neural network ranges. For example, the brain of a shrimp can be compared with an artificial neural network and exhibit no superiority in complexity or in speed of information processing. Therefore, the dot symbolizing shrimp neural system parameters is located within the box area indicating artificial neural network parameters. However, the complexities of their neural systems and speed of data processing for most biological species are much greater than the best parameters achieved by artificial neural networks. The complexity of the human brain is a billion times greater than parameters observed in artificial neural networks.

1.9 Main Advantages of Neural Networks

Neural networks are used widely to solve many practical problems. A Google search of *neural networks application* will yield about 17,500,000 answers. Wow! Of course, these search results include many worthless messages, but the number of serious articles, books, and presentations showing various neural network applications certainly total millions. Why are so many researchers and practicing engineers, economists, doctors, and other computer users interested in using neural networks? The widespread use may be attributed mainly to the following advantages.

- Network learning capability allows a user to solve problems without having to find and review methods, build algorithms, or develop programs even if he or she has no prior knowledge about the nature of the problem. A user needs some examples of similar tasks with good solutions. A collection of successful solutions of a problem allows use of a neural network for learning the results and applying them to solve similar problems. This approach to problem solving is both easy and comfortable.

- Pattern recognition has no easy algorithmic solution. A neural network can be comfortably engaged in the learning process to generate solutions in this area. Theoretical analysis of particular types of images (e.g., human faces) leads to conclusions for which exact algorithms are unavailable, such as those guaranteeing proper differentiation of faces of different persons and reliably recognizing the face of a specific person regardless of position, similar appearance, and other factors. It is possible to use learning neural networks on different images of the same person in different positions and also images of different persons for differentiation. These images serve as learning examples that help in the process of identification.

- Another typical area where a learning neural network can be better than a specific algorithm relates to prediction. The world today is abuzz with forecasting weather, money exchange rates, stock prices, results of medical treatments, and other items. In all prediction problems, up-to-date status and historical data are equally important. It is nearly impossible to propose a theoretical model for all nontrivial problems that can be used for algorithmic forecasting. Neural networks are effective for solving these problems too. Historical facts can serve as learning examples in these tasks. It is possible to develop many successful neural network forecasting models by using relevant history and considering only stationary processes.

- Another advantage is the realization of neural networks as specialized hardware systems. Until recently, neural network applications were based on software solutions. Users had to be involved with all steps of problem solving (i.e., neural network formation, learning, exploiting, and using computer simulation). The situation is slowly changing as hardware solutions for neural networks become available. Numerous electronic and optoelectronic systems are based on neural network structures. The hardware solutions offer high degrees of parallel processing, similar to the biological brain in which many neurons work simultaneously to activate vision, hearing, and muscle control at the same time.

Neural networks are used mostly for pattern recognition. The first known neural network called the perceptron was designed by Frank Rosenblatt and dedicated to automatic perception (recognition) of different characters. Kusakabe and colleagues (2011) discussed similar applications of neural networks on pattern recognition. Another interesting application of neural network is the automated recognition of human actions in surveillance videos (Shuiwang et al., 2013). Automatic classification of satellite images is another interesting application of neural networks (Shingha et al., 2012). Optical character recognition is perhaps the oldest and most common application.

Automatic noise recognition using neural network parameters is gaining popularity quickly (Haghmaram et al., 2012). The ability of neural networks to automatically solve recognition and classification problems is often used in diagnostic applications. A very good overview of neural network applications is found in Gardel et al. (2012). In general, objects recognized by neural networks vary hugely (Nonaka, Tanaka, and Morita, 2012; Deng, 2013); examples are mathematical functions and nonlinear dynamic system identification. Many neural network applications are connected with computer vision and image processing.

A typical example of such research related to medical applications is described in a paper by Xie and Bovik (2013). Another example of medical image processing by means of neural networks can be found in a paper by Wolfer (2012). Neural networks are used for many nonmedical types of analyses. Latini et al. (2012) demonstrated the application of neural networks to satellite image processing for geoscience purposes.

As noted above, forecasting is another typical application for neural networks. Samet et al. (2012) used artificial neural networks for prediction of electrical arc furnace reactive power to improve compensator performance. Liu et al. (2012) used neural-based forecasting to predict wind power plant generation. Thousands of examples of neural network applications exist. Many can be found by using Internet search engines. The important point is that neural networks have proven to be useful tools in many areas of scientific and professional activities. For that reason, it is useful to understand their structures, operation characteristics, and practical uses.

1.10 Neural Networks as Replacements for Traditional Computers

Based on the previous section, neural networks have many uses and can solve various types of problems. Does that mean we should give up our "classical" computers and use networks to solve all computational problems? Although networks are "fashionable" and useful, they present several serious limitations that will be discussed in the following chapters. Readers will also learn about network structures, methods of learning to use networks, and applications to specific tasks. Certain tasks cannot be handled by neural networks.

The first category of tasks not suitable for neural networks involves symbol manipulation. Neural networks find any information processing task involving symbols extremely difficult to handle and thus should not be used for elements based on symbol processing. In summary, it makes no sense to create a text editor or algebraic expression processor based on a neural network.

The next class of problems not suitable for a neural network involves calculations that require highly precise numerical results. The network always works qualitatively and thus the results generated are always approximate. The precision of such approximations is satisfactory for many applications (e.g., signal processing, picture analysis, speech recognition, prognosis, quotation predictions, robot controls, and other approximations). However, it is absolutely impossible to use neural networks for bank account services or precise engineering calculations.

Another situation in which a neural network will not produce effective results is a task that requires many stages of reasoning (e.g., deciding the authenticity or falseness of sequences of logical statements). A network solves a specific type of problem and generates an immediate result. If, however, a problem requires argumentation involving many steps and documentation of the results, an artificial network is useless. Attempts to use networks to solve problems beyond their capability leads to frustrating failures.

1.11 Working with Neural Networks

Readers should not jump to conclusions about the limitations of neural networks based on the statements above. A neural network alone cannot make symbolic calculations, but it can support systems that operate on symbols by handling functions symbol-based systems cannot handle alone. Good examples of such networks include those designed by Teuvo Kohonen, the classical NetTALK products, and the invention of Terrence Sejnowski that changes orthographic text into a phonemic symbol sequence used to control speech synthesizers.

While neural networks are not useful for terminals used to process customer transactions in banks, they are very effective for dealing with debtor credibility issues and establishing conditions for negotiating contracts. In summary, the neural network is useful for many applications in many fields worldwide. Its possibilities are simply not as universal as those of the classical computer.

Enthusiasts can easily list the results generated by neural networks that turned out to be far superior to those solved by classical computers. Proponents of classical computing, on the other hand, can easily show that the results produced by neural networks were incorrect. Both groups are correct—in a way. We shall try to explain both sides of this argument to find the truth in the following chapters by describing the teaching techniques of neural networks, various types of learning methods, simple programs, and ample illustrations that we hope will enable readers to make their own judgments.

In this chapter, we explained the genesis and benefits of neural networks in an effort to foster reader interest in such devices. In the following chapters, we treat neural networks as devices to help achieve practical goals (e.g., obtaining favorable stock market projections). We will show you how interesting the networks are because their designs are based on the structure and functioning of the live brain.

We will also describe significant successes that may be achieved by engineers, economists, geologists, and medical practitioners who use artificial networks to improve efficiency in their respective fields. We will also discuss the studies of the human brain that led to the invention of artificial neural networks as self-educating systems. In each chapter, the most important theoretical information is clearly categorized by descriptive headings. This enables readers to read or skip the important but less colorful mathematical techniques.

By accessing our programs on the Internet (http://home.agh.edu.pl/~tad//index.php?page= programy&lang=en), you will be both a witness and an active participant in unique experiments that will provide even more understanding of neural networks and the functioning of your own brain—a mysterious structure abounding in various capabilities that Shakespeare (1603) described as "a fragile house of soul."

Do you know why it is worthwhile to study neural networks? If the answer is yes, we invite you to read the remaining chapters! This book is current and exhaustive. We did our best to include the most important and up-to-date information about neural networks. We did not, however, cover the small but onerous details in which each branch of calculation technology abounds and are usually expressed as mathematical formulae. We decided to treat seriously the principle written on the cover of Stephen Hawking's *A Brief History of Time* (1988, 1996). Hawking wrote that each equation included in his text diminished the number of readers by half.

It is important to us that this book appeals to a large audience, among whom are readers who will find neural networks amazing and useful devices. Therefore, we are not going to include even a single equation in the text of this book. Even one reader discouraged by the inclusion of equations represents a heavy loss.

References

Callaghan, P.T., Eccles, C.D., Xia, Y. 1988. NMR microscopy of dynamic displacements: k-space and q-space imaging. *Journal of Physics E.*, Scientific Instruments, vol. 21(8), pp. 820–822.

Friston, K. 2009. Causal Modeling and Brain Connectivity in Functional Magnetic Resonance Imaging. *PLOS Biology,* vol. 7(2), DOI: 10.1371/journal.pbio.100003.

Hawking, S. 1988, 1996. *A Brief History of Time.* New York: Bantam.

Kusakabe, K. Kimura Y. and Odaka K. 2011. Character recognition using feature modification with neural networks learning feature displacement in two opposite directions. *IEICE Transactions on Information and Systems*, vol. J94-D, no.6, pp. 989–997.

Latini, D., Del Frate, F., Palazzo, F. et al. 2012. Coastline extraction from SAR COSMO-SkyMed data using a new neural network algorithm. In *Proceedings of IEEE International Geoscience and Remote Sensing Symposium*, pp. 5975–5977.

Liu, Z., Gao, W., Wan, Y.H. et al. 2012. Wind power plant prediction by using neural networks. In *Proceedings of IEEE Energy Conversion Congress and Exposition*, pp. 3154–3160.

Rosenblatt, F. 1958. The Perceptron: A probabilistic model for information storage and organization in the brain. *Psychological Review*, American Psychological Association, vol. 65, no. 6, pp. 386–408.

Samet, H., Farhadi, M.R., and Mofrad, M.R.B. 2012. Employing artificial neural networks for prediction of electrical arc furnace reactive power to improve compensator performance. *Proceedings of IEEE International Energy Conference*, pp. 249–253.

Shakespeare, W. 1603. *Hamlet, Prince of Denmark.* Act I, Scene 3. http://www.shakespeare-online.com/plays/hamlet_1_3.html

Van Essen, D.C., Smith, S.M., Barch, D.M., Berhens, T.E.J., Yacoub, E., Ugurbil, K. 2013. The WU-Minn Human Connectome Project: An Overview. *NeuroImage* 80, pp. 62–79. http://www.humanconnectomeproject.org/ accessed on April 2, 2014

Wolfer, J. 2012. Pulse-coupled neural networks and image morphology for mammogram preprocessing. In *Proceedings of Third International Conference on Innovations in Bio-Inspired Computing and Applications.* IEEE Computer Society, pp. 286–290.

Xie, F. and Bovik, A.C. 2013. Automatic segmentation of dermoscopy images using self-generating neural networks seeded by genetic algorithm. *Pattern Recognition*, 46, 1012–1019.

Chapter 2

Neural Net Structure

2.1 Building Neural Nets

Who has not started to explore the world by breaking an alarm clock into pieces or smashing a tape recorder just to find out what was inside? Before we explain how a network works and how to use it, we will try to precisely and simply describe how one is built. As you know from the previous chapter, a neural network is a system that makes specific calculations based on simultaneous activities of many connected elements called neurons. The network structure was first observed in biological nervous systems, for example, in the human cerebellum depicted in Figure 2.1.

Neural networks are also built from a lot of neurons, but they are artificial—far more simple than the biological neurons and connected in a less complicated (more primitive) way. The artificial neural network model of a real nervous system structure would appear unclear and difficult to control. Figure 2.2 shows how an artificial neural net based on the identical structure scheme of a real nervous system. You can see that the structure does not appear easy to study; the structure is very complex, like a forest.

Artificial neural nets are built so that their structures may be traced easily, and production and use are economical. In general, the structures should be flat (not three-dimensional) and regular, with layers of neurons having well-defined objectives and linked according to simple (but wasteful) requirement to connect "everyone with everyone." Figure 2.3 illustrates a common neural net [general regression neural network (GRNN) type]. Its structure is rational and simple in comparison to a biological network. We shall discuss three factors that influence neural networks properties and possibilities:

1. The elements used to build a network (how artificial neurons look and work)
2. How the elements are connected with each other
3. Establishing the parameters of a network by its learning process

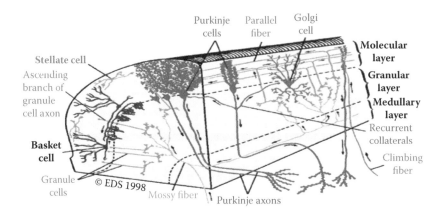

Figure 2.1 Cerebellar cortex showing that an organism's nervous system is built of many connected neurons. The same pattern is applied in artificial neural nets.

2.2 Constructing Artificial Neurons

The basic building materials we use to create a neural network are artificial neurons and we must learn about them precisely. In the previous section, we illustrated biological neurons. Figure 2.4 is a simplified depiction of a neuron. To make the point that not all neurons look exactly like that, Figure 2.5 shows a biological neuron dissected from rat cerebral cortex.

It is hard to distinguish between an axon that delivers signals from a specific neuron to all the others, and a dendrite that serves another purpose from the maze of fibers in the figure. Nevertheless, the figure portrays a real biological neuron that resembles the artificial neuron

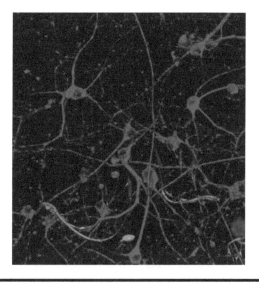

Figure 2.2 Artificial neural net with structure based on three-dimensional brain map. (Source: http://www.kurzweilai.net/images/3D-nanoelectronic-neural-tissue.jpg)

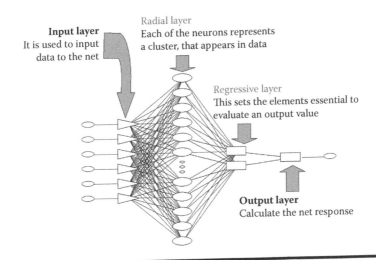

Input layer
It is used to input
data to the net

Radial layer
Each of the neurons represents
a cluster, that appears in data

Regressive layer
This sets the elements essential to
evaluate an output value

Output layer
Calculate the net response

Figure 2.3   Common neural net (GRNN type).

presented in Figure 2.6. A comparison of Figures 2.4 through 2.6 will demonstrate the degree to which neural network researchers simplified biological reality.

However, despite the simplifications, artificial neurons have all the features required from the view of tasks they are supposed to carry out. Let us look at some common features of artificial neurons.

They are characterized by many inputs and a single output. The input signals xi (i = 1, 2,…,n) and the output signal y may take on only numerical values, generally ranging from 0 to 1 or from −1 to +1). The fact that the tasks to be solved contain information (e.g., the output of a decision to recognize an individual after analyzing a photo) is the result of a specific agreement. Generally each input and output is associated with a specific meaning of a signal. Additionally, signal scaling is used, so that the selected signal values within a network would not be out of an agreed range (e.g., from 0 to 1).

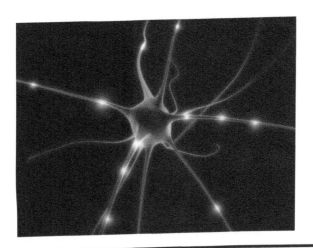

Figure 2.4   Structure of a biological nerve cell (neuron). (Source: http://cdn.thetechjournal. com/wp-content/uploads/HLIC/8905aee6a649af86842510c9cb0fc5bd.jpg)

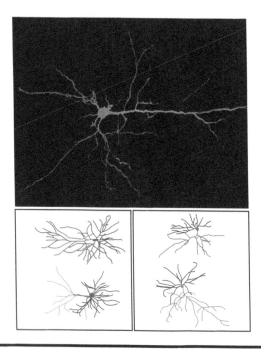

Figure 2.5 Microscopic views of real neurons. (Source: http://newswire.rockefeller.edu/wp-content/uploads/2011/12/110206mcewen.1162500780.jpg)

Figure 2.6 General scheme of artificial neuron shows the extent of simplification.

Artificial neurons perform specific activities on input signals, and consequently produce output signals (only one by a single neuron) meant for forwarding to other neurons or onto the network's output. Network assignment, reduced to the functioning of its basic neuron element, is based on the fact that it transforms an input data xi into a result y by applying rules that are both learned and assigned at the time of network creation. Figure 2.7 illustrates these neuron properties.

Figure 2.7 Basic signals in a neuron.

Figure 2.8 Neuron with weighted coefficient.

Neurons have the ability to learn via coefficients called synaptic weights (Figure 2.8). As noted in Chapter 1, artificial neurons reflect the complex biochemical and bioelectric processes that take place in real biological neuron synapses. The synaptic weights that constitute the basis of teaching a network can be modified (i.e., their values can be changed). Adding adjustable weight coefficients to a neuron structure makes it a learnable unit. Artificial neurons can be treated as elementary processors with specific features described below.

Each neuron receives many input signals xi and on the basis of the inputs, determines its answer y with a single output signal. A weight parameter called wi is connected to separate neuron inputs. It expresses a degree of significance of information arriving to a neuron using a specific input xi.

A signal arriving via a particular input is first modified with the use of the weight of the input. Most often a modification is based on the fact that a signal is simply multiplied through the weight of a given input. Consequently, in further calculations, the signal participates in a modified form. It is strengthened (if the weight exceeds 1) or restrained (if the weight value is less than 1). A signal from a particular input may occur even in the form opposite signals from the other inputs if its weight has a negative value. Inputs with negative weights are defined by neural network users as inhibitory inputs; those with positive weights are called excitatory inputs.

Input signals (modified by adequate weights) are aggregated in a neuron (see Figure 2.9). Networks utilize many methods of input signal aggregation. In general, aggregation involves simply adding the input signals to determine internal signals. This is referred as cumulative neuron stimulation or postsynaptic stimulation. This signal may be also defined as a net value.

Sometimes a neuron adds an extra component independent of input signals to the created sum of signals. This is called bias and it also undergoes a learning process. Thus, a bias can be considered an extra synaptic weight associated with inputs and it is provided an internal signal of constant value equal to one. A bias helps in the formation of a neuron's properties during the learning phase since the aggregation function characteristics need not pass through the beginning of the coordinate system. Figure 2.10 depicts a neuron with a bias.

A sum of internal signals multiplied by weights plus (possibly) a bias may be sometimes sent directly to its axon and treated as a neuron's output signal. This works well for linear systems

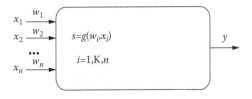

Figure 2.9 Aggregation of input data is the first internal function of a neuron.

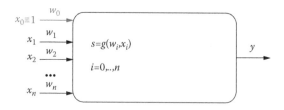

Figure 2.10 Application of bias parameter.

such as adaptive linear (ADALINE) networks. However, in a network with richer abilities such as the multilayer perceptron (MLP), a neuron's output signal is calculated by means of some nonlinear function. Throughout this book, we shall use the symbol $f()$ or $\varphi()$ to represent this function. Figure 2.11 depicts a neuron including both input signal aggregation and output signal generation.

Function $\varphi()$ is called a characteristic of a neuron (transfer function). Figure 2.12 illustrates various characteristics of neurons. Some of them are chosen in such a way that an artificial neuron's behavior would be the most similar to a real biological neuron's behavior (a sigmoid function), but characteristics also could be selected in a manner that would ensure the maximum efficiency of computations carried on by a neural network (Gauss function). In all cases, function $\varphi()$ constitutes an important element between a joint stimulation of a neuron and its output signal.

A knowledge of the input signals, weight coefficients, input aggregation method, and neuron characteristics allowed to unequivocally define the output signal at any time usually assumes

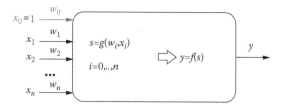

Figure 2.11 Complete schematic of neuron internal functions.

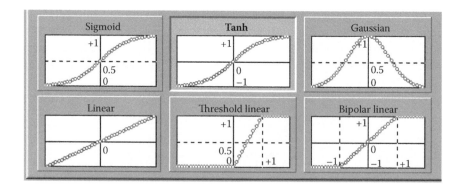

Figure 2.12 Often-used neuron characteristics.

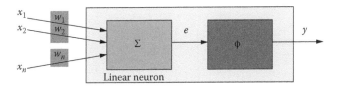

Figure 2.13   Structure of a neuron as a processor—the basis for building neural networks.

that the process occurs immediately, contrary to what happens in biological neurons. This helps the artificial neural networks reflect changes in input signals immediately at the output. Of course, this is a clearly theoretical assumption. After input signals change, even in electronic realizations, some time is needed to establish the correct value of an output signal by an adequate integrated circuit.

Much more time would be necessary to achieve the same effect in a simulation run because a computer imitating network activities must calculate all values of all signals on all outputs of all neurons of a network. That would require a lot of time even on a very fast computer. We will not pay attention to neuron reaction time in discussions of network functioning because the reaction time is an insignificant factor in this context. Figure 2.13 presents a complete structure of a single neuron.

The neuron presented in this figure is the most typical "material" used to create a network. More precisely, such typical network material constitutes neurons defined as multilayer perceptrons (MLPs). The most crucial elements of the material are presented in Figure 2.14. Note that the MLP neuron is characterized by the aggregation function consisting of simple summing of input signals multiplied by weights and uses a nonlinear transfer function with a distinctive sigmoid shape.

Radial neurons are sometimes used for special purposes. They involve an atypical method of input data aggregation, use a specific (Gaussian) characteristic, and are taught in an unusual manner. We will not go into elaborate details about these specific neurons that are used mainly to create special networks called radial basis functions (RBFs). Figure 2.15 shows a radial neuron to allow a comparison with the typical neuron shown in Figure 2.14.

2.3 Attempts to Model Biological Neurons

All artificial sigmoid and radial neurons described in this chapter and elsewhere in this book are simplified models of real biological neurons, as noted earlier. Now let us see the true extent of simplification of artificial neurons in reality. We shall use the example of research of Goddard et al. (2001) to illustrate this point.

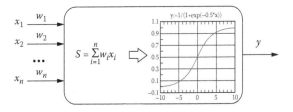

Figure 2.14   Most common neural network component: the MLP neuron.

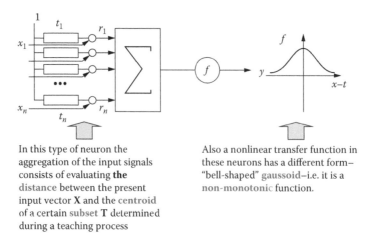

In this type of neuron the aggregation of the input signals consists of evaluating **the distance** between the present input vector **X** and the centroid of a certain subset **T** determined during a teaching process

Also a nonlinear transfer function in these neurons has a different form– "bell-shaped" gaussoid–i.e. it is a non-monotonic function.

Figure 2.15 Structure and peculiar properties of radial neuron.

For many years, de Schutter tried to model in detail the structure and working of a single neuron known as the Purkinje cell. His model utilized electric systems that, according to Hodgkin and Huxley (Nobel Prize in 1963), modeled bioelectrical activities of individual fibers (dendrites and axons) and cell membranes of neuron soma. He was successful in generating with extraordinary accuracy the shape of a real Purkinje cell after considering Neher's and Sakamann's research (Nobel Prize in 1991) on the functioning of so-called ion channels.

The modeled cell structure and replacement circuit used in Goddard et al. (2001) model are shown in Figure 2.16. The model turned out to be very complicated and involved costly calculations. For example, it required 1,600 so-called compartments (cell fragments treated as homogeneous parts containing specific substances in specific concentrations), 8,021 models of ion channels, 10 different complicated mathematical descriptions of ion channels dependent on voltage, 32,000 differential equations, 19,200 parameters to estimate when tuning the model, and a precise description of the cell morphology based on precise microscopic images.

It is no surprise that many hours of continuous work on a large supercomputer were needed to simulate several seconds of "life" of such a nerve cell. Despite this issue, the results of the modeling are very impressive. One result is presented in Figure 2.17.

The results of these experiments are unambiguous. This attempt at faithful modeling of the structure and action of a real biological neuron was successful but simply too expensive for creating practical neural networks for widespread use.

Since then, researchers used only simplified models. Despite the extent of simplification they represent, we know that neural networks can solve certain problems effectively and even allow us to draw interesting conclusions about the behavior of human brain.

2.4 How Artificial Neural Networks Work

From the earlier description of neural networks, it follows that each neuron possesses a specific internal memory (represented by the values of current weights and bias) and certain abilities to convert input signals into output signals. Although these abilities are rather limited (a neuron is a low-cost processor within a system consisting of thousands of such elements),

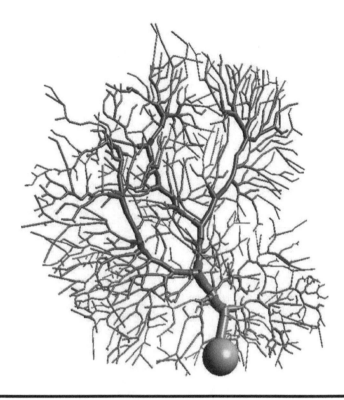

Figure 2.16 de Schutter's model of Purkinje cell neuron that clearly resembles biological original. (Source: http://homepages.feis.herts.ac.uk/~comqvs/images/purkinje_padraig.png)

neural networks are valuable components of systems that perform very complex data process-ing tasks.

As a result of the limited amount of information gathered by a single neuron and its poor com-puting capabilities, a neural network usually consists of several neurons that act only as a whole. Thus, all the capabilities and properties of neural networks noted earlier result from collective performances of many connected elements that constitute the whole network. This specialty of computer science is known as massive parallel processing (MPP).

Let us now look at the operational details of a neural network. It is clear from the above dis-cussion that the network program, the information constituting the knowledge database, the data calculated, and the calculation process are all completely distributed. It is not possible to point to an area where specific information is stored even though neural networks may function as memo-ries, especially as so-called associative memories and have shown impressive performance. It is also impossible to relate certain areas of a network to a selected part of the algorithm used, for example, to indicate which network elements are responsible for initial processing and analysis of input data and which elements produce final network results.

We will now analyze how a neural network works and what roles the single elements play in the whole operation. We assume that all network weights are already determined (i.e., the teach-ing process has been accomplished). Teaching a network is a vital and complex process that will be covered in subsequent chapters. We will start this analysis from the point where a new task is presented to a network. The task is represented by a number of input signals appearing at all input

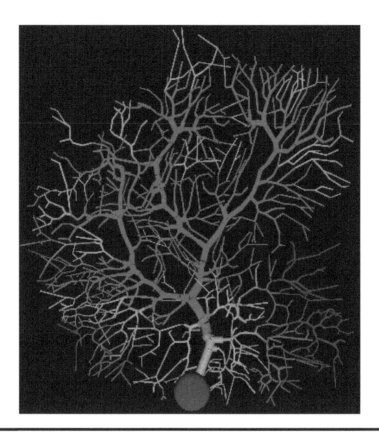

Figure 2.17 Example result obtained by de Schutter. (Source: http://www.tnb.ua.ac.be/models/ images/purkinje.gif)

ports. In Figure 2.18, these signals are represented by red (tone) dots. The input signals reach the neurons in the input layer. These neurons usually do not process the signals; they only distribute them to the neurons in the hidden layer (Figure 2.19).

Note that the distinct nature of the input layer neurons that only distribute signals rather than process them is generally presented graphically by various types of symbols (e.g., a triangle instead of a square).

The next stage involves activation of the neurons in the hidden layer. These neurons use their weights (hence utilizing the data they contain) first to modify the input signals, aggregate them, and then, accordingly to their characteristics (shown in Figure 2.20 as sigmoid functions), calculate the output signals that are directed to the neurons in the output layer.

This stage of data processing is crucial for neural networks. Even though the hidden layer is invisible outside the network (its signals cannot be registered at the input or output ports), this layer is where most of the task solving is performed. Most of the network connections and their weights are located between the input and the hidden layers. We can say that most of the data gathered in the teaching process is located in this layer.

The signals produced by the hidden layer neurons do not have direct interpretations, unlike input or output signals—every single signal has a meaning for the task being solved. However, using a manufacturing process analogy, the hidden layer neurons produce semiproducts, that is, signals characterizing the task in such a way that it is relatively easy to use them

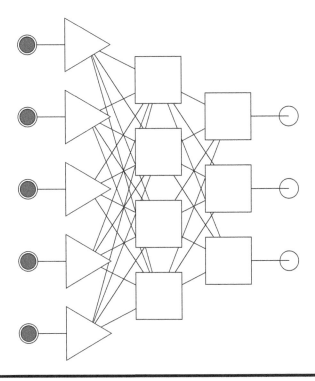

Figure 2.18   Neural network starts working when signals carrying a new task appear at input ports.

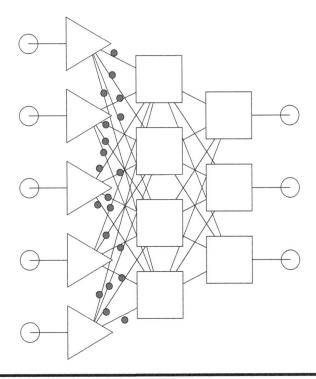

Figure 2.19   Unprocessed input signals are sent to all neurons in a hidden layer.

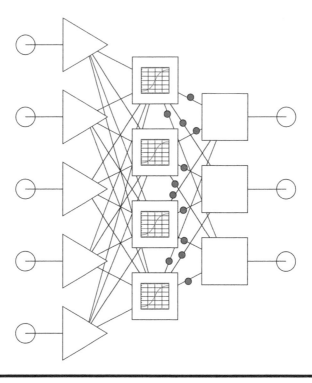

Figure 2.20 After processing signals, neurons from a hidden layer produce intermediate signals and direct them to neurons in an output layer.

later to assemble the final product (the final solution determined by output layer neurons; see Figure 2.20).

Following the performance of the network at the final stage of task solving, we can see that the output layer neurons take advantage of their abilities to aggregate signals and their characteristics to build the final solution at the network output ports (Figure 2.21). In summary, a network always works as a whole and all its elements contribute to performing all the tasks of the network. The process is similar to a hologram reproduction where one can reproduce a complete picture of a photographed object from pieces of a broken photographic plate.

One of the advantages of network performance is its unbelievable ability to work properly even after a failure of a significant portion of its elements. Frank Rosenblatt, a neural network researcher, taught his networks certain abilities (such as letter recognition) and then tested them as he damaged more and more of their elements. The networks were special electronic circuits. Rosenblatt could damage a significant part of a network and it would continue to perform properly (Figure 2.22). Failure of a higher number of neurons and connections would deteriorate the quality of performance in that the damaged part of the network would make more mistakes (e.g., recognize *O* as *D*) but it would not fail to work.

Compare this behavior to the fact that the failure of a single element of a modern electronic device such as a computer or television can cause it to stop working. Thousands of neurons within a human brain die every day for many reasons, but our brains continue to work unfailingly throughout our lives. Details of this fascinating property of the neural network are described in a paper by Tadeusiewicz et al. (2011).

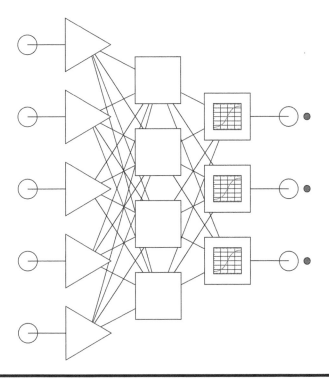

Figure 2.21   Neurons from an output layer use information from neurons in a hidden layer and calculate final results.

2.5 Impact of Neural Network Structure on Capabilities

Let us consider now the relationship between the structure of a neural network and the tasks it can perform. We already know that the neurons described previously are used to create networks. A network structure is created by connecting outputs of neurons with inputs of other neurons based on a chosen design. The result is a system capable of parallel and fully concurrent processing of diverse information.

Considering all these factors, we usually choose layer-structured networks and connections between the layers are made on a one-to-one basis. Obviously the specific topology of a network (the numbers of neurons in layers) should be based on the types of tasks the network is to perform.

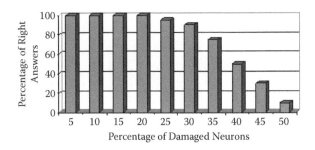

Figure 2.22   Neural networks work properly even if some elements are damaged.

In theory the rule is simple: the more complicated the task, the more neurons in a network are needed to solve it. A network with more neurons is simply more intelligent. In practice, however, this concept is not as unequivocal as it appears.

The vast literature about neural networks contains numerous works proving that the decisions related to a network's structure affect its behavior far less than expected. This paradoxical statement derives from the fact that behavior of a network is determined fundamentally by the network teaching process and not by its structure or number of elements it contains. This means that a well-taught network that has a questionable structure can solve tasks more efficiently than a badly trained network with an optimal structure. Many experiments were performed on network structures created by randomly deciding which elements to connect in what way. Despite their casual designs, the networks were capable of solving complex tasks.

Let us take a closer look at the consequences of the statement about random design because they are interesting and important. If a randomly designed network can achieve correct results despite its structure, its teaching process allowed it to adjust its parameters to operate as required based on a chosen algorithm. This means the system will run correctly despite its fully randomized structure. These experiments were first performed in the early 1970s by Frank Rosenblatt. The researcher rolled dice or drew lots and, depending on the results, connected certain elements of a network together. The resulting structure was completely chaotic (Figure 2.23). After teaching, the network could solve tasks effectively.

Rosenblatt's reports of his experiments were so astonishing that scientists did not believe his results were possible until the experiments were repeated. The systems similar to the perceptron built by Rosenblatt were developed and studied around the world (Hamill et al., 1981). Such networks with random connections could always learn to solve tasks correctly; however, the teaching process for a random network is more complex and time consuming compared to teaching a network whose structure relates reasonably to the task to be solved.

It is interesting that philosophers were also interested in Rosenblatt's results. They claimed that the results proved a theory proclaimed by Aristotle and later extended by Locke. The philosophical concept is *tabula rasa.* The mind is considered a blank page that is filled in by learning and

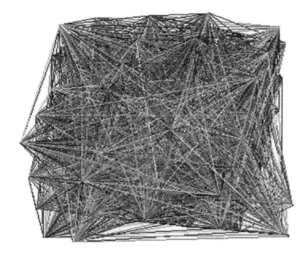

Figure 2.23   Network structure for elements connected to each other using randomization rules.

life experience. Rosenblatt proved that this concept is technically possible, at least in the form of a neural network. Another issue is whether the concept works for all humans. Locke claimed that inborn abilities amounted to nothing and gained knowledge was everything.

We cannot comment on Locke's statement but we certainly know that neural networks gain all their knowledge only by learning adjusted to the task structure. Of course, the network structure must be complex enough to allow "crystallization" of the needed connections and structures. A network that is too small will never learn anything because its "intellectual potential" would be inadequate.

The important issue is the number of elements, not the structure design. For example, no one teaches relativity theory to a rat although a rat may be trained to find its way through complicated labyrinths. Similarly, no human is programmed at birth to be a surgeon, an architect, or a laborer. Careers and jobs are choices. No statements about equality will change the fact that some individuals have remarkable intellectual resources and some do not.

We can apply this idea to network design. We cannot construct a network with inborn abilities although it is easy to create a cybernetic moron that has too few neurons to learn. A network can perform widely diverse and complex tasks if it is big enough. Although it seems that a network cannot be too large, size can create complications as we will see in Section 2.13.

2.6 Choosing Neural Network Structures Wisely

Despite studies indicating that a randomly constructed network can solve a problem, a formalized neural structure is obviously more desirable. A reasonably designed structure that fits the problem requirements at the beginning can significantly shorten learning time and improve results. That is why we want to present some information about construction of neural networks even though it may not provide solutions for all kinds of construction problems.

Choosing a solution to a construction problem without sufficient information is very difficult if not impossible. Placing a neural network constructor in a situation that allows it to adopt any structure freely is similar to the problem of the abecedarian computer engineer who is confused by the "press any key" system message. Which key? You may laugh about that but we hear a similar question from our graduate students: what is "any structure" of a neural network?

We must note a few facts about common neural network structures. Not all aspects of all structures are completely understood. Designing a neural network requires both cerebral hemispheres to deal with the logical and creative issues. We start by classifying commonly used neural network structures into two major classes: neural networks with and without feedback. Neural networks without feedback are often called feed-forward types. Networks in which signals can circuit for unlimited time are called recurrent.

The feed-forward networks follow a strictly determined direction of signal propagation. Signals go from defined input, where data relevant to the problem arrives in the neural network, to output where the network produces a result (Figure 2.24). These types of networks are the most common and useful. We will talk about them later in this chapter and elsewhere in this book.

The recurrent networks are characterized by feedback (Figure 2.25). Signals can circuit between neurons for a very long time before they reach a fixed state. In some cases, these networks do not produce fixed states. In Figure 2.25, the connections presented as red (outer) arrows are feedbacks so the network depicted is recurrent.

Recurrent network properties and abilities are more complex than feed-forward networks. Furthermore, their computational potentials are astonishingly different from those of other types of neural networks. For instance, they can solve optimization problems. They can search for best

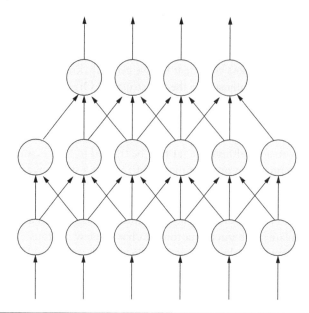

Figure 2.24 Example structure of a feed-forward neural network. Neurons represented by circles are connected to allow transmission signals only from input to output.

possible solutions—a task that is almost impossible for feed-forward networks. Among all recurrent networks, a special place belongs to those named after John Hopfield. In Hopfield networks, the one and only type of connection between neurons is feedback (Figure 2.26).

Some time ago, the solution of the famous traveling salesman problem by a Hopfield network was a global sensation. Given a set of cities and the distance between each possible pair, the traveling salesman problem is to find the best possible way of visiting all the cities exactly once and returning to the starting point. A solution of this problem using neural networks was presented for the first time in a paper by Hopfield and Tank (1985). Afterward, the problem has been discussed

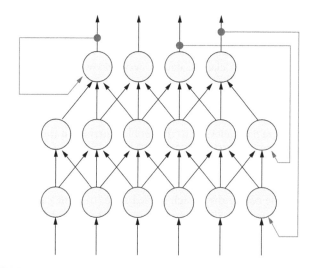

Figure 2.25 Example structure of a recurrent neural network.

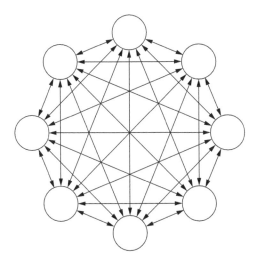

Figure 2.26   Hopfield neural network. All connections are of feedback type.

many times in numerous papers (e.g., Gee and Prager, 1995). One recently published paper about using neural networks for solving the traveling salesman problem was authored by Wang, Zhang, and Creput (2013). The event opened a path for Hopfield networks to manage the important NP-complete (nondeterministic polynomial time) class of computational problems, but this is something we will discuss later. Despite this sensational breakthrough, Hopfield networks did not become as popular as other types of neural networks, so we will cover them in Chapter 11.

Building a neural network with feedbacks is far more difficult than constructing a feed-forward net. Controlling a network involving multiple simultaneous dynamic processes is also much more difficult than controlling a network where signals uniformly go from input to output. For this reason, we will start with one-directional signal flow networks and then progress to recurrent nets.

If we focus on feed-forward networks, the best and most common way to characterize their structure is a layer model in which we assume that neurons are clustered in sets called layers. Major interlinks exist between neurons in adjacent layers. This kind of structure is mentioned early in the chapter, but is worth another look (Figure 2.27).

As noted earlier, links between neurons from adjacent layers may be constructed in many different ways but the most common configuration is all-to-all linkage. The learning process will cut off unneeded connections automatically by setting their coefficients (weights) to zero.

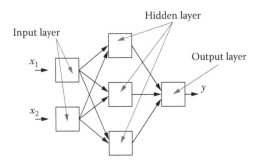

Figure 2.27   Layered structure of simplest neural network.

2.7 "Feeding" Neural Networks: Input Layers

Among all layers that constitute a neural net, we begin with the input layer whose purpose is to collect and convert data outside the network (tasks to be completed, problems to be solved) to inputs. The input layer decision is fairly easy. The number of elements in the layer is determined strictly by the amount of incoming data to be analyzed for a specific task or problem. However, sometimes decisions about which and how many data should be fed to a neural net become quite complex.

Assume, for example, that we want to predict how stock indices will behave. It is well known that some researchers achieve encouraging results that surely produce increased income for those willing to take risks by selling or buying stocks based on outputs produced by neural nets. However, publications revealing data used as inputs are harder to find. Neural nets are applied after they master learning routines.

Users receive outputs in the forms of colorful graphs showing how well the stocks performed. Inputs are described vaguely, for example, "The network utilized information about earlier stock returns and financial analysis documentation." Obviously, preparation and results are explained, but the actual operation of such networks remains an interesting secret.

Another important yet subtle issue is that numeric inputs and outputs are usually limited. Most implementations assume all neuron inputs to be digits from 0 to 1 (or better, from −1 to +1). If we require results outside that range, we need scaling (Figure 2.28).

The problem with scaling inputs is actually less important than dealing with results as shown in the next section. Inputs may be assigned any signal with any value. However, outputs are defined by neuron characteristics. Neurons can produce only signals for which they are programmed. To preserve unitary interpretation of all signals in a neural network and assign importance weights, we usually scale output data. Scaling also aids normalization of input variables.

It is difficult to guarantee network equivalency of input signals. The main problem is that the values of some important variables are naturally very small, whereas other less important variables produce high values. Inputs of a neural net used by a doctor to help diagnose patients could be

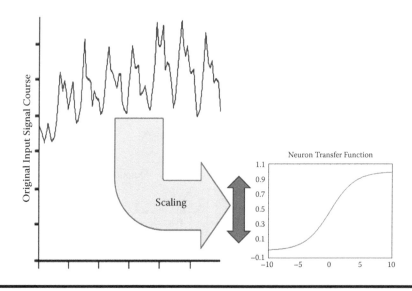

Figure 2.28 Scaling of original input signal for proper representation in a neural network.

levels of erythrocytes (red blood cells) and body temperature. Both variables are equally important to the network although the doctor may be influenced by one value or the other. However, human body temperature is generally a low number (36.6 degrees Celsius for a healthy man) and even its slight changes up or down may indicate serious health issues.

The number of red blood cells is normally about 5 million. A difference of a million cells is not a cause for alarm. Remember scaling? A neuron seeing two inputs at different levels would ignore the difference. Normalization or scaling allows us to treat every input according to its importance defined by the neural net creator rather than its numerical value.

2.8 Nature of Data: The Home of the Cow

The next problem is more difficult. Data provided to a neural network or generated by it as a result of solving a problem may not always be numerical nature. Not everything in our world can be measured and described numerically. Many data to be used as inputs into or outputs from a neural network have a qualitative, descriptive, or nominal nature. This means that their values are represented by names instead of numbers. As an example, assume your task is to design a neural network to distinguish whether certain animals may or may not be dangerous to humans. (We have published similar problems on the Internet.)

The task needs inputs, for example, the part of the world where the animal lives. If an animal is big, has horns, and gives milk, it is probably a cow. What determines whether it is dangerous is the continent where it lives. European and Asian cows are calm and mellow as a rule. Some American cows reared on open pastures are dangerous. Therefore, to decide whether an animal is or is not dangerous, the task involves a variable that indicates an animal's origin. However, how do we distinguish Asia from America as inputs of a neural network?

A solution for the input problem is use of a representation called *one of N* where *N* denotes the number of different possible values (names) that the nominal variable may adopt. Figure 2.29 shows a coding system for the *one of N* method in which $N = 3$. The principle is simple and involves using for every nominal variable as many neurons in an input layer as different values of a specific variable may adopt (which is simply N). If, for example, we assume that an animal may come only from Asia, America, or Europe, we must designate a set of three neurons to represent the origin variable. We then we want to inform a network that in this case one origin variable is

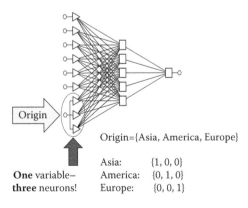

Figure 2.29 Nominal input data coding method.

the America name. We assign a signal of value 0 to the first input, 1 to the second input, and 0 again to the third input.

You may ask: why complicate things? Perhaps a better idea is to code Asia as 1, America as 2, and Europe as 3, then assign the values to one input of the network. If the signal on the input assumes values ranging from 0 to 1, let Asia be 0, America be 0.5, and Europe be 1. Why has no one thought of this earlier?

The hypothetical solution proposed above is unsatisfactory. Neural networks are very weak in the area of analyzing values shown to them. If you adopt the 1, 2, 3 coding system, a neural network in the learning phase will assume Europe is three times more valuable or larger than Asia and that is nonsensical. Even worse will be the application of scaling to the problem. That will indicate that America can be converted to Europe (by multiplying by 2) and Asia cannot be converted because 0 multiplied by any number always totals 0.

In brief, all nominal values have to be represented with the *one of N* technique even though this will increase the number of inputs, connections, and layers of a network. Of course this is inconvenient, because every connection in a network is related to a weight coefficient whose value must be determined in the course of teaching. Additional inputs and connections require more teaching. In spite of this inconvenience, no better solution exists at present. A designer must multiply inputs related to every nominal variable by using the *one of N* schema until a better method is devised.

One more point must be considered: an exception to the *one of N* rule that arises when $N = 2$. One binary nominal variable may be gender for which we can code male = 0, female = 1 or vice versa, and a network will cope with it. However, this kind of binary data is the exception that proves the rule that nominal data should be coded by the *one of N* method.

2.9 Interpreting Answers Generated by Networks: Output Layers

The second component we will discuss in this chapter is the output layer that generates the solutions to the problem considered. The solutions take the form of output signals from the network. Thus, their interpretation is vital because we must understand what the network wants to tell us.

Determining the number of exit neurons is simpler than deciding the number of entrance signals because we usually know how many and what kinds of solutions we need. Thus we have no need to deal with the steps of adding or dropping signals required for designing input layers. Coding procedures are similar for both the input and output layers. The numerical variables should be scaled to allow the neurons at the output layer to produce a number that represents the correct solution to a problem. The nominal values to be presented as outputs should follow the *one from N* method. However, a few typical problems arise in the output layer, as discussed below.

The first problem arises directly from use of the *one from N* method. Recall that the signal with maximum value (usually 1) in this method can have only one neuron on exit—a name represented as a value of a nominal variable. All remaining neurons representing one variable group should have values equal to zero. This ideal situation in which the nominal variable at the output layer is correctly indicated is shown in Figure 2.30. The convention used is that the network is (in some sense) a reversal of the task in Figure 2.29. In that case, the input requirement was the name of the continent where the classified animal lives as the first step in determining whether the animal is dangerous. An animal entry must indicate the continent where it lives.

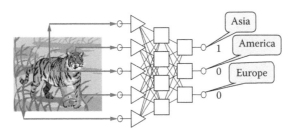

Figure 2.30   Ideal situation: output of a network producing nominal variable.

The situation shown in Figure 2.30 is theoretical; it could happen in practice only as a result of a favorable coincidence. In practice, considering the limited precision of computations performed by networks (discussed below), neuron outputs often include a nominal variables with non-zero signals as shown Figure 2.31. What should we do about this?

To obtain clear and unequivocal answers in such situations, some additional criteria may be useful in working with network outputs. These additional criteria for post-processing of results are known as the threshold of acceptance and threshold of rejection. The exit signals computed by the neurons belonging to output layer of the network are, according to this concept, quantified by comparison of their current values with thresholds as shown in Figure 2.32.

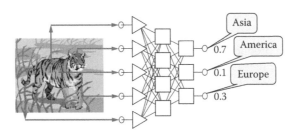

Figure 2.31   Real situation that can arise when working with nominal variables as network outputs.

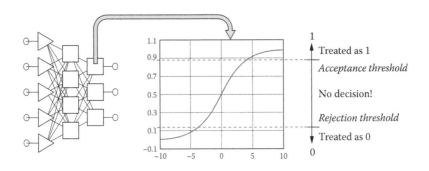

Figure 2.32   Result of output signal post-processing showing unambiguous result values despite inaccurate neuron output values.

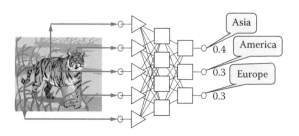

Figure 2.33   Situation in which the only proper network answer is "identification not possible."

The values of the threshold of acceptance and threshold of rejection parameters can be chosen to meet user needs. Experience shows that it is better to set high requirements for a network without trying by force to determine unequivocal values of exit variable nominals, for example, in situations of low clarity as in Figure 2.33. It is also wise to admit that a network is not able to achieve an unequivocal classification of the input signal than to accept a network decision that is probably false.

2.10 Preferred Result: Number or Decision?

While using a neural network, we must remember that results returned by the network even if they are numeric values (that may be subject to appropriate scaling) are always approximate. The quality of the approximation can vary, but significant figures should be accurate.

Accuracy is good if a product returned by a neuron has accuracy higher than two significant figures, which also means that the fault can reach several percent. That is the nature of the tool. Awareness of such limitations dictates an appropriate interpretation of the output signals so that they can be useful and also induces thinking about which neural calculations model should be used. Generally, neural networks can form regressive and classification models. In a regressive model, the output of the network must generate a specific numeric value that represents a solution of the problem. Figure 2.34 presents an interpretation of such a model.

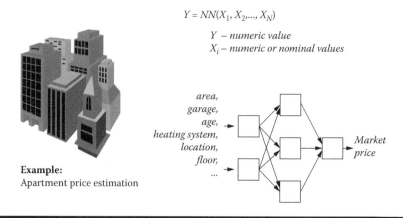

Figure 2.34   Example of a neural network regressive model.

In Figure 2.34, the task of the neural network is to estimate the price of an apartment. At the input, we load data that can be numeric values (e.g., area in square meters) and data that are nominal (e.g., whether an apartment has an assigned garage). Conversely, we expect the output to be a numeric value indicating the amount that may be gained from a sale. As all apartment buyers and sellers know, a market price depends on many factors. No one can present strict economic rules for predicting absolutely accurate apartment prices. Accurate prediction is seemingly impossible because price is determined by a combination of market factors, decisions made by buyers and sellers, and timing. Still it appears that a neural network after long training (based on historical buy and sell transaction data) can form a regressive model of the problem so efficient that real prices for successive transactions may differ from predicted prices by only a few percentage points.

The alternative classification model requires information for classifying an object described by input data to one of the predefined classes. Of course, in this type of problem, a nominal output variable will be assigned (Figure 2.35). The example in the figure concerns the classification of individuals of companies seeking bank loans. Potential borrowers must be classified by a bank worker in one of two categories:

1. Clients who are trustworthy and reliable, who will repay loans with interest and thus generate bank profits.
2. Fraudulent applicants and potential bankrupts who will not repay their loans, thus exposing the bank to losses.

How can one distinguish one category from the other? While no strict rules or algorithms exist for this question, a correct answer can be provided by a neural network taught with historical data. Banks grant many loans and compile complete data on clients who have and have not repaid their loans and thus have a lot of relevant history information.

Years of experiences in neural network exploitations proved that it is most convenient to interpret the tasks given to a neuron network computer in a way that would allow answers utilizing the classification model. For example, we can specify that a network will state the profitability of an investment as low, average, or high or classify as borrower as reliable, risky, or totally unreliable. However, demanding that a network estimate the amount of profit, determine a risk level, or limit

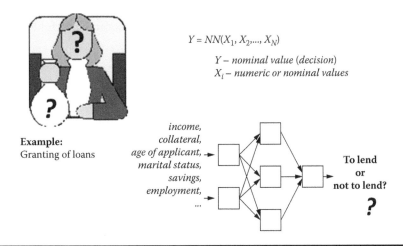

Figure 2.35 Example of a neural network classification model.

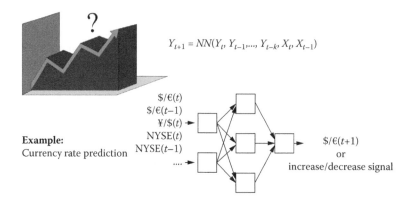

Figure 2.36 Currency rate estimation using a neural network.

the amount loaned to a customer will inevitably lead to frustration because in general a neural network cannot perform these tasks. That is why the number of the outputs of a network usually exceeds the number of questions posed. This happens because we must add a few artificial neurons to service all output signals to allow the predicted range of output signal values to be divided into certain distinct subranges essential for the user. We should not force a network to return a specific "guessed" value as an output. Instead, each output neuron is responsible for signalizing a certain answer within a specific range and usually that is all we need.

Such classification networks are easy to build and teach. Constructing a neural network intended to "squeeze out" specific answers to mathematical problems is time consuming and yields minimal practical application. These issues are illustrated by Figure 2.36, which presents a "classic" neural network problem: prediction of currency rates.

Currency rate estimation is one of many problems that require the creator of a neural network to choose between regressive and classification models. As shown in Figure 2.36, the problem can be solved in two ways: A designer can build a prognostic model that attempts to determine how many euros a dollar will be worth tomorrow or he or she can be satisfied with a model that will only indicate whether the exchange rate will rise or fall tomorrow. The second task is far easier for a network to solve and the prediction of exchange rate rise or fall can be useful for an individual who wants to exchange currency before traveling abroad.

2.11 Network Choices: One Network with Multiple Outputs versus Multiple Networks with Single Outputs

Another issue related to the design of output layers of neural networks can be solved in two different ways. It is possible to create a network producing any number of outputs to generate sufficient data to solve a problem. Increasing outputs is not always an optimal solution because the teaching of a multiple-output network, while estimating weight values, requires specific compromises that always have negative effects on results.

One example of such a compromise is deciding the role of a neuron in the calculation of the values of several output neurons that receive output signals from neurons while setting a problem for a specific neuron of the hidden layer. It is possible that the role of a given hidden neuron, optimal from the view of generating one output signal from an entire network, will be significantly different from its optimal role for another output.

In such cases, the teaching process will change the weight values in this hidden neuron by adapting it each time to a different role. This will necessitate more teaching that may not be completely successful. That is why it is better to divide a complex problem into smaller subproblems. Instead of designing one network to generate multiple outputs, it is more useful to build several networks that will use the same set of input data but contain separate hidden layers and produce single outputs.

The rule suggested in Figure 2.37 cannot be treated as dogma because some multiple-output networks learn better than those with single outputs. This paradox may not have to be solved. The potential "conflict" (described above) connected to functioning of the hidden neurons and assignment of their roles for calculating several different output values may never occur.

On the contrary, during the teaching process a designer can sometimes observe a specific synergy in setting the parameters of a hidden neuron that are optimal from the view of the "interests" of several output layer neurons. One can achieve success faster and more efficiently with multiple-output networks than with individual networks tuned for each separate output signal.

To decide which solution works best, we recommend testing them both, then making a choice. Our observations, based on experience in building hundreds of networks for various uses and years of examining works by our students, shows that significantly more often a collection of single-output networks is an optimal solution although biological neural networks are more often organized as multi-output aggregates.

Let's consider a network with two outputs: A and B.

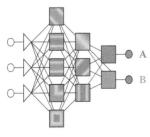

For one network with two outputs, neurons belonging to hidden layer must be collected containing knowledge necessary for calculating values for both outputs: A and B.

Sometimes it can be profitable, especially when there is synergy between the outputs. While working on output A we simultaneously collect knowledge useful when calculating values on output B.

However when collecting hidden layer values useful for calculating A, we break values necessary for B calculation and vice versa.

It is better to built two separate networks:

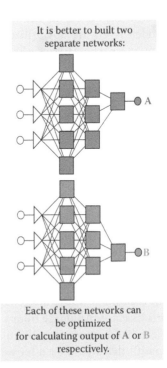

Each of these networks can be optimized for calculating output of A or B respectively.

Figure 2.37 Comparison of one network with two outputs and two separate networks.

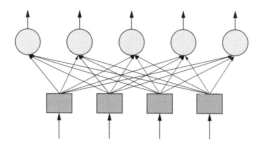

Figure 2.38   Single-layered network.

You already know that every feed-forward network requires at least one input layer and one output layer. However, single-layered networks (see Figure 2.38) utilize only one learning layer. It is, of course, an output layer because input layers of networks do not learn. Many networks, especially those solving more complex problems, must contain additional layers connecting inputs and outputs. They are installed between input and output layers and designated hidden layers. The name sounds mysterious. For that reason we will explain in what sense these layers are hidden

2.12   Hidden Layers

Hidden layers are the tools used to process input signals (received by the input layer) to the output layer in such a way to allow the required response (problem to be solved) to be found easily. Hidden layers are not utilized in every network. If they are present, they cannot be observed by users who assign tasks to a network and then make sure the network performs them correctly.

The user has no access to enter the neurons of hidden layers. He or she must use the input layer neurons to transmit signals to hidden layers. Furthermore, the user cannot access outputs. The effects of hidden layer neurons are revealed only indirectly, via the responses they produce and transmit to the output layer neurons. These layers are "hidden" in the sense that their activities are not directly visible to network users.

Although they are not accessible, these additional layers in neural networks handle a very important function. They create an additional structure that processes information. The simplest way to explain their role is to use the example of network implementation frequently used for pattern recognition tasks. A digital image is produced at the input (first) layer of the network.

The image cannot be a typical camera photo or traditional image loaded into a scanner or frame grabber. The reason is very simple. In a system fed by a simple image at the input (see Figure 2.30), the input layer neurons corresponds to the size and organization (grouping of neurons in corresponding rows and columns) of the image.

Briefly, each point of the image is assigned to the input of a neuron network that analyzes and reports its status. An image from a digital camera or scanner is a set of millions of pixels. It is impossible to build a network with millions of input neurons because it would require billions of connections (!) that would need set weight values. Such a structure is impossible. However, you can imagine a system that processes simplistic digital images consisting of small numbers of pixels arranged in the form of simple characters such as letters as inputs (Figure 2.39).

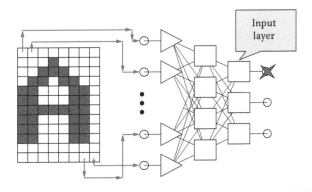

Figure 2.39   Example of a network that recognizes simple images.

The output of the network that is expected to provide certain decisions may be organized so that the outputs of individual neurons assign certain decisions, for example, "A was diagnosed" or "B was diagnosed." The sizes of the signals at these outputs will be interpreted in terms of the degree of certainty of the decision. Note that it is therefore possible for a network to generate ambiguous responses ("x is related to A to the extent of 0.7 and to B to the extent of 0.4 points"). It is one of the interesting and useful features of neural networks that they can be associated with fuzzy logic systems. More comprehensive discussion of this topic goes beyond the scope of this book.

Hidden layer neurons act as intermediaries. They have direct access to the input data and can see the image presented at input. Based on their outputs, additional layers make certain decisions based on certain images. It appears that the role of the hidden layer neurons is to devise pre-processed sets of input data for use by the output layer neurons in determining the final result.

The utility of the intermediate layers arises because certain input transformations make the solution of a network task much easier to achieve than attempts to solve the same task in a direct way. Using a pattern recognition task as an example, it is difficult to find a rule that allows identification of an object when only bright and dark pixels appear in an image. Finding the correct recognition rule that functions at that low level is difficult because the subjects may vary widely in shape but convey the same meaning.

A single object (e.g., the letter A) can look different when scanned from a manuscript, printed on a page, and photographed on a fluttering banner. A printed document containing exactly the same characters can be represented as two completely different pixel images due to pixel values at selected points. A slight movement can change a digital picture in a dramatic way if specific pixels are only white or black. Another difficulty with digital images of low resolution arises when completely different objects display very large sets of identical pixels on digital images.

The expectation that a "one-jump" neural network will overcome these discrepancies between the raw image and the final recognition decision may be unrealistic in some situations. The reasoning is correct because experience confirms that no learning process can ensure that a simple network with no hidden layer will be able to solve every task. Such a network without hidden layers would produce a mechanism by which some selected and established sets of pixels would be treated as belonging to different objects and at other times would link different sets pixels to the same object. This simply cannot be done.

What is not possible for a network with few layers can generally be achieved by a network containing a hidden layer. For complex tasks, neurons in the hidden layer would find certain auxiliary values that significantly facilitate solution of a task. In a pattern recognition task, hidden layer neurons can detect and encode a structure describing the general characteristics of the image and objects within the image. These characteristics should be more responsive to the demands of the final image recognition than the original image. For example, they can be to an extent independent of the position and scale of recognized objects. Examples of features that describe the objects in images of letters (to facilitate their recognition) may be:

■ The presence or absence of closed contour drawing letters (letters O, D, A, and a few others; letters such as I, T, S, N, and others do not have these characteristics)
■ Whether the character has a notch at the bottom (A, X, K), at the top (U, Y, V, K), or at the side (E, F)
■ Rounded (O, S, C) or severe (E, W, T, A) shape

Obviously you can find many more differentiating features of letters that may or may not be insensitive to common factors affecting their recognition (font changes, handwriting, letter size changes, tilting, and panning). However, it should be emphasized that the creator of a neural network does not have to explicitly ask what characteristics of a picture may be found because the network can acquire relevant identification skills during the learning process.

Of course, we have no guarantee that a neural network designed to recognize letters taught its hidden layers to detect and signal precisely the characteristics cited above. A neural network would not detect the characteristics for differentiating letters mentioned above without sufficient training. The experiences of many researchers confirm that neural networks can recognize characteristics that effectively facilitate recognition when performing recognition tasks, although the user of a network cannot understand the relevance of characteristics encoded in hidden layers.

Hidden layers allow a neural network to perform more intelligently by utilizing elements that can extract descriptive image features precisely. Note that the nature of the extracted features is determined by the structure of the network only through the process of learning. In a network designed to recognize images, all features that will be extracted by hidden layer neurons may adapt automatically to the types of recognizable images. If we ask the network to detect masked rocket launchers in aerial photographs, it becomes clear that the main task of the hidden layer will become independent of the position of the object because the shape of the suspect can occur in any area of the image and should always be recognized in the same way.

If a network has to recognize letters, it should not lose information about their positions. A network that will detect an A somewhere on a page is not very useful because the user wants to know where the A is and in what context. In this case, the objective of the hidden layer is to extract features that may allow reliable identification of letters regardless of their size or typeface (font). Interestingly, both these tasks can be achieved after appropriate training by the same network. Of course, a network taught to recognize tanks cannot read printed material and a network trained to identify fingerprints cannot handle face recognition.

2.13 Determining Numbers of Neurons

It follows from the above that the broadest possibilities for future use involve networks structured with at least three layers: (1) an input layer that receives signals, (2) a hidden layer that elicits the relevant characteristics of input signals, and (3) an output layer that makes decisions and provides a solution. Within this structure, certain elements must be determined: the numbers of input and output elements and the methods of connecting successive layers. However, certain variable

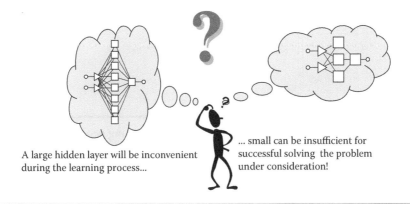

A large hidden layer will be inconvenient during the learning process...

... small can be insufficient for successful solving the problem under consideration!

Figure 2.40   The most important problem for neural network design concerns the number of hidden neurons.

elements may need to be considered: (1) the number of hidden layers and (2) the number of elements within the hidden layer or layers (Figure 2.40).

Despite many years of development of this technology, no precise theory of neural networks has yet been formulated. Network elements are usually chosen arbitrarily or by trial and error. It is possible that a designer's concept of how many hidden neurons to use or how they should be organized (as one hidden layer or several layers) will not operate correctly. Nevertheless, these issues should not exert a critical impact on the total operation because the learning process should provide opportunities to correct possible structure errors by choosing appropriate connection parameters. Still, we warn our readers about two types of errors that may trap designers and researchers of neural networks.

The first error is designing a network with too few elements—no hidden layer or too few neurons. The learning process may fail because the network will not have any chances to imitate in its inadequate structure all the details and nuances of the problem to be solved. Later, we will provide examples demonstrating that a network that is too small and too primitive cannot deal with certain tasks even if it is taught thoroughly for a very long time. Neural networks are somewhat like people. Not all of them are capable of solving certain types of problems. Fortunately, we have an easy way to check how intelligent a network is. We can see its structure and can count its neurons. Thus the measure of a network's capability is merely counting its hidden neurons. The task with humans is more difficult!

Despite the ability to build bigger or smaller networks, it sometimes happens that the intelligence of a network is too low to achieve a specific task. A "neural dummy" that does not have enough hidden neurons will never succeed in its assigned tasks no matter how much teaching it undergoes.

Conversely, network intelligence should not be excessive. The effect of excessive intelligence is not a greater capacity for dealing with assigned tasks. The result is astonishing. Instead of diligently acquiring useful knowledge, the network begins to "fool" its teacher and consequently fails to learn. This may sound incredible but it is true. A network with too many hidden layers or too many elements in its hidden layers tends to simplify a task and "cuts corners" whenever possible. To explain this phenomenon we will briefly describe a network's learning process (Figure 2.41).

You will learn about the details of this process in later chapters. In simple terms, one teaches a network by providing it with input signals for which correct solutions are known because they are included in the learning data. For each given set of input data, the network tries to offer an output solution. Generally, the network's suggestions differ from correct solutions included in the teaching data. After comparing the network solution with the correct exemplar solution in the teaching

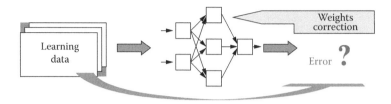

Figure 2.41   Very simplified schema of a neural network learning process.

data, the extent of the error made by the network becomes clear. On the basis of mistake evaluation, the network's teaching algorithm changes the weights of all its neurons so that the error will not be repeated in the future.

This simple model of a learning process indicates that a network tries to make no errors when presented with teaching data. Therefore, a network that learns well seeks a rule for processing input signals that would allow it to derive correct solutions. When a network discovers this rule, it can perform tasks from the teaching data it receives and similar tasks that may be assigned. We consider a successful network one that demonstrates an ability to learn and generalize learning results.

Unfortunately, a network that is too intelligent (has excessive memory in the form of large numbers of hidden neurons together with their adjustable weight sets) can easily avoid mistakes during learning by memorizing a whole collection of teaching data. It then achieves great success in learning within an astonishingly short time because it gives correct answers for all questions. However, in this method of "photographing" teaching data, a network that learns from provided examples of correct solutions makes no attempt at generalizing acquired information. Instead, it tries to achieve success by meticulously memorizing rules like "this input implies this output."

Such incorrect operation of a network becomes obvious when the network quickly and thoroughly learns an entire teaching sequence (set of examples that demonstrate how it should perform assigned tasks) but fails embarrassingly in its first attempt to handle a task from similar class but slightly different from the tasks presented during learning. Teaching a network to recognize letters yields immediate success because it recognizes all letters shown. However, it will fail completely to recognize a letter in a different handwriting or font (all outputs are zero) or recognize them incorrectly. In such cases, an examination of the network's knowledge reveals that it memorized many simple rules like "if two pixels are lit and there are five 0s, letter A should be recognized." Such crude rules do not stand the test of a new task, and networks utilizing them fall short of expectations.

The described symptom of learning by memorizing is not displayed by networks with smaller hidden layers because limited memory forces a network to do its best. By using the few elements of its hidden layer, it works out rules for processing input signals that enable it to generate the required answer. In such cases, the learning process is usually considerably slower and more tedious because the network needs more examples presented more times—a few hundred or a few thousand. However, the final effect is usually much better. After a correctly conducted learning process is complete and a network effectively handles base learning examples, we may assume that it will also cope with similar (not identical) tasks presented during a test. The assumption is often (but not always) true and serves as a base for our expectations for using a network to solve problems.

In summary, do not expect miracles. The presumption that an uncomplicated network with a few hidden neurons will succeed in a complicated task is unrealistic. Conversely, too many hidden layers or too many neurons can cause a significant decline in learning. Obviously, the optimal requirements for hidden layers lie somewhere between these extremes.

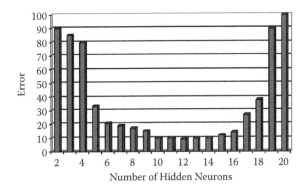

Figure 2.42 **Exemplary relation between hidden neurons and errors made by a network.**

Figure 2.42 shows (on the basis of computer simulations) the relationship of network errors and numbers of hidden neurons. It proves that many networks operate with almost the same efficiency despite different numbers of hidden neurons. Thus it is not so difficult to hit such a broad target. Nevertheless, we must avoid extreme (too large or too small) networks. Especially undesirable are excessive) hidden layers. It is not surprising that networks with fewer hidden layers often produce better results. This is because they can be taught more effectively than better (theoretically) networks with more hidden layers where teaching is buried in unneeded details. The best practice in most situations is to use networks with one or (only as an exception) two hidden layers, and fight the temptation to use networks with more hidden layers—by fasting and taking cold baths!

References

Gee, A.H., and Prager, R.W. 1995. Limitations of neural networks for solving traveling salesman problems, *IEEE Trans. Neural Networks*, vol. 6, pp. 280–282.

Goddard, N., Hood, G., Howell, F., Hines, M., and De Schutter, E. 2001. NEOSIM: Portable large-scale plug and play modelling. *Journal of Neurocomputing*, vol. 38, pp. 1657–1661.

Hamill, O.P., Marty, A., Neher, E., Sakmann, B., and Sigworth, F.J. 1981. Improved patch-clump techniques for high-resolution current recording from cells and cell-free membrane patches. *Pflugers Archive European Journal of Physiology*, vol. 391 (2), pp. 85–100.

Hodgkin, A.L., and Huxley, A.F. 1952. A quantitative description of ion currents and its application to conduction and excitation in nerve membranes. *Journal of Physiology, London,* vol. 117, pp. 500–544.

Hopfield, J.J. 1982. Neural networks and physical systems with emergent collective computational abilities. *Proc. of National Academy Scientific, USA*, vol. 79, pp. 2554–2558.

Hopfield, J.J. 1985. Neural computation of decisions in optimizing problems. *Biological Cybernetics,* vol. 52, pp. 141–152.

Hopfield, J.J., and Tank, D.W. 1985. "Neural" computation of decisions in optimization problems, *Biol. Cybern:* vol. 52, pp. 141–152.

Rosenblatt, F. 1958. The Perceptron: A probabilistic model for information storage and organization in the brain. *Psychological Review*, American Psychological Association, vol. 65, No. 6, pp. 386–408.

Tadeusiewicz, R. and Figura I. 2011. Phenomenon of tolerance to damage in artificial neural networks. *Computer Methods in Material Science*, 11, 501–513.

Wang, H., Zhang, N., and Creput, J.-C. 2013. A massive parallel cellular GPU implementation of neural network to large-scale Euclidean TSP. *Proc. 12th Mexican International Conference on Artificial Intelligence*, MICAI 2013, LNCS vol. 8266, pp. 118–129.

Questions and Self-Study Tasks

1. What are some of the most significant differences between artificial neural networks and natural biological structures such as human and animal brains? Which differences result from capitulation (inability to build enough complicated artificial neurons and settling for substitutes)? Which differences are results of conscious deliberate choices by neural network creators?

2. Discuss the concept of synaptic weight, taking into account its role in artificial neural networks and also its biological inspiration. In electronic circuit modeling, neural networks weights are sometimes discrete (can only take certain values, e.g., integers) rather than arbitrary. How do you think weight exerts an impact on neural network functioning?

3. Introduce an artificial neuron scheme to transform input information into output signals. Demonstrate the differences between these transformation processes in particular types of neurons (linear, MLP, RBF).

4. Discuss the step-by-step operation of an artificial neural network. Why are hidden layers so named?

5. Discuss reactions between neural network structures and the functions the networks perform. Which are most popular neural network structures and what are their properties? Explain the ability of a randomly structured network to perform serious computational tasks.

6. What do you think about the ability of neural networks to show great fault tolerance when they encounter damages to the elements and destruction of their whole structures?

7. Why do neural networks require differentiation of quantitative and qualitative data? There is an opinion that networks that use qualitative data as inputs or outputs need more time for learning because they include more connections for which weights must be established. Is this opinion justified?

8. A network whose output data is encoded via the *one of N* method may not provide precise answers to questions. What could be the result? Should the lack of precision be seen as an advantage or a disadvantage?

9. Can time series analysis and related forecast tasks (see Figure 2.36) be considered more similar to regression tasks (Figure 2.34) or classification tasks (Figure 2.35)? What are the arguments for similarity to (a) regression and (b) classification?

10. Do Figure 2.37 and the text related to it lead to the conclusion that the application of a single network with many outputs is always ineffective? Specifically, if we must solve a problem whose expected output is in the form of qualitative data encoded by the *one of N* method, may we use *N* networks with one output each instead of one network with *N* outputs?

11. Advanced exercise: Assume you want to solve a certain classification with a neural network utilizing input data of questionability applicability and have doubts that the data will yield valuable information in the context of the classification under consideration. The issue is whether to use the doubtful input in a neural network because it could turn out to be useless. You could build your network without using a decision rule for the questionable data, or perhaps it would be better not to mix data to solve task variables that may be worthless. What is your choice? Justify your answer.

12. Advanced exercise: Books and articles describing neural networks sometimes propose the use of a genetic computer algorithm that somewhat simulates natural biological evolution. During evolution, the "fittest" network (having the best capabilities to produce a superior solution) will survive. The algorithm method can be used to select the best inputs for a network, estimate an optimal number of hidden layers, and evaluate the best hidden neurons in each layer. Study more about this method and develop an opinion whether it is or is not effective. Present arguments for both positions.

Chapter 3

Teaching Networks

3.1 Network Tutoring

A neural network's activity cycle can be divided into various stages of learning during which the network acquires information needed to determine what it should do and how, and the stages of regular work when the network must solve specific new tasks based on the acquired knowledge. The key to understanding how a network works and its abilities is the learning process. This chapter details the exact process. Subsequent chapters will cover the activities of already taught networks of various types.

Two variations of learning can be distinguished: one that requires a teacher and one that does not. We are going to talk about learning without a teacher in the next chapter. This chapter will focus on learning with a tutor. Such learning is based on giving a network examples of correct actions that it should learn to mimic. An example normally includes a specific set of input and output signals given by a teacher to show the expected response of the network for a given configuration of input data. The network watches the connection between input data and the required outcome and learns to imitate the rule.

While learning with a tutor you always have to deal with a pair of values: a sample input signal and a desired output (required response) of the network to the input signal. Of course, a network can have many inputs and many outputs. The *pair* in fact represents a complete set of input data and output data that should work as a full solution for a task. The two components (data for a task and output solution) are always required.

The *teacher* and *tutor* terms require explanations at this point. A tutor is not necessarily a human being who teaches a network, even though humans work with and instruct networks. In practice the role of a tutor is taken over by a computer that models the specific network. Unfortunately neural networks are not very smart. Effective learning of a difficult task requires hundreds or sometimes even hundreds of thousands of steps! No human would have the strength and patience to tutor a device that learns so slowly. That is why a teacher or tutor in this context means a computer program supplied by a human with a so-called learning set.

What is a learning set? Figure 3.1. contains a table showing sample data concerning pollution rates in various US cities. Any other type of data could be used. It is important to use real-life data

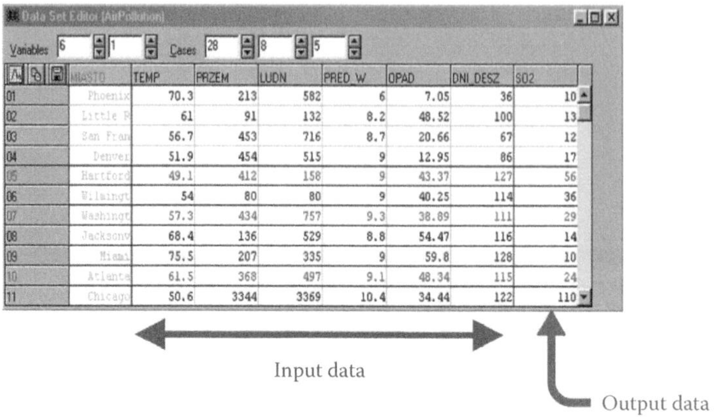

	MIASTO	TEMP	PRZEM	LUDN	PRED_W	OPAD	DNI_DESZ	SO2
01	Phoenix	70.3	213	582	6	7.05	36	10
02	Little R	61	91	132	8.2	48.52	100	13
03	San Fran	56.7	453	716	8.7	20.66	67	12
04	Denver	51.9	454	515	9	12.95	86	17
05	Hartford	49.1	412	158	9	43.37	127	56
06	Wilaingt	54	80	80	9	40.25	114	36
07	Washingt	57.3	434	757	9.3	38.89	111	29
08	Jacksonv	68.4	136	529	8.8	54.47	116	14
09	Miami	75.5	207	335	9	59.8	128	10
10	Atlante	61.5	368	497	9.1	48.34	115	24
11	Chicago	50.6	3344	3369	10.4	34.44	122	110

Figure 3.1 Example of a learning set.

taken from a real database. I demonstrated that, leaving the elements of an original window (from a program operating on this database) in the figure.

Among the data collected in the database, we can isolate those that will be used as outputs for the network. Look at the range of columns of the table marked by an arrow at the bottom of the figure. The data in the figure should allow us to predict levels of air pollution. The data cover population figures, industrialization levels, weather conditions, and other factors. Based on these data to be used as inputs, the network will have to predict the average level of air pollution in every city.

For a city for which pollution level information has not been compiled, we will have to guess. That is where a network taught earlier will go to work. The learning set data—known pollution data for several cities—has been placed in an appropriate column of the table, which is marked with a red arrow (indicating output data) on Figure 3.1.

Therefore, you have exactly the material you need to teach the network shown in Figure 3.1: a set of data pairs containing the appropriate input and output data. We can see the causes (population, industrialization, and weather conditions) and the result (air pollution value). The network uses these data and will learn how to function properly (guessing the values of air pollution in cities for which proper measurements have not yet been made) via a learning strategy.

Exemplary learning strategies will be thoroughly discussed later. In the meantime, please pay attention to another detail of Figure 3.1. The letters in one column of the table are barely visible because they appear in gray instead of black. This shading suggests that the data portrayed are somewhat less important. The column contains names of particular cities. Based on this information, the database generates new data and results given, but for a neural network the column information is useless. Air pollution has no relationship to the name of a city, so even though these facts are available in the database, we are not going to use them to teach networks. Databases can contain a lot of information data that is not needed to teach a network.

We should remember that the tutor involved in network learning will usually be a collection of data that is not used "as is," but is adjusted to function as a learning set after cautious selection and proper configuration (data to be used as inputs and data to be generated as outputs). A network should not be littered with data that a user knows or suspects is not useful for finding solutions to a specific problem.

3.2 Self-Learning

Besides the schema of the learning with a tutor described earlier, a series of methods of learning without a teacher (self-learning networks) are also in use. These methods consist of passing only a series of test data to the input of networks, without indicating desirable or even anticipated output signals. It seems that a properly designed neural network can use only observations of entrance signals and build a sensible algorithm of its own activity based on them, most often relying on the fact that classes of repeated (maybe with certain variety) input signals are automatically detected and the network learns (spontaneously, without any open learning) to recognize these typical patterns of signals.

A self-learning network requires a learning set consisting of data provided for input. No output data are provided because in this technique, we need to clarify the expectations from the network analysis of some data. For example, if we apply the data in Figure 3.1 to learning without a teacher, we would use only columns described as input data instead of giving the information from the column noted with the red pointer to the network.

A self-learning network could not have chance to predict in which city the air pollution would be greater or smaller because it cannot gain such knowledge on its own. However, by analyzing the data on covering different cities, the network may favor (with no help) a group of large industrial cities and learn to differentiate them from small country towns that serve as centers of agricultural regions.

The network will develop this distinction from given input data by following a rule that industrial cities are similar and agricultural towns also share many common characteristics. A network can use a similar rule (without help) to separate cities with good and bad weather and determine many other classifications based only on values of observed input data.

Notice that the self-learning network is very interesting from a view of the analogy between such activities of networks and the activities of human brains. People also have abilities to classify encountered objects and phenomena ("formation of notions") spontaneously. After the execution of the suitable classification, people and networks recognize another object as having characteristics of a previously recognized class.

Self-learning is also very interesting based on its uses. It requires no external knowledge that may be inaccessible or hard to collect. A network will accumulate all necessary information and pieces of news without outside help. Chapter 9 will describe exactly and demonstrate across suitable programs the bases of self-learning of networks.

Now you can imagine (for fun and stimulation of the imagination rather from real need) that a self-learning network with a television camera can be sent in an unmanned space probe to Mars. We are unaware of conditions on Mars. We do not know which objects our probe should recognize or how many classes of objects will appear!

Even without that information, the network will adjust (see Figure 3.2). The probe lands and the network begins the process of self-learning. At first it recognizes nothing and only observes. However, over time, the process of spontaneous self-organization will allow the network to learn to detect and differentiate various types of input signals that appear as inputs: rocks from stones and plant forms from other living organisms. If we give the network sufficient time, it will educate itself to differentiate Martian men from Martian women even though the network creator did not know that Martian people existed!

Of course the self-learning Mars landing vehicle is a hypothetical creation even though networks that form and recognize various patterns exist are in common use. We may be interested in determining how many forms of some little known disease can in fact be found. Is a condition one sickness unit or several? How do the components differ? How can they be cured?

Figure 3.2 Hypothetical planetary landing module powered with a self-learning neural network can discover unknown (alien) forms of life on mysterious planets.

It will be sufficient to show a self-learning neural network the information on registered patients and their symptoms over a long period. The network will later yield information on how many typical groups of symptoms and signs were detected and which criteria can be used to classify patients into different groups. Applications of neural networks to goals like these can lead to a Nobel Prize!

This method of self-learning, of course, has many defects that will be described later. However, self-learning has many undeniable advantages. We should be surprised that the tool is not more popular.

3.3 Methods of Gathering Information

Let us take a closer look at the process of learning with a teacher. How does a network gain and gather knowledge? A key factor is the assignments of weights to each neuron on entrance, as described in Chapter 2.

To review, every neuron has many inputs, by which it receives signals from other neurons and from network data to add its calculations. The parameters called weights are united with the entry data. Every input signal is first multiplied by the weight and only later added to the other signals. If we change values of the weights, a neuron will begin to function within the network in another way and ultimately the entire network will work in another way. The art of learning of a network relies on the choice of weights in such a manner that all neurons will perform the exact tasks the network demands.

A network may contain thousands of neurons and every one of them may handle hundreds of inputs. Thus it is impossible for all these inputs to define the necessary weights simultaneously and without direction. We can, however, design and achieve learning by starting network activities with a certain random set of weights and gradually improving them. In every step of the process of learning, the values of weights from one or several neurons undergo changes. The rules for change are set in such a way that every neuron individual can qualify which of its own weights must change, how (by increase or decrease), and how much.

The teacher passes on the information about the necessary changes of weights that can be used by the neuron. Obviously, what does not change is the fact that the process of changing the weights (as the only memory trace in the network) runs through every neuron of the network spontaneously and independently. In fact, it can occur without direct intervention by the person supervising this process. What is more, the process of the learning of one neuron is independent from how another neuron learns. Thus, learning can occur simultaneously in all neurons of a network (of course only in a suitable network with an adequate electronic system, and not via a simulation program). This characteristic allows us to achieve very high speeds of learning and a surprisingly dynamic increase of qualifications of a network that literally grows wiser and wiser in front of us!

We once again stress a key point: a teacher need not get into the details of the process of learning. It is sufficient for the teacher to give a network an example of a correct solution. The network will compare its own solution obtained from the example originating from the learning set with the solution that was recorded in the learning set as a model (most probably correct). Algorithms of learning are constructed so that the knowledge about the value of an error is sufficient to allow a network to correct values of its weights. Every neuron separately corrects its own weights on all entries under the control of the specific algorithm after it receives an error message.

Figure 3.3 depicts a very simple but efficient mechanism. Its systematic use causes the network to perfect its own activities until it is able to solve all assignments from the learning set and on the grounds of generalization of this knowledge. It can also handle assignments that will be introduced to it at the examination stage.

The manner of network learning described earlier is used most often, but some assignments (e.g., image recognition) do not require a network to have the exact value of a desired output signal. For efficient learning, it is sufficient to give a network only general information on a subject, whether its current behavior is correct, or not. At times, network experts speak about "rewards" and "punishments" in relation to the way all neurons in a network find and introduce proper corrections to their own activities without outside direction. This analogy to the training of animals is not accidental.

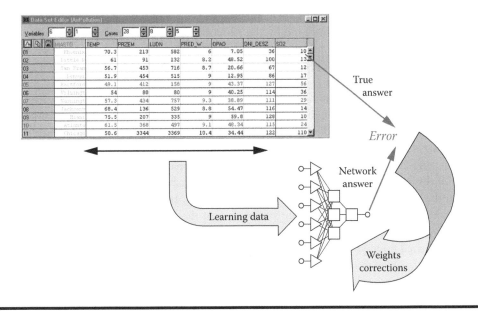

Figure 3.3   Typical steps of neural network learning.

3.4 Organizing Network Learning

Necessary changes of values of weight coefficients in each neuron are counted according to special rules (sometimes called paradigms of networks). The numbers of different rules that are used today and their varieties are extreme because most researchers try to demonstrate their own contributions to the field of neural networks as new rules of learning.

We now consider two basic rules of learning without using mathematics: (1) the rule of the quickest fall lying at the bases of most algorithms of learning with a teacher and (2) the Hebb rule defining the simplest example of learning without a teacher (see Section 3.10).

The rule of the quickest fall relies on the receipt by every neuron of definite signals from the network or from other neurons. The signals result from earlier levels of processing the information. A neuron generates its own output signal using its knowledge of earlier settled values of all amplification factors (weights) of all entries and (possibly) the threshold.

Methods of marking the values of output signals by neurons based on input signals were discussed in detail in Chapter 2. The value of the output signal of a neuron at each step of the process of learning is compared with the standard answer of the teacher within the learning set.

In the case of divergence that will appear almost certainly at the initial stage of the learning process, the neuron finds the difference between its own output signal and the value of the signal the teacher indicates is correct. The neuron then (by the method of the quickest fall to be described shortly) decides how to change the values of the weights to decrease the error.

It is useful to understand the area of an error. You already know that the activity of a network relies on the values of weight coefficients of the constituent neurons. If you know the set of all weight coefficients appearing in all neurons of the entire network, you know how such a network will act. Particularly you can show a network all examples of assignments and solutions accessible as part of the learning set. Every time the network produces its own answer to an asked question, you can compare its answer to the pattern of the correct answer found in the learning set, thus revealing the network error.

A measure of this error is usually the difference between the value of the result delivered by the network and the value of the result read from the learning set. To rate the overall activities of networks with defined sets of weight coefficients in their neurons, we usually use the pattern of the sum of squares of errors committed by the network for each case from the learning set. The errors are squared before summing to avoid the effect of mutual compensation of positive and negative errors. This results in heavy penalties for large errors. A twice greater error is a quadruple component in the resulting sum.

Note in Figure 3.4 the yellow (lighter tone) rectangle and cloud first, then the green (darker tone) rectangle and cloud. The figure depicts a situation that could occur in a network so small that it would have only two coefficients of weights. Such small neural networks do not exist, but let us assume that you have such a very small network. We will attempt to analyze its behavior without getting into difficulties arising from multidimensional spaces. Every state of good or poor learning of this network will be joined at some point on the horizontal (light blue) visible surface shown in the figure with its weight coefficient coordinates. Imagine now that you placed weight values in the network that comply with the location of the red point on the surface. Examining such a network by means of all elements of the learning set will reveal the total value of the error. In place of the red point you will put a red arrow pointing up. The height will represent the calculated value of the error according to the vertical axis in the figure.

Next, choose other values of weights, marking their positions on the surface (navy blue) and perform the same steps utilizing the navy blue pointer. Imagine that you perform these acts for all combinations of weight coefficients, that is, for all points of the light blue surface. Some errors will

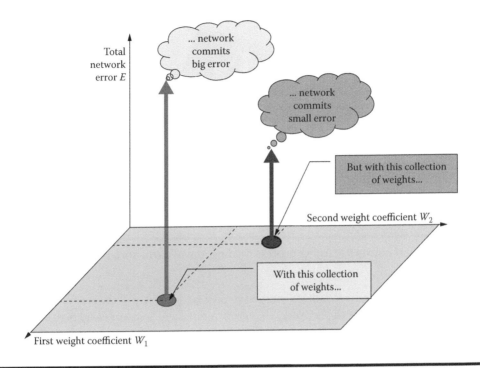

Figure 3.4   Error surface formation.

be greater and other smaller. If you had the patience to examine your network many times, you would see the error surface spread over the surface of the changed weights.

You can see many "knolls" on the surface in Figure 3.5. These indicate where the network committed several errors and should be avoided. The neural network committed smaller errors as shown by the deep valleys. This indicates the network solves its tasks especially well, but how do we find the valleys?

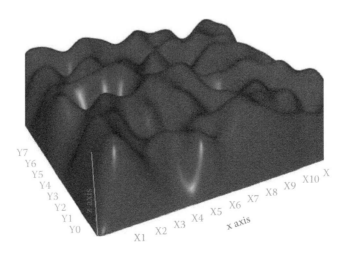

Figure 3.5   Error surface formed during neural network learning.

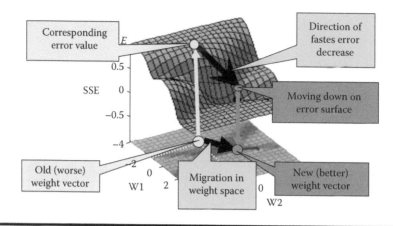

Figure 3.6   Neural network learning process "sliding down" error surface.

The learning of a neural network is a multistage-process. Each step of the process is intended to improve values of weights in the network, changing unsatisfactory sets of weights that may cause large errors for new weights that hopefully will perform better (see Figure 3.6).

Starting at the bottom left corner of the figure, we see an old (vector) set of weights, noted on the parameter surface of the network with a yellow (light tone) circle. For this vector of weights, you find the error and "land" on the surface of the error shown with a yellow arrow in the left upper corner of the figure. The error rate is very high and the network temporarily has incorrect parameters. It is necessary to improve this situation, but how?

A neural network can be taught to find a way to change the weight coefficients to decrease error rates. The direction of the quickest fall of the error is noted in Figure 3.6 as a large black pointer. Unfortunately, the details of the learning method cannot be explained without using complicated mathematics and such notions as the gradient and partial derivative. However, the conclusions yielded by these complex mathematical considerations are simple enough. Every neuron in a network modifies its own weight and possibly threshold coefficients using two simple rules:

1. Weights are changed more strongly when great errors are detected.
2. Weights connected on which large values of input signals appeared are changed more than weights on which input signals were small.

The basic rules may need additional corrections even though the outline of the method of learning is understood. Recognizing an error committed by a neuron and knowing its input signals allow a designer to foresee easily how its weights will change. The mathematics-based rules are very logical and sensible. For example, the faultless reaction of a neuron to a specific input signal should proceed without a change if its weights are correctly calculated.

A network using prescribed methods in practice breaks the process of learning when it is well trained. Small errors require only minimum cosmetic corrections of weights. It is logical to subordinate the size of a correction based on the size of the input signal delivered. Inputs that have greater signals exert more influence on the result of the activity of a neuron. To ensure a neuron operates correctly, it must be "sharpened."

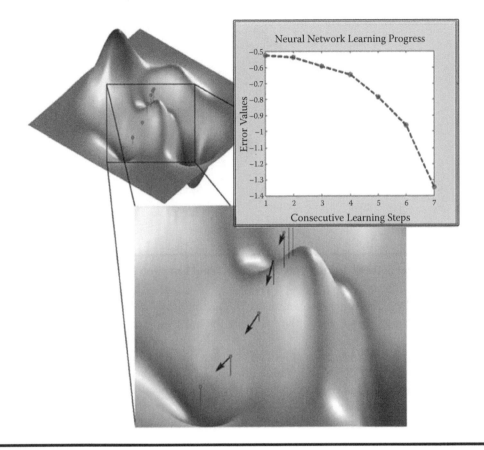

Figure 3.7 Searching for and finding network parameters (weight coefficients for all neurons) guaranteeing minimal error values during supervised learning.

We now return to the process of learning shown in Figure 3.6. After we find the direction of the quickest fall of the error, the algorithm of learning the network makes a change in the weight space and replaces the incorrect vector with a correct one. The migration causes the error to "slide down" to a new point, usually lower, to approach the valley where errors are the fewest and eventually solve assignments perfectly. This optimistic scenario of gradual and efficient migration to the area where errors are minimal is shown in Figure 3.7.

3.5 Learning Failures

Learning is not always a simple and pleasant process as depicted in Figure 3.7. At times, a network "struggles" until it finds a suitable solution. A detailed discussion of difficulties arising from learning would require complicated considerations of differential calculus and analysis of the convergence of algorithms. We will try to explain learning problems without detailing complicated mathematics by telling a story about a blind kangaroo (Figure 3.8).

Imagine a blind kangaroo is lost in the mountains and wants to return to his home. The kangaroo knows only one fact about the location of his house: it is situated at the very bottom

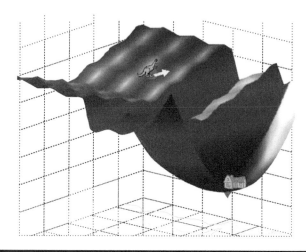

Figure 3.8 Neural network learning presented as a blind kangaroo hike. See discussion in text.

of the deepest valley. The kangaroo cannot see the surrounding mountain landscape just as an algorithm of learning cannot check the values of the error functions at all points for all sets of weights.

The kangaroo can only use his paws to feel which way the ground subsides in the same way a network learning algorithm can determine how to change weights to make fewer errors. The kangaroo thinks he has found the correct direction and hops with all his power, thinking that the hop will deliver him to his home.

Unfortunately a few surprises await the kangaroo and the algorithm for teaching a neural network. Note from Figure 3.8 that an incorrectly aimed jump can lead the kangaroo into a rift that separates him from his house. Another situation not shown in the figure but easy to imagine is that the ground in what appears a promising direction can drop and then suddenly elevate. As a result, the kangaroo's long jump in that direction will make his situation worse, because he will find himself landing higher (farther from the low valley where he lives) than he was at the start of his quest.

The success of the poor little kangaroo depends mostly on whether he can properly measure the length of the jump. If he is too cautious and performs only small jumps, his journey home will take longer. If he jumps too far and the surrounding area has cliffs and rifts, he may be injured.

As a network learns, the creator of the algorithm must decide the sizes of weight changes based on specific values of input signals and the potential sizes of errors. The decision is made by changing the so-called proportion coefficient or learning rate. Apparently, the algorithm designer has a great number of choices but every decision generates specific consequences.

Choosing a coefficient that is too small makes the process of learning very slow. Weights are improved very slightly at every step. Thus many steps must be performed for the network to reach desirable values. Choosing a too large coefficient of learning may cause abrupt changes to the parameters of the network; in extreme cases, this can cause learning instability, as a result of which the network will be unable to find the correct values of weights. Changes made too quickly will make it difficult for a network to reach the necessary solution.

We can view this problem from another point. Large values of the coefficient of learning resemble the attitude of a teacher who is very strict and difficult to please and severely punishes pupils for their mistakes. Such a teacher seldom attains good learning results because he creates confusion and imposes excessive stress on his students. On the other hand, low values of a coefficient of learning resemble a teacher who is excessively tolerant. Her pupils progress too slowly because she fails to motivate them to work.

In the processes of teaching networks and teaching pupils, compromises are necessary. Teaching means balancing the advantages of quick results with safety considerations to achieve stable functioning of the process of learning. A method to accomplish this goal is described in the next section.

3.6 Use of Momentum

One way of increasing the learning speed without interfering with stability is using an additional component called momentum in the algorithm of learning. Momentum enlarges the process of learning by changing the weights on which the process depends and the current errors, and allows learning at an earlier stage.

Figure 3.9 allows a comparison of learning with and without momentum and the process of changing the weight coefficients. We can show only two of them, and thus the drawing should be interpreted as a projection on plane determined by weight coefficient wi and the weight adaptation process wj that takes place in the n dimensional space of the weights. We can see behavior of only two inputs for a specific neuron of the network, but the processes in other neurons are similar.

Red (dark tone) points represent starting points (the setting before the start of learning the values of weight coefficients). Yellow points indicate the values of weight coefficients obtained during the steps of learning. An assumption has been made that the minimum of the error function is attained at the point indicated by the plus sign (+). The blue ellipse shows the outline of the stable error (set of values of weight coefficients for which the process of learning attains the same level of error).

As shown in the figure, introducing momentum stabilizes the learning process as the weight coefficients do not change as violently or as often. This also makes the process more efficient as the consecutive points approach the positive point faster. We use momentum for learning from a rule because it improves the attainment of correct solutions and the execution costs are lower.

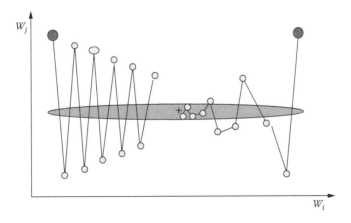

Figure 3.9   Learning process without momentum (left) and with momentum (right).

Other manners of improving learning can involve changing the values of the coefficients of learning—small at the beginning of the process when the network chooses the direction of its activity, greater in the middle of learning when the network must act forcefully to adapt the values of its parameters to the rules established for its activity, and finally smaller at the end of learning when the network fine-tunes the final values of its parameters and sudden corrections can destroy the learning structure. The techniques resemble the elaborate methods of a human teacher who has a large body of knowledge to use to train pupils with limited abilities.

Every creator of an algorithm of learning for a neural network faces the problem of assigning original values of coefficients of weights. The algorithm of learning described earlier shows how we can improve the values of these coefficients during learning. At the instant of onset of learning, the network must have concrete values of coefficients of the weights to be able to qualify the values of output signals of all neurons and to compare them to values given by the teacher for the purpose of qualification of errors. Where should we get these original values?

The theory of the learning process says that at the realization of certain (simple) conditions, a linear network can learn and find correct values of weight coefficients based on initial values we set at the start of the learning process. In the domain of non-linear networks, the situation is not so simple, because the process of learning can "get stuck" in the starting values of the so-called minima of local error functions. In effect, this means that starting from different primary sets of weight coefficients can yield different parameters of the taught network—appropriate or incorrect for resolving the set assignment.

What does the theory say about choosing correct starting points? Here we must support our knowledge with empiricism. A common practice relies on the fact that the primary values of weight coefficients are random. At the beginning, all parameters receive accidental values, so we start from a random situation. This may sound strange but actually makes sense. Because we know where to find minimum error functions, there is no better solution than relying on randomness.

Simulator programs contain special instructions for "sowing" the first random values of coefficients in a network. We should avoid excessively large values of start coefficients. Normal practice is to choose random values from the area between −0.1 and +0.1. Additionally, in many-layered networks, we must avoid coefficients having 0 values because they block the learning process in deeper layers. Weight signals do not pass through 0 values of weights. The result is cutting off part of the network structure from further learning.

Of course, the progress of learning reduces error potential. Learning is rapid at the beginning, then slows somewhat, and finally stops after completion of certain steps. It is useful to remember that learning by targeting training of the same assignment by means of the same network can run differently. Figure 3.10 shows three courses of this process that differ by the speed of progress of learning final effects. The difference results from the size of the coefficient of the error, below which a network cannot operate despite the intensity of further learning. The graphs refer to the same network and the same assignment and differ only in the primary values of coefficients of weights. We can thus say that they show diverse "inborn abilities" of the network.

The neural network learned many times using the same learning set, but starting from different points (determined by random setting of initial weight values). Three courses are plotted: average (most representative), course with maximal end value of post-learning error (pessimistic case), and course with minimal end value of post-learning error (optimistic case). In some networks, (e.g., Kohonen types) an additional learning demand is that original values of weight coefficients be normalized. We will talk about this in Chapter 10.

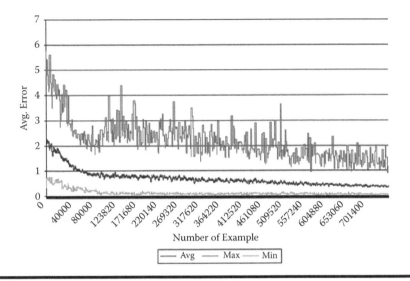

Figure 3.10   Decreasing network error during learning process.

3.8 Duration of Learning Process

Unfortunately, the answer to determining duration of learning is pessimistic. The simplicity of training a network instead of the complex process of programming it extracts a price: a long period of learning. We currently accept the price because no one has found an efficient way to shorten network learning processes. Furthermore, it is difficult to anticipate the time it will take to teach a network until it begins to develop some elements of intelligent behavior. Sometimes the process is speedy but generally it is necessary to use the elements of a learning set for a long time and with great effort before a network begins to understand some of its task.

What is more, as the result of random choice of original values of weight coefficients, the learning results for the same data used as the learning set can differ a little and this fact should be accepted unless a designer time to teach the same network several times and choose the variant that guarantees the best result. A single process of learning for a network with several thousands of elements lasts several hours! For example, a neural network designed for face recognition built from 65,678 neurons in a three layer perceptron structure needs 5 hours and 23 minutes of learning time using a Dell PC with 1.2 GHz clock. The learning set contains 1,024 example images of 128 known persons (8 images per person).

The long learning process is not an isolated result. For example, a compilation published in the *Electronic Design* monthly lists the numbers of presentations of the learning set required to achieve certain tasks as shown in the table below. Other authors noted similar results.

Function	Number of Presentations
Kanji character recognition	10^{13}
Speech recognition	10^{12}
Recognition of manuscript	10^{12}
Voice synthesis	10^{10}
Financial prediction	10^{9}

Source: Wong, W. Neural net chip enables recognition for micro. *Electric Design,* June 22, 2011.

Because of the learning time required, researchers seek methods other than the classical or delta algorithms for teaching networks. The time of teaching a network with the algorithm of the quickest fall (described earlier) grows exponentially as the number of elements increases. This fact limits the sizes of neural networks.

3.9 Teaching Hidden Layers

Finally, we will discuss the teaching of hidden layers of networks. As described in Chapter 2, all layers of a network other than the entrance (input) and exit (output) layers are hidden. The essence of the problem of teaching neurons of the hidden layer arises because we cannot directly set the sizes of errors for those neurons because the teacher provides standard values of signals only for the exit layer. The teacher has no basis for comparison for signals from neurons of the hidden layer.

One solution to this problem is backward propagation (backpropagation) of errors suggested by Paul Werbos and later popularized by David Rumelhart whose name is usually connected to the method. Backpropagation consists of reproducing the presumable values of errors of deeper (hidden) layers of network on the ground of projecting backward the errors detected in the exit layer. The process will be detailed in Chapter 7.

Basically, the technique considers the neurons to which the hidden layer sends output signals and adds the signals, taking into account the values of coefficients of weights of connections between hidden layer neurons and neurons that produced errors. This way the "responsibility" for errors of neurons of the hidden layer burdens those neurons more heavily (with greater weight) because they influence the signals transmitted to the exit layer. By proceeding backward in this manner from the exit neurons to the entry neurons of a network, we can evaluate presumable errors of all neurons and consequently gain sufficient information to make the necessary corrections of weight coefficients of these neurons.

Of course, this method does not allow us to mark errors of neurons of intermediate layers exactly. As a result, corrections of errors during the learning process are less accurate than corrections made in networks without hidden layers. Finding and correcting errors with this technique adds to network learning time. However, the wide range of capabilities of networks with multiple layers means we must accept the tens of thousands of demonstrations involved in a learning set.

Other problems may arise through the repeated presentation of a learning set to a network. The necessary repetition would try the patience of a human teacher who could never deal with the hundreds of thousands or millions of operations required to teach a neural network. At present we have no alternative for presenting the same input signals and patterns to a network as many times as it needs to learn answers.

It is detrimental to show learning set elements always in the same order. Such predictable instruction can allow a network to establish definite cycles of values of weight coefficients and will halt the process of learning and possibly cause network failures. It is vital to randomize the learning process by mixing the elements and presenting them in different orders. The randomization complicates learning but it is crucial for obtaining reasonable results.

3.10 Learning without Teachers

How is it possible to learn without a teacher? We know that a network should be capable of resolving a specific task without having a set of ready examples with solutions. Is this possible? How can we expect a network to perfect its own work without receiving instructions?

In practice, it is entirely possible and even relatively easy to teach a spontaneous self-organizing neural network subject to a number of simple conditions. The simplest idea of self-learning of a network is based on the observations of Donald Hebb, a US physiologist and psychologist. According to Hebb, the processes of strengthening (amplification) of connections between neurons occur in the brains of animals if the connections are stimulated to work simultaneously. The associations created in this manner shape reflexes and allow simple forms of motor and perceptive skills to develop.

To transfer Hebb's theories to neural network operation, computer scientists designed a method of self-learning based on showing a network examples of input signals without telling the network what to do with them. The network simply observes the signals in its environment although it is not told what the signals mean or what relationships exist between them. After observing the signals, a network gradually discovers their meaning and sets dependencies among the signals. The network not only acquires knowledge, but in a way creates it! Let us now discuss this interesting process in more detail.

After processing consecutive sets of input signals, a network forms a certain distribution of output signals. Some neurons are stimulated very intensely, others weakly, and some even generate negative signals. The interpretation of these behaviors is that some neurons "recognize" signals as their own (are likely to accept them), others are indifferent to the signals, while other neurons are simply "disgusted" by them. After the production of output signals of all neurons throughout a network, all weights of the input and output signals are changed. It is easy to see that this is a version of the Hebb postulate in that connections between sources of strong signals are noted and strengthened.

Further analysis of the process of self-learning based on the Hebb method allows us to state that after consistent use of a specific algorithm for start parameters, neurons develop accidental "preferences" that lead to systematic strengthening and detailed polarization. If a neuron has an "inborn inclination" to accept certain types of signals, it will learn after repetition to recognize these signals accurately and precisely. After a long period of such self-learning, the network will create patterns of input signals spontaneously.

As a result, similar signals will be recognized and assembled efficiently by certain neurons. Other types of signals may become "objects of interest" to other neurons. Through this process of self-learning, a network will learn without a teacher to recognize classes of similar input signals and assign the neurons that will differentiate, recognize, and generate appropriate output signals. So little to accomplish so much!

3.11 Cautions Surrounding Self-Learning

The self-learning process unfortunately displays many faults. Self-learning takes much longer than learning with a teacher. For this reason, a controlled process is preferable to spontaneous learning. Without a teacher, we never know which neurons will specialize in diagnosing which classes of signals. For example, one neuron may stubbornly recognize the letter R, another may recognize Ds, and a third may see Gs. No learning technique can make these neurons arrange themselves in alphabetical order.

This creates a certain difficulty when interpreting and using the output of a network, for example, to steer a robot. The difficulty is basic but it may produce troublesome results. We have no guarantee that neurons developing their own random starting preferences will specialize to the extent that they will process different classes of entrance images. It is very probable that several neurons will "insist" on recognizing the same class of signals, for example As, and no neurons will recognize Bs.

That is why a network intended to be self-learning requires more effort than a network solving the same problem with the participation of a teacher. It is difficult to measure the difference exactly. Our past experiments indicate that a network intended to be self-learning must have at least three times as many elements (especially in the exit layer) than the answers it is expected to generate after learning.

A very subtle and essential matter is the choice of the starting weight values for neurons intended to be self-taught. These values strongly influence the final behavior of a network. The learning process deepens and perfects certain tendencies present from the beginning of the process. Thus these innate properties of a network strongly affect the end processes of learning.

Without knowing from the beginning which assignment a network should learn, it is difficult to introduce a specific mechanism to set the start values of weights. However, leaving these decisions to random mechanisms can prevent a network (especially a small one) from sufficiently diversifying its own mechanisms at the start of learning. Subsequent efforts to represent entrance signals of all classes in the structure of a network may prove futile.

However, we can introduce one mechanism for initial distribution of the values of weights in the first phase of learning. This method, known as convex combination, modifies original values of the weights in a way that maximizes the probability of an even distribution of all typical situations appearing in the entrance data set among neurons. If data appearing in the first phase of the learning will not differ from data to be analyzed and differentiated by a network, convex combination will create a convenient starting point to further self-learning automatically and also ensure relatively good quality of solutions to assignments.

Questions and Self-Study Tasks

1. What conditions must be fulfilled by a data set to allow it to be used as a teaching set for a neural network?

2. How does teaching a network with a teacher differ from teaching without a teacher?

3. On what grounds does the algorithm of teaching calculate the directions and changes of weights in the steps of teaching?

4. How should we set the starting values of weight coefficients of a network to start its learning process?

5. When does the teaching process stop automatically?

6. Why do network teaching efforts fail and how can we prevent failures?

7. Describe the steps of generalizing knowledge obtained by a neural network during teaching.

8. Where can we obtain the data necessary to fix the values of changes of weight coefficients of neurons in hidden layers during teaching?

9. What is momentum and what can we do with its help?

10. How much time is required to teach a large network? What factors determine the time required?

11. Why do we speak about "discovering knowledge" of self-learning networks instead of "teaching" them?

12. Advanced exercise: Suggest a rule that allows us to change the coefficient of teaching (learning rate) in a manner that will accelerate the speed of learning in safe situations and slow it at the moment when the stability of the teaching process is endangered. Note: Consider changes of the valued of errors committed by a network in subsequent steps of teaching.

Chapter 4

Functioning of Simplest Networks

4.1 From Theory to Practice: Using Neural Networks

The intent of the previous chapters was to provide a theoretical basis of neural network design and operation. Starting with this chapter, readers will gain practice in using neural networks. We will use simple programs to illustrate how neural networks work and describe the basic rules for using them. These programs (along with data required for start-up) can be found at http://www.agh.edu. pl/tad* on the Internet.

This address will lead you to a site that accurately describes step by step all the required actions for using these programs legally and at no cost. You need these programs to verify information about neural networks contained in this book. Installing these programs in your computer will enable you to discover various features of neural networks, conduct interesting experiments, and even have fun with them.

Don't worry. Minimal program installation experience is required. Detailed installation instructions appear on the website. Note that updates of the software will quickly make the details in this book outdated. Despite that possibility, we should explain some of the procedures.

Downloading the programs from the site is very easy and can be done with one mouse click. However, obtaining the programs is not enough. They are written in C# language and need installed libraries in .NET Framework (V. 2.0). All the needed installation software is on the site.

The first step is the installation of the libraries (Figure 4.1). You may have some of these libraries installed on your computer already and conclude that this step is unnecessary. If you are certain about that, you can skip the .NET Framework step, but we suggest you perform it "just in case."

---

* All software programs available from http://www.agh.edu.pl/tad may be used legally and without cost under the terms of an educational license from Microsoft*. The license allows free use and development of the .Net technology on condition it is not used for commercial purposes. You can use the software for experiments described in the book with no limits and also use it for your own programs. You are prohibited legally from selling the software.

If the appropriate programs are installed on your computer already, the install component will determine that it has no need to install them. However, the site may contain newer versions of the libraries than the ones you have, in which case the installer will go to work. It is always smart to replace old software with newer versions. The new software will serve many purposes beyond those described in this book.

After you install the necessary .NET Framework libraries on which further actions depend according to the site guidelines, the installer will run again. This will allow you to install all example programs automatically and painlessly. You will need them for performing experiments covered in this book. When the installation is finished, you will be able to access the programs via the start menu used for most programs. Performing .NET experiments will help you understand neural networks theoretically and demonstrate their use for practical purposes.

To convince unbelievers that this step is simple, Figure 4.1 shows the difficult part of installation: the installer asks the user (1) where to install the programs and (2) who should have access. The best response is to keep the default values and click on Next. More inquisitive users have two other options: (1) downloading the source code and (2) installing the integrated development environment called Visual Studio.NET.

The first option allows you to download to your computer hard drive the text versions of all the sample programs whose executable versions you will use while studying this book. It is very interesting to check how these programs are designed and why they work as they do. Having the source code will allow you—if you dare—to modify the programs and perform even more interesting experiments. We must emphasize that the source codes are not necessary if you simply want to use the programs. Obviously, having codes will enable you to learn more and use the resources in more interesting ways. Obtaining the codes is not a laborious process.

The second option, installing Visual Studio.NET, is addressed to ambitious readers who want to modify our programs, design their own experiments, or write their own programs. We encourage readers to install Visual Studio.NET even if they only want to view the code. It is worthwhile to spend a few more minutes to make viewing of the code easier. Visual Studio.NET is very easy to install and

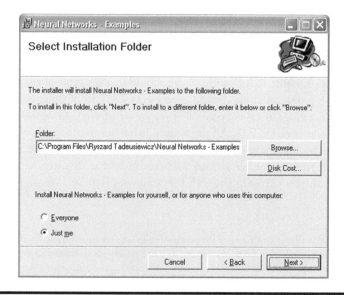

Figure 4.1 The installer will ask only two questions.

use. After installation, you will be able to perform many more actions such as adding extern sets, diagnosing applications easily, and quickly generating complicated versions of the software.

Remember that the installations of source codes and Visual Studio.NET are totally optional. To run the example programs that will allow you to create and test neural network experiments described in this book, you need only install .NET Framework (first step) and example programs (second step).

What's next? To run any example, you first choose an appropriate command from the Start/Programs/Neural Networks Examples menu. After making your selection, you may use your computer to create and analyze every neural network described in this book. Initially your system will use a network whose shape and measurements we designed. After you are immersed in the source code, you will be able to modify and change whatever you want. The initial program will make networks live on your computer and allow you to teach, test, analyze, summarize, and examine them. This manner of discovering the features of the neural networks—by building and making them work—may be far more fulfilling than learning theory and attending lectures.

The way a network works depends on its structure and purpose. That is why we will discuss specific situations in subsequent chapters. Because the simplest network function to explain is image recognition, we will start our discussion there. This type of network receives an image as an input and after categorization of the image based on previous learning, it produces an output. This kind of network was presented in Figure 2.39 in Chapter 2. A network handles the task of classifying geometric figures by identifying printed and handwritten letters, planes, silhouettes, or human faces.

How does this type of network operate? To answer that, we start from an absolutely simplified network that contains only one neuron. What? You say that a single neuron does not constitute a network because a network should contain many neurons connected to each other? The number of neurons does not matter and even so small a network can produce interesting outputs.

4.2 Capacity of Single Neuron

As noted earlier, a neuron receives input signals, multiplies them by factors (weights assigned individually during the learning process) that are summed and converge to a single output signal. To review, you know already that summed signals in more complicated networks converge to yield an output signal with an appropriate function (generally nonlinear). The behavior of our simplified linear neuron involves far less activity.

The value of the output signal depends on the level of acceptance between the signals of every input and the values of their weights. This rule applies ideally only to normalized input signals and weights. Without specific normalization, the value of an output signal may be treated as the measure of similarity between assembly of the input signals and the assembly of their corresponding weights.

You can say that a neuron has its own memory and stores representations of its knowledge (patterns of input data as values of the weights) there. If the input signals match the remembered pattern, a neuron recognizes them as familiar and answers them with a strong output signal. If the network senses no connection between the input signals and the pattern, the output signal is near 0 (no recognition). It is possible for a total contradiction to occur between the input signals and weight values. A linear neuron generates a negative output signal in that case. The greater the contradiction between the neuron's image of the output signal and its real value, the stronger its negative output.

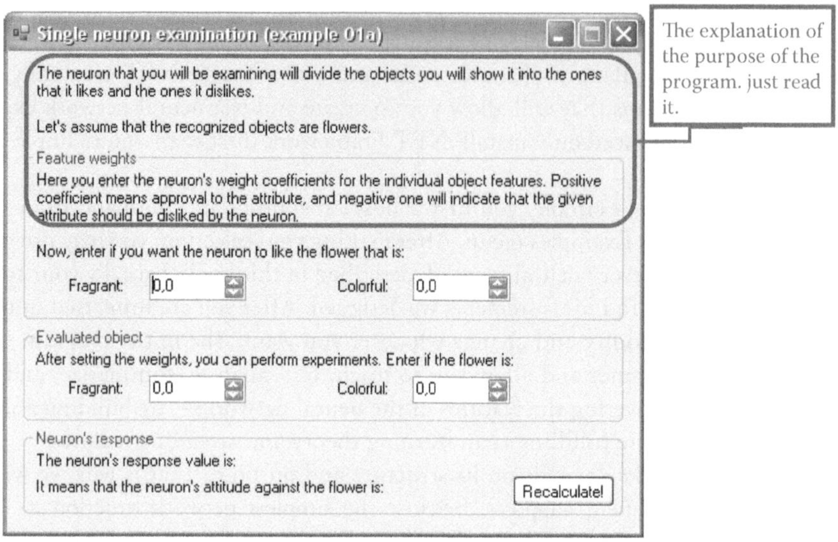

Figure 4.2 Window of the Example 01a program just after start.

We encourage you to install and run a simple program named Example 01a to perform a few experiments. You will learn even more about networks if you try to improve the program. After initializing Example 01a, you will see the window in Figure 4.2. The text in the top section explains what we are going to do.

The blinking cursor signals that the program concerning flower characteristics is waiting for the weight of the neuron's input (in this case the fragrant value). You can enter the value by typing a number, clicking the arrows next to the field, or using the up and down arrows on the keyboard. After inserting the value for the fragrant feature, go on to the next field that corresponds to the second feature—color.

Let us assume that you want your neuron to like colorful and fragrant flowers, with more weight for color. After receiving an appropriate answer, the window of the program will resemble Figure 4.3.

This program and every other one you will use allows you to change your decision and choose another input. The program will try to update the results of its calculations. After we input the feature data (which in fact are weight values), we can study how the neuron works. You can input various sets of data as shown in Figure 4.4 and the program will compute the resulting output signal and its meaning. Remember that you can change the neuron's preferences and the flower description at any time.

If you use a mouse or arrow keys to input data, you do not have to click the recalculate button every time you want to see the result; calculations are made automatically. When you input a number from the keyboard, you have to click the button because the computer does not know whether you finished entering the number or left to get a tuna sandwich.

The next stage is to experiment with a neuron in an unusual situation. The point of the experiment shown in Figure 4.5 is to observe how the neuron reacts to an object that differs from its remembered ideal colorful and fragrant flower. We showed the neuron a flower full of colors with no fragrance. As you can see, the neuron liked this flower as well!

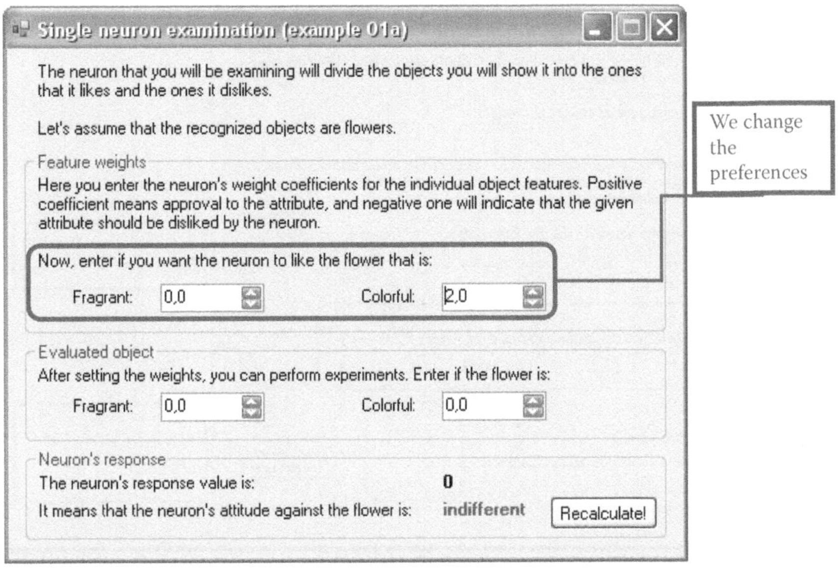

Figure 4.3   Initial stage of user's communication with Example 01a program.

Changing the parameters of the flower allows us to observe what the neuron will do in other circumstances. The examples of such experiments are shown in Figure 4.6 and Figure 4.7. We tested the behavior of the neuron when the flower had a pleasing fragrance and little color. The network liked it anyway. We then tested a colorless flower with an unpleasant smell; that one was not likeable.

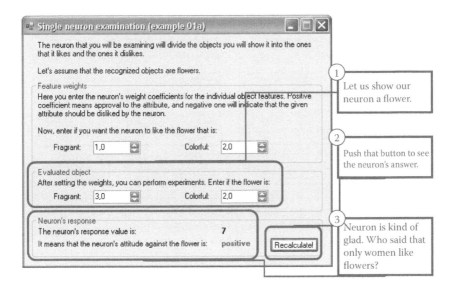

Figure 4.4   Final stage of user's communication with Example 01a program.

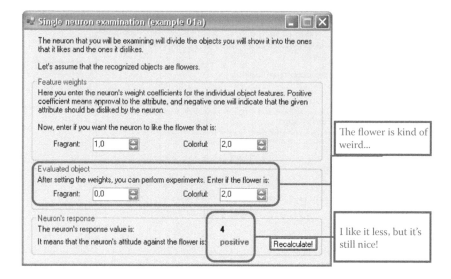

Figure 4.5 Example 01a in an unusual situation.

Now let us test our neuron with a little more complicated task: whether it accepts a flower that smells badly if it is colorful enough. As you can see, the program provides plenty of ways to experiment. You can change the preferences of the neuron to see how it reacts in various situations, for example, it may like a flower that smells bad (the weight for fragrance can be negative).

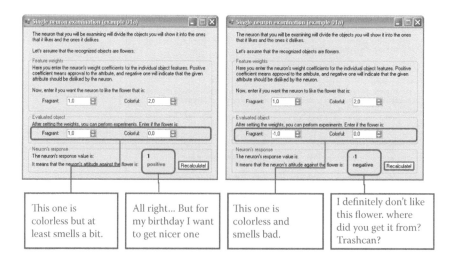

Figure 4.6 Another experiment with Example 01a program.

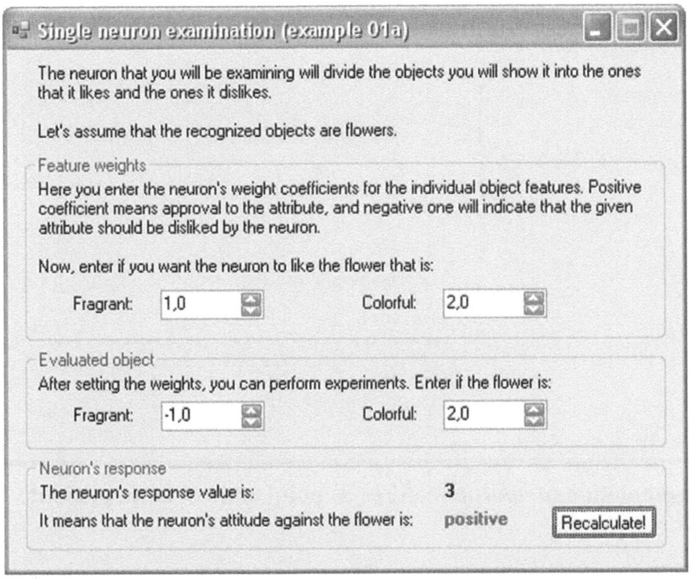

Figure 4.7   Yet another experiment with Example 01a program.

4.3 Experimental Observations

You will find "playing" with the Example 01a program a worthwhile exercise. As you input various data sets, you will quickly see how a neuron works according to a simple rule. The neuron treats its weight as a model for the input signal it wants to recognize. When it receives a combination of signals that corresponds to the weight, the neuron "finds" something familiar and reacts enthusiastically by generating a strong output signal. A neuron can signal indifference by a low output signal and even indicate aversion via a negative output because its nature is to react positively to a signal it recognizes.

Careful examination will indicate that the behavior of a neuron depends only on the angle between the vector of weight and the vector of the input signal. We will use Example 01b to further demonstrate a neuron's likes and dislikes by presenting an ideal flower as a point (or vector) in input space.

When you set the preferences of a neuron, you tell it, for example, to like fragrant and colorful flowers. Fragrance and color are separate weight vectors. You can draw two axes. On the horizontal axis, you can note the values of the first feature (fragrance) and indicate the values of the second feature (color) on the vertical axis (Figure 4.8). You can mark the preferences of the neuron on the axes. The point created where these coordinates meet indicates the neuron's preferences.

A neuron that values only the fragrance of a flower and is indifferent to color will be represented by a point located maximally to the right (high value of first coordinate) but on the horizontal axis set at a low number or zero. A puttyroot flower has beautiful colors and a weak and sometimes unpleasant smell. The puttyroot would be located high on the vertical axis (high color value) and to the left of this axis to indicate unpleasant or weak smell. Flower color is valued on the vertical axis and fragrance on the horizontal axis. You can treat any object you want a neuron to mark by using this technique.

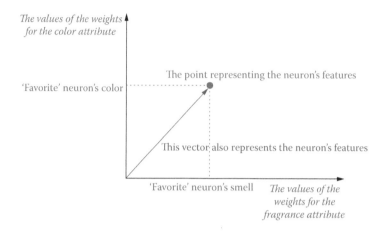

The values of the weights for the color attribute

The point representing the neuron's features

'Favorite' neuron's color

This vector also represents the neuron's features

'Favorite' neuron's smell

The values of the weights for the fragrance attribute

Figure 4.8   Representation of neuron features as point and vector in attribute space.

A lily of the valley has a wonderful smell and would be represented by the point located maximally to the right. However, its color is not a strong asset so color would be valued low on the axis. The beautiful and unpleasant smelling gillyflower would be rated high on the color axis and low on the fragrance side. The sundew would appear at the bottom left segment of the system; it looks like rotting meat and has a similar smell intended to attract insects. Majestic and fragrant roses would be valued at the top right corner.

On a neural network, it is convenient to mark objects (ideal flowers and flowers to be analyzed) as points on a coordinate system and as vectors. You can acquire needed vectors by joining the points with the beginning of the coordinate system. This is how Example 01b works. Similar to Example 01a, it can be found in on the start menu. Certain features should be noted:

■ The value of the output depends mostly on the angle between the input vector (representing input signals) and the weight vector (ideal object accepted by the neuron). It is illustrated in Figure 4.9.

■ If the angle between the input and weight vectors is small (the vectors are located next to each other), the value of neuron output is positive and high.

■ If the angle between the input and weight vectors is large (they create an angle greater than 90 degrees), the value of neuron output is negative and high.

■ If the angle between the input and weight vectors is close to 90 degrees, the value of neuron output is low and neutral (near zero).

■ If the length of the input vector is far smaller than the length of the weight vector, the value of neuron output is neutral (near zero) independent of the direction of the output vector.

All these characteristics of neuron behavior can be tested via the Example 01b program. Although the graphics are not as good as those in Figure 4.9, they can be understood and serve the purpose of demonstrating what a neuron does.

Example 01b is easy to operate. You simply need to click in the area on the left chart. First, click with the right button to set the location of chosen point corresponding to the neuron's weight factors (see Figure 4.10). You will see the point and its coordinates. Of course, you can change

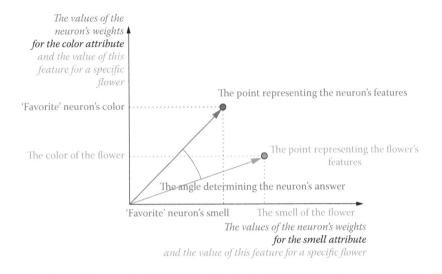

The values of the neuron's weights **for the color attribute** and the value of this feature for a specific flower

The point representing the neuron's features

'Favorite' neuron's color

The point representing the flower's features

The color of the flower

The angle determining the neuron's answer

'Favorite' neuron's smell   The smell of the flower

The values of the neuron's weights **for the smell attribute** and the value of this feature for a specific flower

Figure 4.9   Mutual position of weights vector and input signal vector as factors determining value of neuron response.

values at any time by clicking again in another part of the chart or modifying the coordinates as we did in the Example 01a program.

Now click on the chart with the left button to locate the position of the flower and watch the answer appear. If the neuron likes the flower (you can see what the neuron thinks of the flower from the value of the output signal on the right), the appropriate point is marked on the chart with red box (like a mountains on a map; see Figure 4.11). If the judgment is negative,

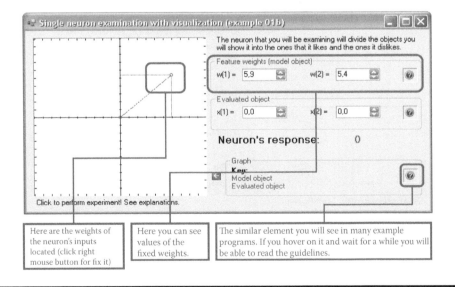

Figure 4.10   Window of Example 01b program with model object marked.

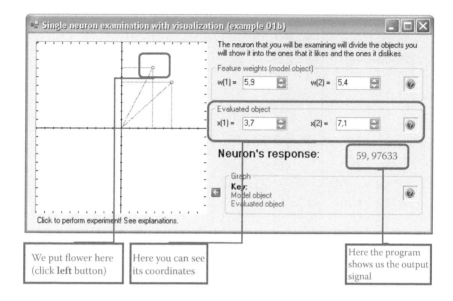

Figure 4.11 Input vector location for which output signal is positive.

the point is marked with blue box (like a seabed on a map; see Figure 4.12). When the reaction of the neuron is neutral, the corresponding point is light blue (Figure 4.13). You will soon be able to imagine how the areas corresponding to the decisions in the input space will appear. Also, you can drag the mouse pointer over the chart with one of the buttons pressed to see the results change.

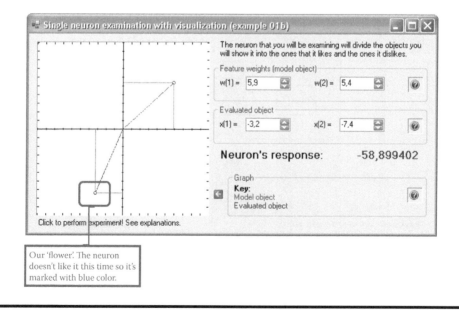

Figure 4.12 Input vector location for which output signal is negative.

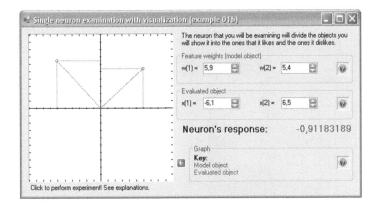

Figure 4.13   Input vector location for which output signal is neutral.

4.4 Managing More Inputs

The examples above are clear and simple because they concern a single neuron with only two inputs. Real applications of neural networks typically involve tasks requiring many inputs. Problems solved by neural networks often depend on huge numbers of input data and many cooperating neurons must work cooperatively to generate an appropriate solution to a problem.

This point is difficult to illustrate. It would involve an input space of 10 or more dimensions! We suggest an alternative: the Example 01c program (Figure 4.14). The system asks the user to enter the number of neuron inputs. You can accept the default value (5) and click Next. As in Examples 01a and b, you then input the weights that define the model of the signal to which your neuron should react positively. Fill in the *w(i)* column shown in Figure 4.15, then enter the values of the input signals in the *x(i)* column. The program will then calculate the output. Simple, isn't it?

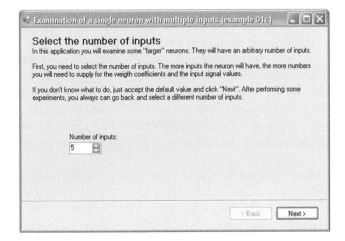

Figure 4.14   Beginning of conversation with Example 01c program.

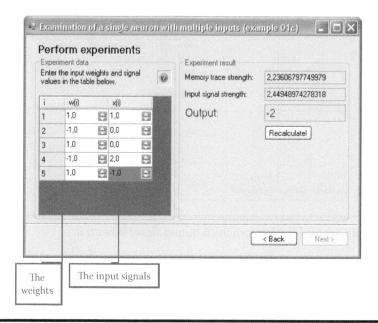

Figure 4.15 Subsequent part of conversation with Example 01c program.

During experiments you will notice that high values of the output signals are returned in two situations: (1) when input signals correspond to the weights of the neuron as expected or (2) by entering huge input values where weights are positive. The first way of obtaining high output is intelligent, sophisticated, and elegant. The same (sometimes even better) effects can be obtained by using brute force and the second method.

When entering input signals, you should try to make them of the same strength using the parameter estimate given by the computer. This will enable you to correctly interpret and compare your results. Similarly, when comparing the behaviors of two neurons with different weight values to find identical input signals (they should have the same value of memory trace strength), the difference is the length of the weight vector. In a network with a great number of neurons, the meaning of the strength of the input signals radically decreases when stronger (better tuned) or weaker (worse tuned) input signals reach every neuron.

When we consider only one neuron, dissimilar values of input signals make results harder to interpret. That is why we should agree on choosing input values so that the sum of their squares is between 5 and 35, for example. The range is an estimate; great precision is not needed here. Because the program calculates the strength as a square root from the sum of squares of the coordinates (the formula for the length of a vector), the strength of the signals should be between the square root of 5 and the square root of 35—roughly between 2 and 6.

Why should we choose these values? While we were designing the program, we observed that entering small random integer values for five inputs of the neuron yielded more or less accurate values. If you prefer, you can choose any other value and it will work. The same suggestion for choosing values is useful for applying weights. Results are easier to check if the input signals "match" the values.

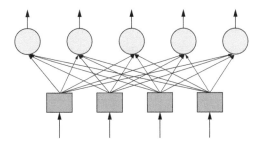

Figure 4.16   Structure of single-layered neural network.

4.5 Network Functioning

Consider a network consisting of multiple neurons organized in a single layer. They are not connected to each other and each neuron handles input and output; see Figure 4.16. The input signals you apply will enter every neuron. The output signals of the neurons will be treated as the entire network's response to a given task. How does this work?

Every neuron has its own set of weights that make it ready to recognize certain characteristics of the input signals. Every neuron has different weights and recognizes different patterns of signals. When input signals are entered, every neuron will calculate its output signal independently. Some will generate high outputs because they recognize patterns and others will produce small outputs based on less recognition.

By analyzing the output signals, you can identify patterns the network "suggests" based on your observations of high output values. You can also evaluate how sure the network is of its decision by comparing the output signal of the "winning" neuron with the signals generated by other neurons.

Sometimes the ability of a network to detect uncertain situations is useful for limited types of problems. An algorithm that makes decisions based on incomplete data must be used wisely.

4.6 Construction of Simple Linear Neural Network

The network described in the Example 02 program recognizes three categories of animals (mammals, fish, and birds). This simple program will help you start a simple exercise with a very small neural network. We encourage you though to write a more complicated program to solve a simple but real problem.

The example network contains only three neurons. Recognitions are made based on five features (inputs). The following information about animal characteristics is input:

How many legs does it have?
Does it live in water or does it fly?
Is it covered with feathers?
Does it hatch from an egg?

For every neuron, the values of weights are set to match the pattern of a specific animal. Neuron 1 should recognize a mammal and utilizes the following weight values set:

Weight Value	Characteristic
4	Mammal has four legs
0.01	Mammal sometimes lives in water (e.g., seal); water is not typical milieu
0.01	Mammal sometimes flies (e.g., bat); flying is not typical activity
–1	Mammal has no feathers
1.5	Mammal is viviparous (major characteristic)

The weights of Neuron 2 are set to recognize birds using the same technique and different values:

Weight Value	Characteristic
2	Bird has two legs
–1	Bird does not live in water
2	Bird usually flies; ostriches are exceptions
2.5	Bird has feathers (major characteristic)
2	Bird hatches from egg

The weights of Neuron 3 for identifying fish are set in the following way:

Weight Value	Characteristic
–1	Fish has no legs
3.5	Fish lives in water
0.01	Fish cannot fly; flying fish are exceptions
–2	Fish is not covered with feathers or similar structures
1.5	Fish generally hatches from egg; viviparous fish are exceptions

After the program starts, it displays information on a screen about weights for every input of every neuron (Figure 4.17) and allows us to perform interesting experiments as described in the next section.

4.7 Use of Network

The program presented previously assumes that a network has three outputs associated with the recognition of three kinds of objects (animals): mammals, birds, and fish. The network has a single layer that contains only these three neurons. Later we will cover networks containing more neurons than the number of outputs. The simple construction of a neural network allows it to accommodate any number of outputs.

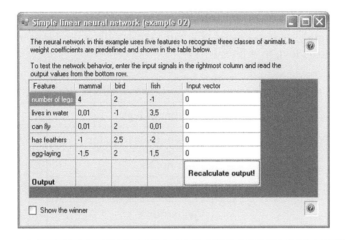

Figure 4.17   Beginning of work of Example02 program.

Our example involved the input of only five signals corresponding to certain features for recognizing objects. Obviously you can increase this number if your problem involves greater numbers of input data. All input signals are connected to every neuron according to the "lazy rule" that states: if you don't feel like analyzing which input signal influences which output signal, the best choice is to connect everything to everything else. This concept has become common practice.

Despite the "lazy rule," it is useful to think about input signals before entering them. Some contain numeric information (e.g., how many legs an animal has); others involve Boolean information (whether an animal lives in water, flies, is covered with feathers, or is viviparous). You should consider how you will represent logical values in a network because neurons operate, as we know, on the values of signals and not on symbols like true or false.

If you are a computer scientist, you may suspect that the idea of true and false can be expressed in binary form: 1 = true, 0 = false. If you are a great computer scientist who uses Assembler and dreams about microprocessor registry, hexadecimal memory records, and Java applets, this type of relation is obvious, total, and correct. We must confess that work in the area of neural networks will make you modify your habits as described below.

Remember that zero in a neural network is a useless signal to transfer because it carries no new information. Neurons work by multiplying signals by weights and then summing the result. Multiplying anything by zero always produces the same result regardless of the inner knowledge (value) of a neuron. By using zero as an input signal, you forego opportunities to learn and influence network behavior. That is why our program uses the convention of +1 = true and –1 = false. Such bipolar signals fulfill their tasks very well.

Another advantage of a bipolar neural network is the ability to use any values of input signals that may reflect the convictions of the user about the importance of certain information. When inserting data for a codfish, a crucial fact is that the fish lives in water so you may input +2 instead of +1. For other situations, you can input values smaller than one. You may have doubts about entering +1 in response to whether flying fish can fly if you entered +1 for an eagle that is a superb flier. In that case you can input +0.2 for the flying fish to indicate the uncertainty. Another example is the answer to a "has tail" signal for a snake. Based on snake anatomy, the answer may be +10.

Because we know how to handle network input signals, we can try a few simple experiments by inputting data for a few randomly chosen animals to check whether the network recognizes them correctly. In a network consisting of many elements, the normalization of input signals (considering signal strength) is not as crucial. The same result will be produced by the neuron if you describe an animal (e.g., fox), in this way:

Weight Value	Characteristic
4	Number of legs
–1	Does not live in water
–1	Does not fly
–0.9	Is not covered with feathers
–1	Viviparous

And the same result will be produced by the neuron if you describe such an animal like this:

Weight Value	Characteristic
8	Has 4 legs; legs are vital and thus counted twice
–6	Hates water
–3	Never flies
–5	Has no feathers; has fur (major characteristic)
–9	Does not lay eggs; is viviparous (major characteristic)

This simple network can recognize typical situations correctly. It will classify mammals, fish, and birds (Figure 4.18, Figure 4.19, and Figure 4.20) and also works well in atypical situations. For example, it will recognize a seal, bat, and even a platypus (a strange animal from Australia that hatches from an egg) as mammals. The network can also identify a non-flying ostrich as a bird and classify a flying fish correctly. Try it!

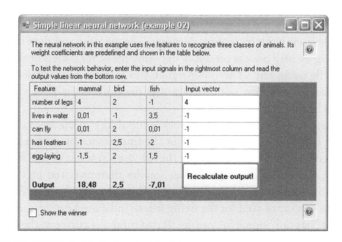

Figure 4.18   Network recognition of a typical mammal.

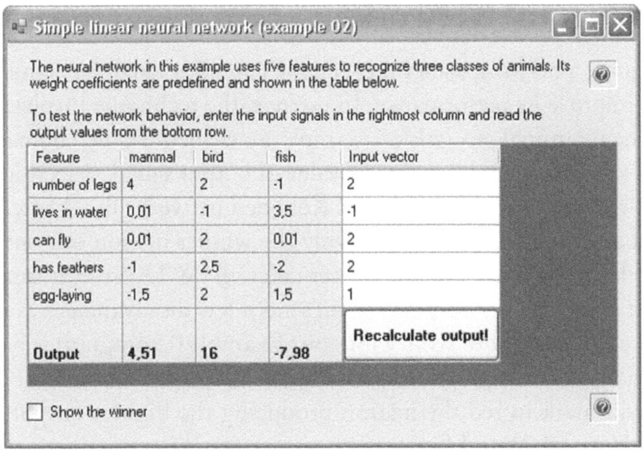

Figure 4.19   Program working to identify a bird.

However, the network will be puzzled by a snake because the snake has no legs, lives on the ground, and hatches from eggs. When faced with a snake, every neuron in the network will decide the snake is not a decent animal and will thus generate a negative output. In the context of our classification, the output makes sense.

The three-neuron network is very primitive and sometimes makes mistakes. For example, it repeatedly recognizes turtle as a mammal (it has 4 legs, lives on land, but hatches from eggs) and classifies lungfish as mammals (they live on land during droughts). This demonstrates the need for a designer to set weights carefully and completely and monitor outputs consistently.

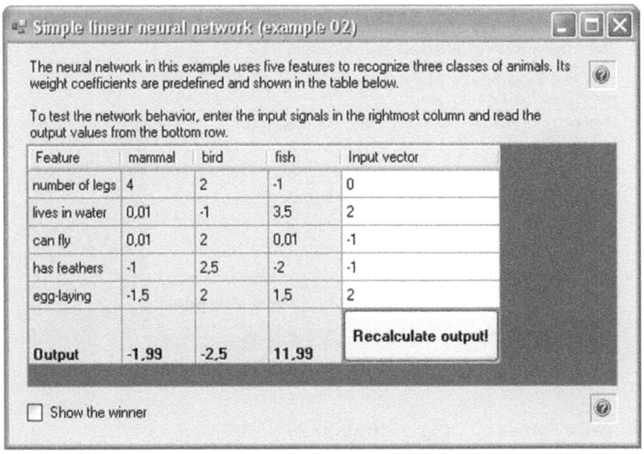

Figure 4.20   Program working to identify a fish.

4.8 Rivalry in Neural Networks

In practical applications, a network sometimes requires an additional mechanism known as *rivalry* between neurons to improve its performance. In essence, the technique involves a competition that produces a winner. In our animal recognition example, an element would compare all the output signals select a winner—the neuron with a highest value of output signal. Selecting a winner may have consequences (as we will see in the discussion of Kohonen networks in Chapter 10). In most cases, the output signals of a network are polarized. Only the winner neuron can output its signal; every other output is zeroed. This is known as the winner-takes-all (WTA) rule. It simplifies the examination of networks that involve many outputs but presents a few disadvantages as noted.

We can introduce the element of rivalry into our Example 02 program simulating the recognition of animals. At the start of the program, select `Show the winner`. After processing the input data, the program will mark in red the neuron producing the highest output value (the winner). Examples appear in Figure 4.21 and Figure 4.22.

Note that we assume that only the positive value is a basis for a decision during a neuron competition. If every output signal is smaller than the value marked in the program as a threshold (set as you wish), the output signal should be a no-recognition signal.

We suggest you use program Example 02 to perform experiments involving rivalry of neurons. Despite the simplicity of a linear network, it functions effectively and provides answers as text instead of numbers that require further interpretation. These networks have limits as well that will be covered in subsequent chapters.

4.9 Additional Applications

The purpose of the network described in this chapter was to recognize some sets of information treated as a set of features of recognized objects. However, it is not the only application for a simple single-layered network consisting of neurons with linear characteristics. Networks of this type are

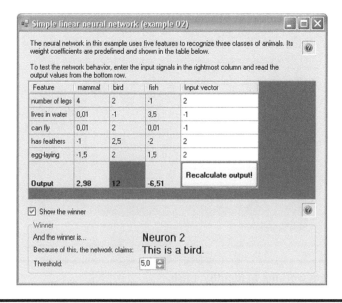

Figure 4.21 Example 02 operating with rivalry option enabled.

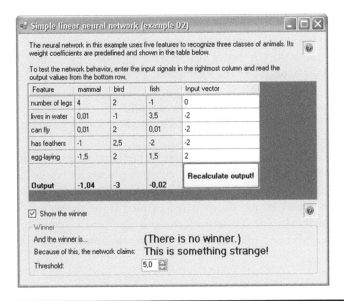

Figure 4.22 Network with enabled rivalry option trying to recognize a snake.

often used for purposes such as signal filtering (especially as adaptive filters with properties that change according to current needs).

These networks also have numerous applications in signal transformation (speech, music, video, and medical diagnosis such as electrocardiogram, electroencephalogram, and electromyelogram instruments). Such networks can extract a spectrum of a signal or arrange input data using the principal components analysis method. These are only a few of many examples. Even a simple one-layer network can handle many types of applications.

All decisions of a network are made by a set of weights for every neuron. By setting the weights differently, we change the way a network works. In the same way, changing a program makes a computer work differently. In the examples described previously, we used a set of weights chosen arbitrarily. We had to determine a weight value for every neuron. This, of course, may be interpreted as a change of a work program for a network.

For a network containing few neurons that allows simple and obvious interpretation of the weight factors (as in our example of animal recognition), this "manual" programming can produce good results. However, in practical applications, networks contain many elements. It is thus impossible to determine the parameters of a single neuron and follow its operation. That is why more useful and flexible networks choose their own weights in the process of learning. Chapter 5 is dedicated to a vital aspect of neural network design: teaching.

Questions and Self-Study Tasks

1. Which of the following properties do a neuron's weights and the input signals need to generate an output signal? Strong and positive? Strong and negative? Close to zero?

2. How can you make a neuron to favor one of its inputs (e.g., make the color of a flower more important than its fragrance)?

3. How can you interpret the positive and the negative values assigned to every input of a neuron?

4. How can you interpret the positive and the negative output signals of a neuron?

5. Does a neuron having all negative input values always generate a negative output signal?

6. Is there any limit to the number of neuron input signals?

7. Does the network modeled in the Example 02 program recognize a dolphin as a mammal or a fish?

8. What can be achieved by rivalry of neural network?

9. What animal group will a bat be assigned to by the network modeled in the Example 02 program?

10. Does the network modeled in the Example 02 program recognize that dinosaurs were not mammals, birds, or fish? They were reptiles but the example has no reptile category. Which animals known to the network do dinosaurs most closely resemble?

11. Does a network competition always have a winner? Is the answer good or bad?

12. Advanced exercise: In a neural network recognizing animals, add additional classes such as predators or herbivores and extra data describing features (sharpness of teeth or bills, speed, etc.).

Chapter 5

Teaching Simple Linear One-Layer Neural Networks

5.1 Building Teaching File

This chapter explains how to teach the simplest neural networks. Theoretical knowledge often gained from reading algorithm descriptions is completely different from hands-on practical knowledge gained from designing an activity and seeing the results. Chapter 4 covered research involving the simplest networks. We built a simple linear network and conducted some research to demonstrate how neurons and networks behave. The experiments in this chapter will expand your knowledge of linear networks.

We will explain linear networks and discuss the limitations imposed by their simple structures. For our purposes, linear networks are easier to teach, they perform certain tasks very well, and their results are easy to analyze. Chapter 6 will cover the more complex nonlinear networks.

We will start with the easiest of the easy tasks: teaching a single neuron. To achieve this, we will use the Example 03 program that allows us to teach a simple linear neuron (Figure 5.1) and conduct simulation research. However, before we input data and attempt to modify the program, some introductory remarks are appropriate.

During the experiments involving the work of a single neuron serving as an entire network, we input all the needed signals; this gave us full control over the experiment. Working with a larger network performing more difficult tasks is a far different endeavor. Sometimes hundreds or thousands of experiments are needed before a reasonable result appears from the initial chaos. Of course, only a masochist will enter the same data thousands of times to teach a network how to generate a correct task solution.

Therefore, we assume that a teaching process is based on a set of teaching data created by and saved on a computer. The set should include input signals for all the neurons in the network and the models of the correct (required) output signals. The teaching algorithm will use

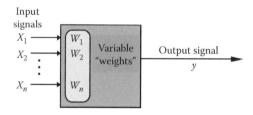

Figure 5.1 Structure and basic elements of teaching an artificial neuron.

these signals to simulate real network behavior. In our programs, the format of teaching data will be as follows:

- Explanatory comments
- Set of input signals
- Set of models of correct output signals

We assume that the input signals will include five element vectors (including five signals for five inputs of the analyzed neuron) and only one model of the correct output signal because we can temporarily use only one neuron. These network parameters are placed in the first line of the teaching sequence file. A teaching sequence can be as long as you wish. In fact, the more examples with correct solutions you show a network, the better the results. Hence, the file containing all this information may be very large. For a program to teach one neuron, we recommend the use of the following file:

```
5, 1
A typical object that should be accepted
3, 4, 3, 4, 5
1
A typical object that should be rejected
1, -2, 1, -2, -4
-1
An untypical object that should be accepted
4, 2, 5, 3, 2
0.8
An untypical object that should be rejected
0, -1, 0, -3, -3
-0.8
```

The above text is a teaching file for Example 03 and may be found in a file called `Default teaching set 03.txt`. Example 03 will offer you the teaching file at the start. Of course, you can create your own file with data for teaching a network and connect it to the program described below. A teaching file is required to enable your neuron to recognize different sets of target standards or you can train it to build a model to approximate some relationship between input and output signals, for example, resulting from medical observations or physical measurements.

Remember that this neuron is linear and is able to learn only how to transform signals similarly to mathematical methods. As for example, correlation and multidimensional linear regression methods. You will learn about wiser neurons and more common nonlinear networks later. For now, we suggest you use our programs to ensure that your neurons work correctly. Later you can work with your own teaching data tailored to your own tasks.

5.2 Teaching One Neuron

We first load the Example 03 program and try to start it. It loads the data from the `Default teaching set 03.txt` data and tries to classify objects correctly. Object data are recorded in file in the correct order in the form of input signals for the neuron. A neuron can notice an incorrect operation because the `Default teaching set 03.txt` file has models of the correct answers recorded by the teacher. The program then modifies the weights of the modeled neuron according to the procedures described in an earlier chapter.

This feature teaches the neuron to perform better when given a defined task. During simulated teaching, the screen will display the progress of the process step by step, show how the weights change, and reveal errors. At the beginning, errors are large, of course, as shown in Figure 5.2.

If you are testing the network as you read this (you can go to this phase at any time by clicking Next), you may check its knowledge. However, you will see at the start that the assumption that the neuron should already know the shown objects is incorrect (Figure 5.3).

To allow a neuron to work effectively, it may require more learning. By clicking the Back button, we can return to the previous Teaching window and teach the neuron by clicking the Teach more! button several times. After analyzing errors again, you may find they have not decreased significantly after further teaching (cf. Figure 5.4). You can stop teaching and try to estimate network knowledge by using the example again. The results should be better (Figure 5.5). The results of advanced teaching are shown in Figure 5.6.

During advanced teaching, the network definitely rejects objects that are only similar to the objects from teaching set and should be rejected as shown in Figure 5.5. During teaching, you can review the history of the process that appears on request in the form of a changing network error

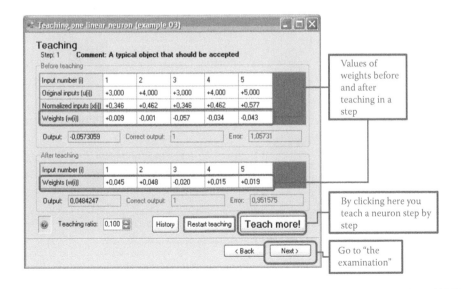

Figure 5.2   Beginning of teaching a neuron.

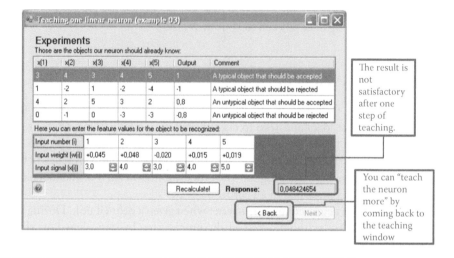

Figure 5.3 Failure of a poorly trained neuron; weak recognition of object by network.

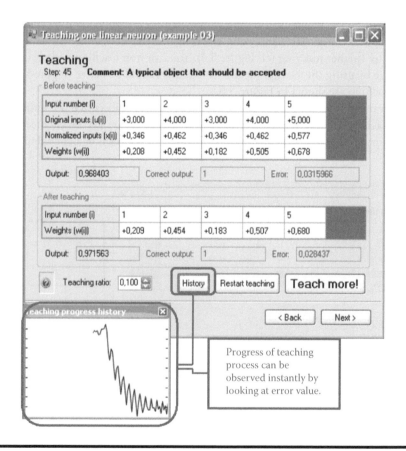

Figure 5.4 Advanced stage of teaching characterized by small values of errors at every step and minimal decreases after teaching.

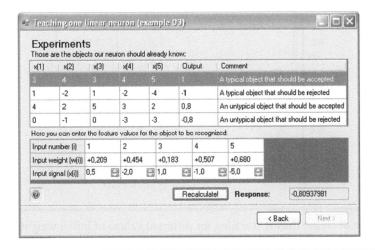

Figure 5.5   During advanced teaching process, the network easily passes examination by reject-ing objects that should be rejected.

value chart. This useful and instructive chart can be used at any time by clicking the History but-ton. The program demonstrates errors as primary elements influencing the teaching process and weight values before and after teaching process correction.

Using a small number of "unshuffled" teaching data will limit the uses of a single-layer net-work. Such networks are not recommended for complex tasks. However, simple tasks like those presented in the `Default teaching set 03.txt` file allow a neuron to learn quickly and effectively. Keep in mind that a correctly trained neuron should create a target standard object in the form of suitable weight values. They must be recognizable so that you can determine immedi-ately whether the teaching process is effective.

We will now describe a dynamic teaching process. The earlier presentations demonstrated sig-nificant progress in the area of improving the neuron performance. As learning speed decreases, we want to work on decreasing network errors. Figure 5.7 shows the typical characteristics of one neuron after error values are changed during teaching.

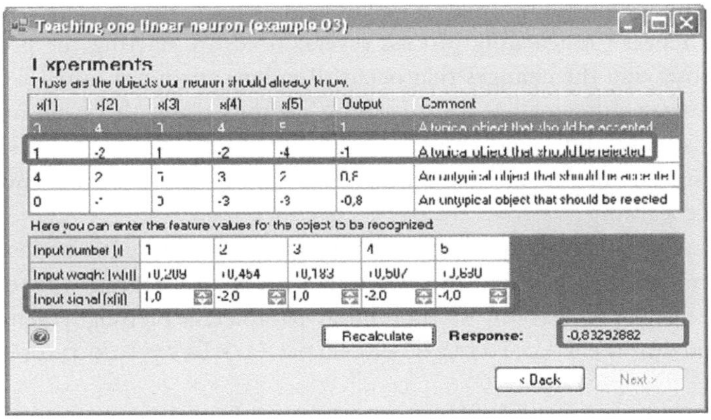

Figure 5.6   Network is able to generalize during advanced teaching period.

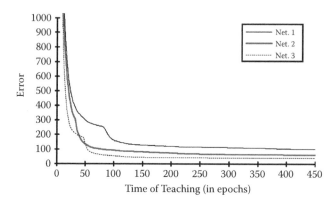

Figure 5.7 Error decrease during teaching for different values of initial weights.

Let us try to check the progress of the teaching process in your experiments. You will obtain different characteristics of teaching in the following experiments despite using the same set of input data. The reason is that a neuron starts from a different randomly drawn initial weight value every time it operates.

The Example 03 program is user friendly. It will allow you to experiment with a neuron by interrupting teaching to examine the neuron and see how it behaves after using trial signals that are similar to the signals it was taught. You can then return to the interrupted teaching process to "tune up" the neuron, then examine it again. You can teach a neuron a few rudiments, examine it, teach it again, check its progress, and so on. We suggest successively longer periods of teaching between examinations because changes over time become less noticeable.

Experiments are worth conducting because they produce substantial and detailed information. Furthermore, they are based on simple examples that demonstrate the most impressive feature of a neural network—its ability to learn and generalize great amounts of data.

5.3 "Inborn" Abilities of Neurons

It is advisable to understand how "inborn" abilities influence teaching effects. To achieve this aim, you should repeat the teaching process several times by starting the program from the beginning and observing the changes that occur. Random setting of initial weight values will enable you to observe different paces of teaching neurons using the same input data. Some neurons learn instantly and some require lengthy teaching. Neurons occasionally produce unsatisfactory results despite intensive teaching. This occurs when they must overcome "inborn preferences" while learning.

This effect may be surprisingly large. We suggest readers conduct a few experiments with the suggested program by changing the range in the text of program where initial random weight values are set.[*] You start by setting initial parameters of weight neuron value other than those assumed in the `InitializeTeaching ()` klasy `ProgramLogic` method.

---

[*] Unfortunately this experiment requires a review of the program text, changing one of its instructions, and then making another compilation; it is suitable for more advanced readers.

Instead of using `examinedNeuron.Randomize( _ randomGenerator, -0.1, 0.1)`, you can apply the `_ examinedNeuron.Randomize( _ randomGenerator, -0.4, 0.4)` instruction.

The initial weight values will undergo a wider range of changes and thus exert more influence on teaching and on the results. By starting the teaching process several times with the same data, you can easily observe how strong the influence of the random initial weight value is. The neuron will learn in a completely different way every time. You will be able to recognize the unpredictability of the learning process and its results as well.

The network used in the experiments described in this chapter is small and simple. Its assigned task is not difficult. If you are solving very complex tasks in a large network, the addition of many random effects (investigated in the described program) can lead to unforeseen network behavior. The effect may amaze users who trust the infallible behavior repetition of numeric algorithms used in typical computer programs.

5.4 Cautions

The simple demonstration suggested above can act as a testing ground for investigating one more important factor influencing the teaching process, namely the influence of teaching ratio value (pace) on the outcome. This factor can be changed in the teaching ratio field of the Example 03 program.

By assigning a larger value, for example, using a ratio of 0.3 instead of the 0.1 used in the program, you can get faster teaching results, but the network may become "nervous" because of sudden weight value changes and unexpected fluctuations. You can try to use a few new values and observe their impacts on the teaching process.

If you set too high a value of a factor, the teaching process becomes chaotic and does not yield positive results, because neurons will be "struggling" between extremes. The final result will be unsatisfactory. Instead of improving its results, a neuron working with values set too high will generate many more errors than expected.

On the other hand, a too-low teaching ratio value will slow teaching considerably. The user will become discouraged by the lack of progress and abandon the method to seek more effective algorithms. All experiment results on artificial neural networks should be interpreted in light of situations that arise in a real teaching process. The teaching ratio value expresses "strictness" of a teacher to a neuron. Low values indicate a lenient teacher who notices and corrects teaching errors but does not demand correct answers. As shown in earlier experiments, such indulgence can yield poor results.

A very high teaching ratio value is equivalent to a too-strict teacher and this extreme may be detrimental also. Very strict punishments imposed on an apprentice after a mistake create frustration. The situation is the same as a neuron "struggling" from one extreme value to another without making real learning progress.

5.5 Teaching Simple Networks

The natural course is to proceed from teaching a single neuron to teaching an entire network. The Example 04 program is designed for this purpose. It is similar to Example 03 designed for a single neuron and is also easy to use. You also need teaching set data to conduct experiments with this program. It is available in the `Default teaching set 04.txt` file. The content of the teaching set appears below:

```
5, 3
```

A typical object that should be accepted by the first neuron is

```
3, 4, 3, 4, 5
1, -1, -1
```

A typical object that should be accepted by the second neuron is

```
1, -2, 1, -2, -4
-1, 1, -1
```

A typical object that should be accepted by the third neuron is

```
-3, 2, -5, 3, 1
-1, -1, 1
```

An untypical object that should be accepted by the first neuron is

```
4, 2, 5, 3, 2
0.8, -1, -1
```

An untypical object that should be accepted by the second neuron is

```
0, -1, 0, -3, -3
-1, 0.8, -1
```

An untypical object that should be accepted by the third neuron is

```
-5, 1, -1, 4, 2
-1, -1, 0.8
```

An untypical object that should be rejected by all neurons is

```
-1, -1, -1, -1, -1
-1, -1, -1
```

The program indicates the state of teaching process and values of particular variables with a little less detail than that shown in Example 03. Using a larger number of neurons generates a too-precise view of each neuron's results. In essence, you would receive too much information and find it difficult to extract the essential data from the results. The insights provided by Example 04 program are more synthetic. Results from three neurons are apparent instantly, as shown in Figure 5.8.

The critical aspect of teaching is progress of the learner. You can view the progress of the teaching process by comparing Figure 5.8 and Figure 5.9 that depict network condition at the beginning and end of teaching, respectively.

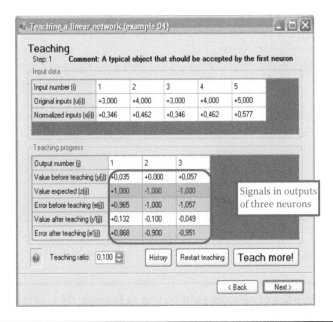

Figure 5.8   Network condition at beginning of teaching in Example 04 program.

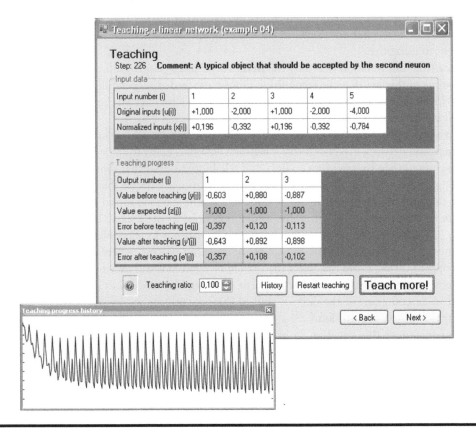

Figure 5.9   Network condition at end of teaching in Example 04 program.

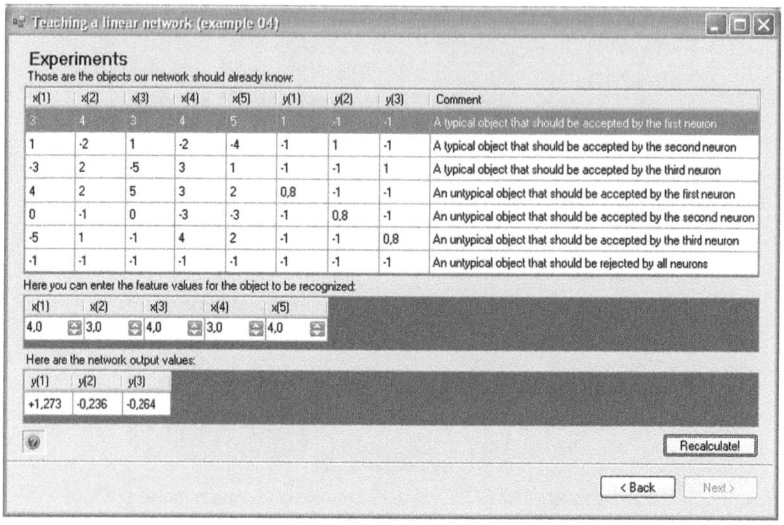

Figure 5.10 Characteristics of network examination in Example 04 program.

The Example 04 program shows network behavior (Figure 5.10) and allows a user to judge whether a network works correctly. The figure indicates that the network after teaching correctly handled an object that was not shown in the teaching data, but is similar to the object the neuron was taught to recognize.

Notice from examination that only the **first** neuron has a positive value of output signal. This clearly points to the fact that the recognition process proceeded successfully. However, the ambiguity of this situation caused Neurons 2 and 3 (that should have rejected the object) to have doubts indicated by their uncertain answers. This situation is typical.

Utilizing the generalization of knowledge concept during teaching usually allows a user to detect uncertain network behavior. From a neuron's view, it is easier to achieve success (correct positive recognition) than to strive for certainty and reliability in cases that should have been rejected.

During the observation of network teaching, you can surely notice that some of the demands made in the form of suitable examples included in teaching data are solved easily and quickly and others are far more difficult to solve. The recognition tasks in the `Default teaching set 04.txt` file are easy for a neuron. However, teaching neurons to reject objects is a more difficult task. Figure 5.11 shows an advanced stage of the teaching process, where recognition of specific objects happens correctly and the object that should be rejected is still causing trouble.

Moreover, repeated unsuccessful attempts of adapting the network to solve this difficult task will lead to deterioration of the current skill of the network for solving elementary tasks. This implies typical object recognition.

If you encounter this situation in practice, instead of struggling and teaching the network unsuccessfully for a long time, consider reformulating the task. It may be more useful to prevent the problem. Usually the removal of one or more troublesome examples from teaching data radically improves and accelerates the process. You can check the extent to which this method improves learning by removing the proper fragment from the `Default teaching set 04.txt` file and teaching the network again without the troublesome element(s). You will certainly notice an improvement in the speed and effectiveness of teaching.

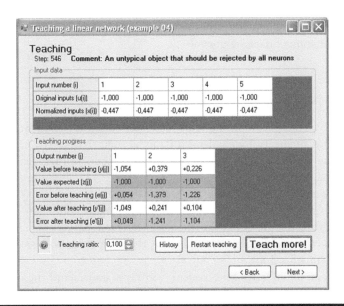

Figure 5.11   Network teaching recognition of inconvenient examples.

5.6 Potential Uses for Simple Neural Networks

The networks we investigated in this chapter are not the largest or most complex neurocomputers ever built. For many readers they will appear almost primitive. However, even simple networks show interesting behaviors and are capable of dealing neatly with fairly complicated tasks. This is simply because collective action of many neurons allows a wide range of varied possibilities. We can certainly see some similarities among single neuron activities and network possibilities. Therefore, we can consider a network a set of cooperating neurons. The behavior of a single neuron can be expanded into an entire network in a very natural manner.

However, networks present some uniquely connected possibilities that individual neurons cannot handle. Networks as simple as those described here enable us to solve multidimensional problems that can create serious difficulties for other mathematical and computational systems. To deal with multidimensional problems, we enlarge network dimensions properly by assuming larger values for a number of inputs and outputs to accomplish some practical tasks.

A network can be designed to model complex systems in which many causes (input signals) influence the production of many results (output signals). You can get an idea of the wide range of these applications by accessing the Google search engine and entering "neural networks modeling." The examples described have been cited almost 30 million times. That indicates huge numbers of practical applications for a single neuron!

Along with creating neuron models of complex systems, we can use simple linear neural networks like those described here for adaptable signal processing. This is another huge area of application revealed by a Google search of "signal processing."

Digital signal processing led to computer and neuron processing for many more types of signals, for example, speech transmission by phone, pictures recorded by camera or video equipment, modern medical diagnostic technologies, and automatic industrial control and measuring equipment. We should take a short look at this interesting discipline, because signal filtration represents a viable application for neural networks. By filtering signal noises that impede perception, accurate analysis and interpretation of data are possible.

5.7 Teaching Networks to Filter Signals

Imagine that you have a signal containing some noise. Telecommunication, automation, electronics, and mechatronics engineers are challenged daily by such signals. If you ask an expert how to clear a signal from noise, he or she will tell you to use a filter. You will learn that a filter is an electronic device that stops noise and allows useful signals to pass. Because filters work well, we have efficient telephones, radios, televisions, and other devices.

However, each expert will confirm that it is possible to create a good filter only when the noise has some property that is not present in the useful signal. If a signal component has this property, it should be stopped by the filter as noise. Otherwise, the component will be allowed to pass. The technique is simple and effective.

However, to design an effective filter system, you must understand the undesirable noise in your signal. You cannot create a filter without this information because the filter must "know" what information to stop and what to pass Without the necessary knowledge, you will not create a filter, because the filter does not know which information should be kept and which should be stopped. In many cases, you may not know the source of the noise or its properties.

If you send a probe rocket far into space and its mission is to gather signals describing an unknown planetoid, you do not know what rubbish may be attached to signals from the probe during its journey over millions of kilometers. Is it possible to create a filter in this situation?

It is possible to separate a useful signal from unknown noise by using adaptive filtration. In this case, adaptive means teaching the signal receiving device the rules for separating signals from noise. Neural networks can be trained to filter select signals from noise. Samples of disturbed signals are treated as input signals for the network and "clean" signals are used as output signals. After some time, the network will learn to differentiate undisturbed output signals from disturbed ones and will work as a filter.

Let us consider a real example. We will use standard sinusoid signals, both "clean" and disturbed. These signals, in the form of a file that allows to teach networks, can be created by the Example 05 program. This program automatically produces a data file called `teaching _ set` that may be used to teach a simple network. The window for modifying the required parameters to generate this file appears when we start the Example 05 program.

Figure 5.12 shows the window. Unfortunately, the program requires you to input network size, expected noise value (noise level measure), frequency, and number of teaching steps.

The number of details needed may discourage you from working with this program, but the process of compiling the necessary values is not as complex as it seems.

Each window in the display shows selected values that have been tested to ensure the program works well and produce interesting effects. Therefore, if you do not have values in mind, you can choose the default settings by clicking the Apply button. When you are more comfortable with the program, you can change the values and observe the results.

The Example 05 program provides a great deal of freedom. The default values can be removed at any time by clicking the Cancel button. You can restore all the settings by using the Default button. Although the program appears unfriendly at the start, its operation is straightforward. The system will let you observe as a network teaches itself to filter signals. The program demonstrates all the steps and depicts the unfiltered signal (Figure 5.12) and the post-filtered signal without

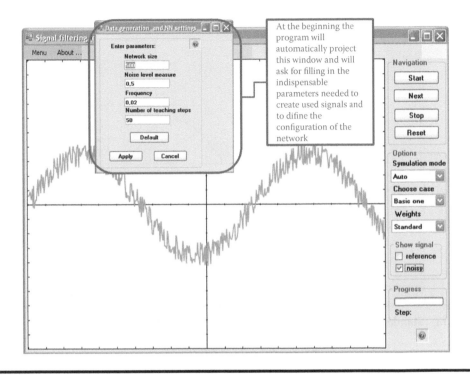

Figure 5.12   Disturbed signal to be filtered by neural network.

noise (Figure 5.13). To access these views, select the reference or noisy option from the Show signal group in the right margin displayed on the screen.

The first results of filtration after few steps are not very promising (Figures 5.14 and 5.15), but the constant teaching of the network (by repeatedly clicking the Next button) trains it to filter signals nearly perfectly (Figure 5.16). The teaching process can proceed automatically or step by step. The program allows you to view the various operations or proceed directly to view the filtered signal by making the appropriate choice of simulation mode.

You may find it helpful in early experiments with the program to observe the individual steps of the teaching process by choosing the manual mode. During experiments, it is possible to modify the number of steps (by using the Menu → Configuration option on the upper edge of the window) and use the automatic mode to specify 50 or 100 steps. The results are very informative and worth the effort.

As you can see from the figures, a network really learns and improves its work. After a fairly short time, it erases disturbances in signals easily. The filter effectiveness resulting from teaching can be evaluated by viewing the signal during the process (Figure 5.17). After sufficient teaching, a network learns to filter signals and performs the task well.

The most difficult task is to teach a network to reproduce a signal in a situation in which the values of the standard signals are small or equal zero. Therefore, it is possible in Example 05 to use two versions of network teaching (1) with the original sinusoid signal and (2) after movement of the sinusoidal signal in such a way that the values processed by the network may be only positive.

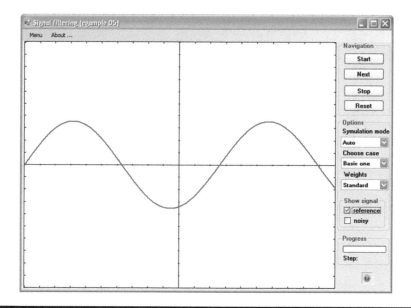

Figure 5.13   Standard signal to be reconstructed by neural network.

You select an option from the Choose case menu on the right side. At the beginning, the "with displacement" results appear to be worse (see Figure 5.18). However, persistent network teaching yields much better results (Figure 5.19). The observation of network behavior under all these conditions will help you detect and analyze the causes of possible failures when you use networks to perform far more complicated tasks.

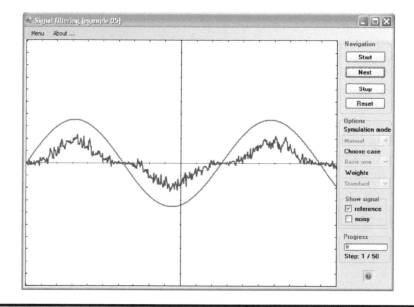

Figure 5.14   Results of signal filtering after one step of teaching.

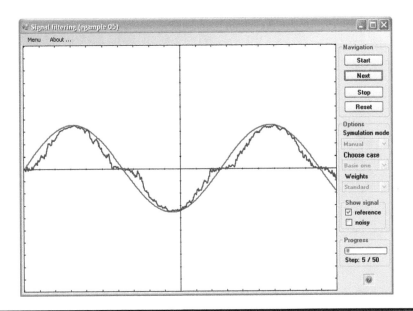

Figure 5.15 Results of signal filtering after five steps of teaching.

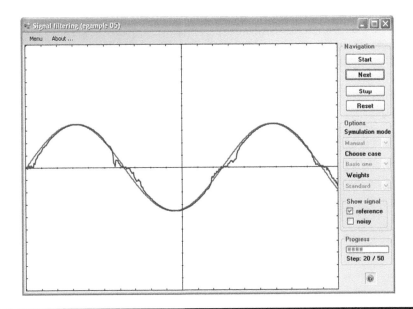

Figure 5.16 Results of signal filtering after 20 steps of teaching.

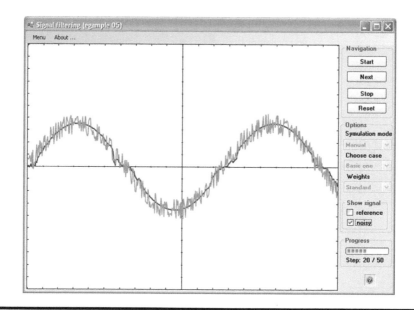

Figure 5.17 Estimation of effectiveness of signal filtration after 20 steps of teaching.

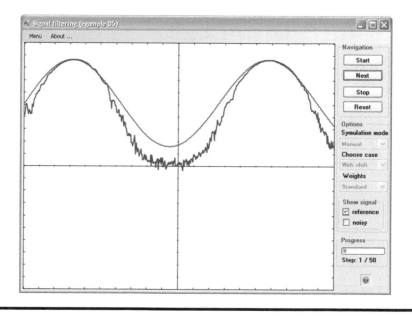

Figure 5.18 Results of filtration of moved signal after one step of teaching.

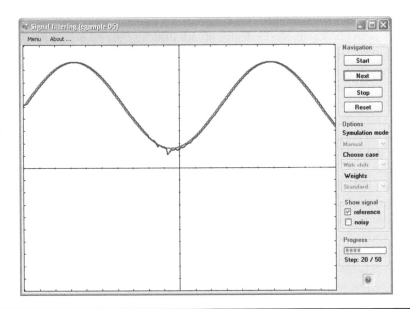

Figure 5.19 Results of filtration of a moved signal after 20 steps of teaching.

Keep in mind that linear networks represent the "kindergarten" level of the neural network field. Think of the linear network as a warm-up for a big event—creating a multilayer network from nonlinear neurons—the subject of the next chapter.

Questions and Self-Study Tasks

1. Why during network teaching of complicated tasks do we use a teaching set saved on a disk instead of using a mouse or keyboard?

2. Figure 5.4 depicts teaching progress history. Why does it exhibit frequent and sudden fluctuations? Did something cause the neuron to "go crazy" from time to time?

3. Based on the experiments described in this chapter, estimate the degree to which the teaching of a specific behavior exerts influence on the final result. Also, estimate the degree to which a neuron's "Inborn abilities" resulting from a random initialization of the network parameters influence its work? Do these analyses allow you to draw some practical conclusions about the influence of your education on your career?

4. Try to determine by several experiments using the Example 03 program the best teaching ratio value for the task solved by the network. In another task described by a completely different teaching set, will the optimal value of teaching ratio be the same or different?

5. When should you use larger teaching ratio values: in tasks that are easy to solve or tasks that are difficult and complicated?

6. Try to invent and use another teaching set cooperating with the Example 04 program. Use the Notepad program of Windows or the specialized Visual Study tool. Save the new content in the `Default teaching set 04.txt` file. Try to master Example 04 until it becomes a valuable tool that enables you to solve various tasks based on a teaching set you randomly select.

7. Prepare a few files with different teaching sets for different tasks and compare the results after a network is taught. Establish the degree of task difficulty (based on the similarities of data sets that the network must distinguish) that influences the duration of teaching and frequency of network errors after teaching is complete. Try to find a difficult task that the network will be unable to learn no matter how much it is taught.

8. Examine how the teaching of the Example 04 program proceeds in relation to initial weight value, teaching ratio, and various modifications of the teaching set.

9. A neural network that learns adaptive signal filtration has at its disposal a signal disturbed by noise and a standard undisturbed signal. Why is the disturbed signal not used as a model during network teaching?

10. Figures 5.18 and 5.19 show that the filtration conducted by Example 05 program is better in the upper part of chart than in the lower section. Why?

11. Advanced exercise: The Example 03 program uses a teaching neural network to create a classifier (a network that receives a specified set of input signals and produces an output signal that could be interpreted as acceptance or rejection of an object described by data). Examine how this program will behave when it is forced to learn a more difficult trick: calculation of a definite output value based on input data values. This network can work as a model of some simple physical or economic phenomenon. The following is an example data set in the form of `Default teaching set.txt`, for which this model can be created. Only two inputs are assumed in an effort to minimize the use of teaching data.

```
2, 1
```

Observation 1

```
3, 4
-0.1
```

Observation 2

```
1, -2
0.7
```

Observation 3

```
4, 2
-0.2
```

Observation 4

```
0, -1
0.3
```

Observation 5

```
4, -5
1.9
```

Observation 6

```
-3, -3
0.6
```

Observation 7

```
-2, -4
1
```

Observation 8

```
3, -2
0.9
```

Observation 9

```
-1, -1
0.2
```

Make sure the program provides correct solutions for a data set other than the one used during teaching, knowing that the teaching data were based on the $y = 0, 1 \times 1 - 0, 3 \times 2$ equation.

12. Advanced exercise: The Example 05 program illustrates the work of an adaptive filter based on teaching a neural network instead of a working program designed for practical uses. The same network can be used to filter other signals, for example, electrocardiogram records. This signal in digital form is not at your disposal so try to use a properly modified network for other signals, for example, filter a sample of sound in the form of a WAV or MP3 file. How can a similar adaptive filter network be used for picture processing?

Chapter 6

Nonlinear Networks

6.1 Advantages of Nonlinearity

Linear systems (both neural networks and other linear devices in general) are well known for their predictable nature and use of simple mathematical descriptions to lead easily to solutions. You may wonder why we leave the comfortable area of linear networks and move on to complex nonlinear networks. The most important reason is that networks of nonlinear neurons are able to solve more varieties of problems. Linear networks can solve only a single class of problem—one in which the correlation between output and input signals is linear. Nonlinear networks are far more flexible.

If you are adept at mathematics, you will understand what the problem is, but don't worry if mathematics is not your strong suit because this book contains no mathematical formulas. And nothing is extraordinary about a network created from linear neurons that deals only with linear functions. One mathematical concept is required here: for a linear transformation, we can use a transformation matrix to obtain an output based only on input signals. Output signals act as vectors. Because that explanation may not be clear, we are going to compare linear and nonlinear transformations by demonstrating their basic properties of homogeneity and additivity (also called superposition).

Homogeneity serves as both a trigger and a result. If an argument is multiplied by a factor, the result is multiplied by some power of the factor. What the cause and result represent in the real world does not matter. If you know a cause, you can predict a result because you understand the rule and the correlation of cause and result.

Multiplicative scaling behavior is, however, not the only possible linear correlation. The real world contains many examples of correlations that do not involve multiplicative scaling. For example, you know that the more you study, the better your grades are; we make a direct correlation between your efforts and your grades. This is a simple type of transformation. However, we cannot say that your grades will be twice as good if you learn twice as much material. In this case, the correlation between efforts and grade is nonlinear because it is not homogeneous.

The other requirement is additivity—another simple concept. When investigating a transformation, you check how it behaves after triggering it and check again after the cause (trigger) is modified. You know the end results for the first and second triggers. The next step is to predict the result if both triggers work simultaneously. If the result is the exact sum of the results we got using triggers separately then the phenomena (and the transformation or function we study) is additive.

Unfortunately, many processes and phenomena that are additive are simply not common in nature. If you fill a pitcher with water, you can put flowers in it. If the pitcher with flowers falls from a table, it will lie there. If you fill a pitcher with water and it falls from the table, you cannot put flowers in it. A pitcher full of water falling from a table will break. The break is thus a nonlinear phenomenon that cannot be predicted as a simple sum of activities that were studied separately.

When creating mathematical descriptions (models) of systems, processes or phenomena, we prefer linear functions because they are easy to use. Linear functions can create simple and efficient networks. Unfortunately, many functions cannot be put into "frames" of linearity. They require complex nonlinear mathematical models. A simpler answer is creating nonlinear neural networks that model the systems, processes or phenomena to be examined. Such neural networks are powerful and efficient tools. A huge multilevel linear network can correlate any types of inputs and outputs as a result of basic mathematical theorems about function interpolation and extrapolation developed by Andrei Kolmogorov, a great Russian mathematician.

We will not go into detail here because the modeling problem is highly theoretical and mathematical. For now, we assure you that the superiority of nonlinear networks over linear ones is a practical problem, not an academic issue. Nonlinear networks can solve many problems that linear networks cannot handle. The program we will study in this chapter will make that point clear. We suggest you experiment with other programs to examine how nonlinear networks work and what they can achieve.

6.2 Functioning of Nonlinear Neurons

We start with a simple program that shows how one nonlinear neuron works. Figure 6.1 illustrates the structure. The Example 06a program that models a nonlinear neuron is analogous to the Example 01c program we used earlier to explore how a linear neuron works. The Example 06a program will demonstrate step by step how a simple nonlinearly characterized neuron works. It starts by asking the user to choose between unipolar and bipolar characteristics (Figure 6.2) from the Neuron type field. You can set the amount of neuron input, but at this point we recommend accepting the default value of 4 and clicking on the Next button.

The concept of the unipolar characteristic is simple: the output signal is always nonnegative (usually 1 or 0 and certain nonlinear neurons can yield output values between these extremes). Bipolar characteristics allow a user to obtain either positive or negative signal values

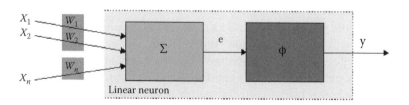

Figure 6.1 **Nonlinear neuron constructed by adding nonlinear transfer function to linear neuron.**

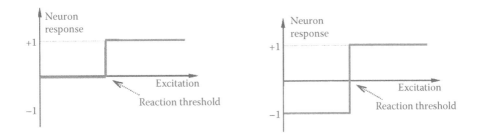

Figure 6.2   Nonlinear neuron characteristics: unipolar (left) and bipolar (right).

(usually +1 or −1, but intermediate values are possible). Figure 6.2 compares unipolar and bipolar characteristics and demonstrates the differences.

We should add one more qualification. Biological neurons such as those in your brain do not recognize negative signals. All signals in your brain must be positive (or zero if you are inactive). Therefore, the unipolar characteristic is more appropriate for achieving biological reality. Technical neural networks are different in that they are intended to act as useful computational tools instead of serving as accurate biological models. We want to avoid situations that allow 0 signals to appear in a network, especially when signals generated by one neuron are treated as inputs for other neurons within the same network. A network learns poorly if it encounters 0 signals. Remember the example of filtering signals discussed in Chapter 5.

The ability of bipolar structures to accept 0 and 1 expands their utility. We also use two other signals labeled +1 and −1. Look more closely at Figure 6.2.

Using the Example 06a program, you will note that nonlinear neurons are more categorical than linear neurons. Figure 6.3 depicts conversations with the program. Neurons and networks react to input signals in a subtle and balanced way. Certain combinations of input signals induce

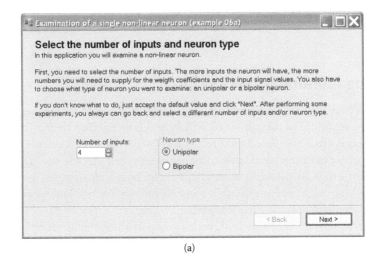

(a)

Figure 6.3   (a) Beginning of conversation with Example 06a program. (b) Next stage of conversation with Example 06a program. (*continued*)

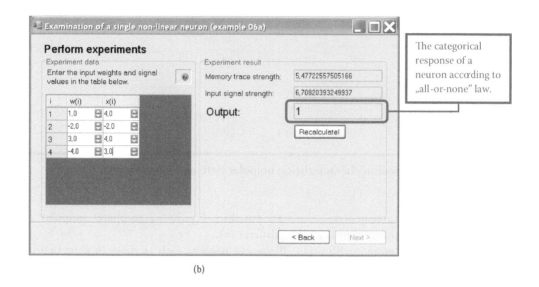

(b)

Figure 6.3 (*continued*) **(a) Beginning of conversation with Example 06a program. (b) Next stage of conversation with Example 06a program.**

a strong reaction (high output signal), whereas other inputs produce far weaker reactions or cause a network to be almost totally unresponsive when output signals approach 0.

Unlike the subtle linear neurons, nonlinear neurons work on an all-or-none principle. They can react negatively to certain combinations of signals by generating –1 outputs. Sometimes a minimal change in input signals is enough to make a neuron output signal become completely positive and change to +1 as shown in Figure 6.4.

While Example 06a is primitive, its operations are similar to those of a biological brain. A few simple experiments like those carried out with linear neurons will help you to understand how the program works and see how this type of network performs like a real nerve cell.

6.3 Teaching Nonlinear Networks

The Example 06a program involved a neuron whose output accepted two values associated with the acceptance (recognition) of certain set of signals or totally rejected them. This acceptance or rejection limitation is often connected with recognition of an object or a situation. Thus the neurons in the network we examined in Example 06a are often called perceptrons. They generate only two output signals: 1 or 0. In neurophysiology, this choice by a biological neuron is known as the everything-or-nothing rule. The Example 06a program follows this rule and we will use it to build all the networks described in subsequent chapters.

We now consider how to teach and work with a group of bipolar neurons by studying a simple single-layer network of bipolar neurons described in the Example 06b program. To teach a network from this program, you can use the `Default teaching set 06b.txt` file linked with example 06b. The file may have the following structure:

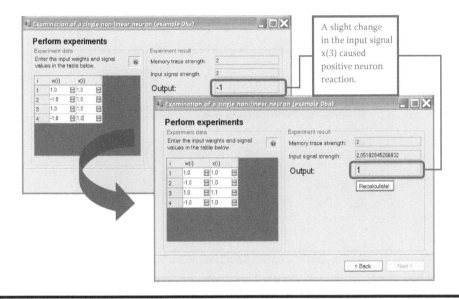

Figure 6.4 **Sensitivity of nonlinear neuron to change of input signal.**

A typical object that should be recognized by the first neuron is

```
3, 4, 3, 4, 5
1, -1, -1
```

A typical object that should be recognized by the second neuron is

```
1, -2, 1, -2, -4
-1, 1, -1
```

A typical object that should be recognized by the third neuron is

```
-3, 2, -5, 3, 1
-1, -1, 1
```

Contents of a similar file were discussed in Chapter 5 so we will not repeat the details here. You can review Chapter 5 if you need clarification. Comparing the above file to the one used earlier, we observe that a small number of examples is sufficient because a nonlinear network can learn very quickly. Usually only one step of learning is sufficient to eliminate errors (Figure 6.5). On average, a nonlinear network is taught fully after six or seven steps and is ready for examination. These networks learn quickly and thoroughly.

The effect of the knowledge generalization in neural networks is an important issue. What would be the benefit if you taught a neural network a series of tasks with the correct solutions and later find that it is unable to solve tasks beyond those it learned earlier? What you really need is a tool that learns to solve tasks from a teaching set and later can be used to solve other tasks by applying knowledge generalization. Knowledge generalization means that learning on a limited number of examples not only gains the knowledge necessary for solving these examples, but also can solve other unknown problems similar to those used during learning.

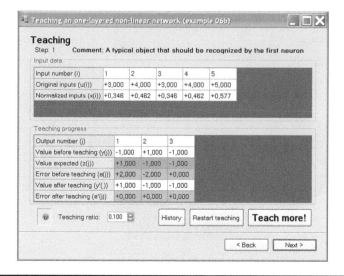

Figure 6.5 A nonlinear network succeeds in removing most errors after the first step of teaching.

Fortunately, neural networks can generalize knowledge (Figure 6.6) and skillfully solve tasks similar to those included in a teaching set if the tasks are based on the similar logic of the relationships between inputs and outputs. Generalization of knowledge is one of the most important features of neural networks. For that reason, we encourage you to change input data on which teaching is based. We recommend that you try to "bully" a nonlinear network in various ways to assess its capabilities and compare its performance with performances of linear networks.

6.4 Demonstrating Actions of Nonlinear Neurons

The outputs of neural networks built from nonlinear neurons can be interpreted easily by drawing the so-called input signal space and indicating which values of the signals trigger positive responses (+1) and which ones trigger negative responses (–1) of neurons. Assume we want to interpret input signal space data.

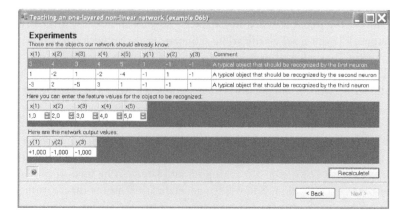

Figure 6.6 Nonlinear network effectively generalizes knowledge gained during teaching.

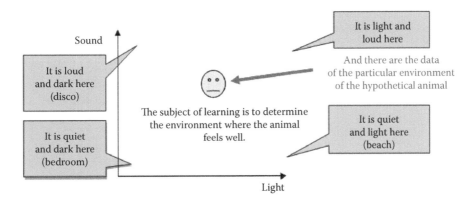

Figure 6.7 Experimental world of a hypothetical animal with a neuron brain containing receptors for sight and sound.

Each point inside the large square created by Example 06c represents a set of data (equivalent to the horizontal and vertical coordinates of the position of a point) composed of input signals of a neural network. The analyzed network is the brain of a hypothetical animal equipped with receptors for sight and sound (Figure 6.7). The stronger the signal received by the sight receptor, the more the point drifts to the right. The stronger the sounds are, the higher the location of the point.

The bottom left corner of the figure represents the conditions of silence and darkness (bedroom). The upper right corner indicates maximum sound and light conditions, for example, in a city's main square at noon. The upper left corner may represent a disco because conditions are dark and loud. The bottom corner is sunny and quiet, like a beach. You can imagine similar analogies for other points in the square. All the situations in the figure can be perceived by the hypothetical animal as positive (the point will show intense red color) or negative (blue); see Figure 6.8.

Imagine that the brain of our modeled animal consists of a single nonlinear neuron. Obviously, the neuron must have two inputs to accommodate the receptors for sight and sound. The two weights must be determined for each receptor. For example, when the first

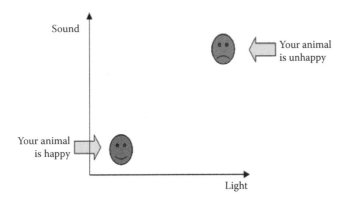

Figure 6.8 Determining wellbeing of hypothetical animal.

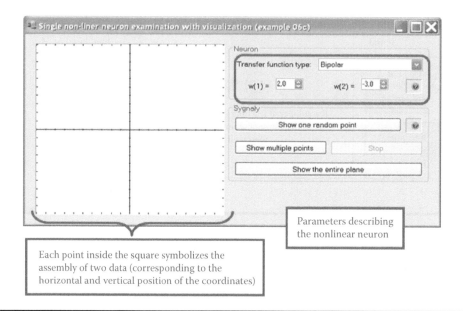

Figure 6.9 Setting neuron parameters in Example 06c program.

weight (sight) is positive, the animal may like lighted surroundings. A negative value may cause the animal to hide in a dark corner. The same procedure can be used with the second weight (sound), allowing you to determine whether the animal prefers peace and quiet or heavy metal concerts.

After your animal is programmed, it will be tested by exposure to different combinations of two input signals. Each initial combination of signals can be treated as an indication of a specified environment where the animal is placed. The properties of this environment are symbolized by a point on the plane of the picture. The value of the first signal (lighting) indicates the *x* axis of the point. The value of the second signal (sound) is the *y* axis. The neuron makes its decision based on the basis of input signals. A +1 indicates a type of environment will be accepted by the animal; −1 indicates rejection by the animal.

Try to prepare a map depicting the preferences of your neuron by coloring the points accepted by the neuron (+1 output) in red and indicated the rejected (−1) points in blue. The Example 06c program will perform this exercise for you. You must first provide all the weights to define the preferences of your neuron (Figure 6.9). You can then check the values (+1 or −1) generated by the neuron at its output at specific points on its input signal plane. The program is very useful because it performs calculations, draws a map, and generates the required input signals for neurons and provides their coordinates (Figure 6.10).

If you want to monitor the positions of new points on the screen, you can press the "Show one random point" button. A currently generated point is already marked by its coordinates projected onto the axes so it can be easily distinguished from the points generated earlier. While checking the position of a new point, you may wonder why the neuron accepted or rejected it. Data for the present point are shown on the line below the picture. Many points will be needed to create a map that would indicate precisely the areas of input signal planes where the responses were positive

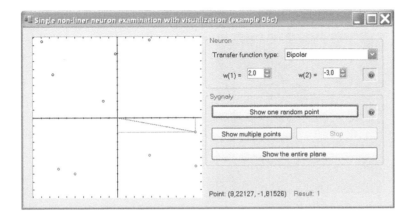

Figure 6.10   Color (in ebook) presentation of neuron response to input signal.

and negative. Pressing the "Show multiple points" button will switch the program into continuous mode in which the subsequent points are automatically generated and displayed on the map. You can always switch back to the previous mode by aborting the process with the Stop button. Eventually, the outline of the areas with the positive and negative responses of the neuron will appear (Figure 6.11).

The border between these areas is clearly a straight line; it may be said that a single neuron performs a linear discrimination of the input plane. However, that statement refers only to what you will see on the screen while conducting the experiments described here.

If you wish to see the map of the neuron response without the effort of generating the points, the Example 06c program allows you to do so by using the "Show the entire plane" button (Figure 6.12). One interesting experiment is to change the nonlinear characteristic of a neuron by choosing another option from the "Transfer function type" list.

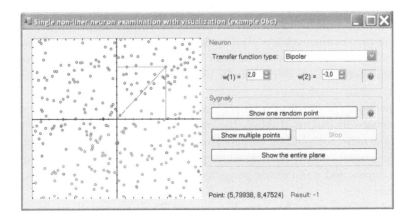

Figure 6.11   Screenshot of Example 06c after generating many points.

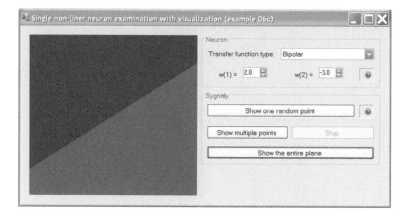

Figure 6.12 Screenshot of the Example 06c showing neuron response map.

6.5 Capabilities of Multilayer Networks of Nonlinear Neurons

One neuron (or one layer of neurons) may distribute two input signals by the boundary line in two-dimensional space as a straight line. By appropriately combining such linear bounded areas and properly juxtaposing them, you can obtain virtually any values of aggregated output signals at any points of input signal space. The neural network literature often contains the somewhat misleading claim of using neurons to generate arbitrarily accurate approximations of all kinds of functions.

This is not possible for a single layer of neurons, as shown by theorems of Cybenko, Hornik, Lapedes, Farber, and others. Scientific reason indicates that the use of multiple layers is necessary in such cases because structural elements forming the desired function built by learning neurons must be collected at the end by at least one resulting neuron (usually linear). This means that networks described as universal approximators in fact contain at least two and often three layers.

Bold statements that networks can approximate any function irritate mathematicians who then attempt to devise functions that neural networks cannot master. The mathematicians are correct in that a neural network does not have a chance with certain types of operations but nature is more generous than mathematicians. Real-world processes (physical, chemical, biological, technical, economic, social, and others) can be described by functions that exhibit certain degrees of regularity. Neural networks are able to handle such functions easily, especially if they consist of multiple layers.

Clearly a network consisting of multiple layers of neurons has much richer potential than the single-layer network discussed above. The areas where neurons will positively react to input signals can have more complicated forms. Two-layer networks contain convex polygons or their multidimensional counterparts called simplexes. Neural networks with more layers may contain both convex and non-convex polygons or even connected areas composed of many separate "islands."

The Example 06D program illustrates this situation. This program allows you to obtain maps such as those built in the previous program faster. Most important, the program works for networks with any number of layers. If you choose a single-layer network, you will see the familiar image of linear discrimination (Figure 6.12).

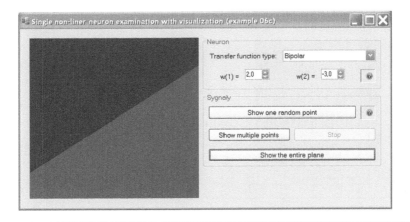

Figure 6.13   Two-layer network showing simplex phenomenon.

If you choose a two-layer network, you will see that the network can cut out the connected subspace convex bounded by planes (simplex) in the input signal space (Figure 6.13). A network with three or more layers has no such limitations. The area highlighted by the network in the input signal space can be complicated, not necessarily convex, and not necessarily connected (Figure 6.14). By using Example 06d, you can examine a lot more areas because the program randomly uses properties of the network. This enables you to view variants of the shapes described above.

It is also possible to change the network parameters, including the number of layers, neuron activation function (select Transfer function type), and number of network outputs. The network has other interesting features beyond the scope of this chapter. We encourage you, however, to try and discover all the potential of this program. If you are interested in programming, we encourage you to analyze its code because it is a good example of the art of programming.

Figure 6.15 and Figure 6.16 produced by this program clearly show how the growing number of network layers increases a system's ability to process input information and implement complex algorithms expressing the relationships of input and output signals. These phenomena did not occur in the linear networks we discussed earlier. Regardless of the number of layers, a linear network realizes only linear processing operations of input data into output data so there is little

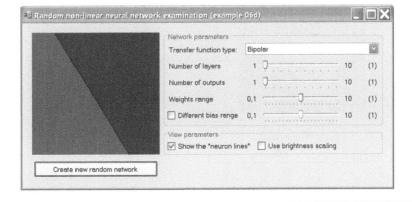

Figure 6.14   Exemplary area of reaction of neural network with single layer.

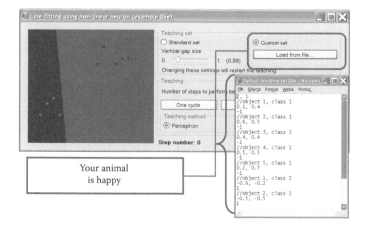

Figure 6.15   Exemplary area of reaction of neural network with two layers.

need to build multilayer linear networks. The picture is quite different for nonlinear networks in which increasing the number of layers is a basic operation intended to improve the functioning of the network.

6.6 Nonlinear Neuron Learning Sequence

We now consider the geometrical interpretation of the learning process of a nonlinear neural network. We start from the simplest case—the learning process of a single neuron. As we know, the action of such a neuron is to divide the region of input signals into two regions, In a flat case (e.g., a typical two-dimensional Cartesian space), the linear function will be a straight line but interesting structures will appear in the n-dimensional space. They are affine varieties of the $n - 1$ order or simply hyperplanes. Such surfaces must be precisely to separate input points for which the network should give contradictory answers.

The Example 06e program will allow you to see how learning of a nonlinear neuron takes place and how the boundary is changed automatically from the random position set at the beginning

Figure 6.16   Exemplary area of reaction of neural network with three layers.

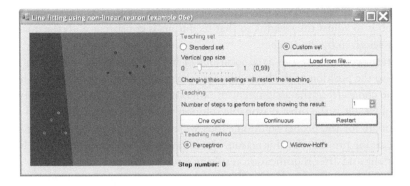

Figure 6.17 Selection of custom set of data from user's file together with example of content of user's data set file for Example 06e.

to the optimum location to separate two groups of points for which the conflicting decisions were applied during the learning process.

The initial screen of the program shows two sets of points (10 objects each) for sequence learning. Points belonging to one set are shown as small black circles. The second set points are shown as white circles. The collection consists of two clearly separate clusters, but to make the task more difficult, each set contains a single "malicious" point located in the direction of the opposite set. Fitting the boundary line, first between sets, and then more precisely between the "malicious" points located close to each other, is the main task of the learning process. The positions of these points may be adjusted freely by creating an input data file in the Example 06e program, then choosing "Custom set" option in the teaching set to load it (Figure 6.17). An example is presented in the `Default teaching set 06e.txt` file.

At the beginning, it will be comfortable to run the program with default parameters (Standard set). A slider option allows a change of set location (Vertical gap size). A closer location makes the neuron's task more difficult. When you select Standard set and run the program, you will see the screen shown in Figure 6.18.

The image shows the points mentioned above and the initial random position of the boundary line at the junction of two half-planes marked with different colors. Of course, the initial position

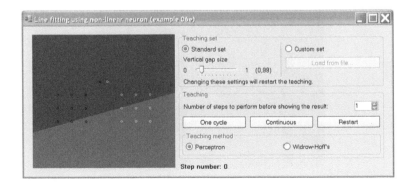

Figure 6.18 Initial state of learning process in Example 06e program after selection of Standard set option for input data.

of the boundary line depends on the initial parameters of the neuron. As usual with learning tasks, the neuron's job is to adjust the weights so that its output is consistent with the qualifying points of the training set given by the teacher.

On the screen, you can see the fixed locations of both sets of points on which the neuron is trained, and also the position of the boundary line that changes during learning. The initial position of this line comes from the assignment of random values to all neuron weights. Such initial randomizing of weight is the most reasonable solution since we have no idea which weight values will be appropriate for the proper solution. Thus we cannot propose a more reasonable starting point for the learning process. For this reason, we cannot predict the location of the line separating our points initially and after modification resulting from learning.

By observing how the line gradually changes position and "squeezes" between the delimited sets of points, you can learn a lot about the nature of learning processes for neurons with nonlinear characteristics. Each time you click the "One cycle" button, learning of the desired number of steps in the cycle occurs.

You can change the number of learning steps performed in a single cycle before the next display of the boundary line. This feature is very practical because learning is characterized by rapid progress at the beginning (consecutive learning steps easily shift the boundary line); subsequent progress is much slower. We recommend setting smaller numbers (1, 5, or 10) at the beginning. Later you will have to set "jumps" of 100 and of 500 steps of the learning process between consecutive shows (Figure 6.18).

You do not have to constantly click the "One cycle" button. Pressing the "Continuous" button will instruct the program to follow one cycle until the button is pressed again. The program displays how many learning steps were performed. See the "Step number" feature at the bottom of the application window that allows you to monitor the learning process.

As seen in Figure 6.18, the initial position of the boundary line is far from the target location. As expected, one side of the boundary line displays all points belonging to one set and the other side indicates all points of the second set. The first learning stage (Figure 6.18) is very short—only three shows—but produces noticeable improvement. This trend continues through subsequent steps as more points are separated (Figure 6.19). Unfortunately, Step 51 reveals deterioration of

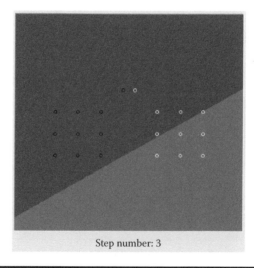

Step number: 3

Figure 6.19   Changes of border line at initial phase of learning process.

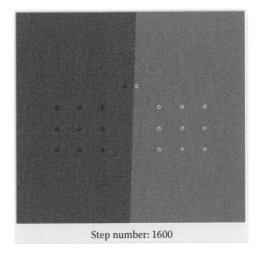

Step number: 1600

Figure 6.20 Changes of border line at final phase of learning process.

learning and more points are located on the wrong side of the boundary line. The network performance deteriorated after it encountered the "malicious" points that are very difficult to separate from points in a set of easily distinguishable data. The next 10 steps fix this crisis in the learning process and generate significant improvement.

Figure 6.20 indicates that learning is finished and was successful because the final line (on the boundary of the red and blue half-plane) separates the set of points ideally. Note that after a network reaches a correct solution, continued learning will not yield anything new. For example, the lines shown after 1600 and 3600 steps of learning are the same. This is natural, because after learning a neuron does not modify the proper (determined by point qualification) values of the weighting factors.

6.7 Experimentation during Learning Phase

Example 06e allows you to conduct experiments in various ways. After you set up the data of interest and the desired parameters, you can change the positions of the individual points or even entire learning data sets. You can also apply one of the learning methods for nonlinear neurons described in the literature: the perceptron based on output signal and its confrontation with the learning data set or the Widrow–Hoff technique that assumes that learning is performed only for linear parts (net value-based learning). You can select one of these from the Teaching method list.

By conducting your own research, you can demonstrate that the Widrow–Hoff method named for its inventors is more robust in some cases. After a few attempts, you will find that almost ideal separation will be achieved more quickly by the Widrow–Hoff method than by the perceptron. The Widrow–Hoff method never stops learning. After finding a correct solution, it reviews it, repairs it, and continues the process.

People behave similarly. Aleksander Gierymski, a famous Polish painter, was never satisfied with his work. After painting masterpieces, he was obsessed with improving them. He erased objects, added new ones, and continued modifying his paintings until they became worthless.

The only remaining works of this great artist were rescued by his friends who forcibly took them—unfinished—from his atelier!

Questions and Self-Study Tasks

1. List at least three advantages that justify the use of nonlinear neurons in solving complex computing tasks.

2. Do linear neurons have unipolar or bipolar characteristics (transfer functions)?

3. What are the benefits of the bipolar transfer functions of neurons? Are they present in the brains of humans and animals? Why?

4. Two commonly used neuron transfer functions are shown in Figure 6.20. Which one is unipolar and which is bipolar?

5. What is the generalization of knowledge phenomenon observed in neural network learning?

6. What limitations must be taken into account for tasks that can be solved by neural networks of (a) a single layer, (b) a double layer, and (c) three layers?

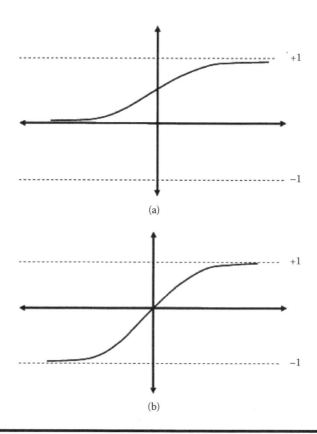

Figure 6.21 Neuron transfer function for question 4.

7. Based on experiments with the classification of points belonging to two classes of sketch graphs, show how the error rates of networks change as they learn.

8. What conclusions do you draw by analyzing the shape of the graph obtained by answering Question 7?

9. Why do repeated learning attempts by the same network based on the same training data usually result in variations of learning processes?

10. Advanced exercise: Try to justify the theorem (which is true) that linear networks with multiple layers can achieve only the same simple mapping of input data to output results as a one-layer network. The conclusion (also true) is that a multilayer structure for a linear network produces no advantage.

11. Build a program that will teach multilayer neural networks to recognize classes built from points placed arbitrarily on the screen by clicking the mouse at certain positions.

12. Build a program that allows a network to classify the input points in five (rather than two) classes as shown in the program used in this chapter.

Chapter 7

Backpropagation

7.1 Definition

In Chapter 6, we discussed some aspects of functioning and teaching a single-layer neural network built from nonlinear elements. Let us continue the analysis now, showing how multilayer nonlinear networks work. They present more significant and interesting possibilities, as we saw from working with the Example 06 program.

You now know how to build multilayer networks from nonlinear neurons and how a nonlinear neuron can be taught, for example, by modifying Example 06. However, you have not yet encountered a basic problem of teaching such multilayer neural networks built from nonlinear neurons: the so-called hidden layers (Figure 7.1). What is the impact of this problem?

The rules of teaching that you encountered in earlier chapters were based on a simple but very successful method: each neuron of a network individually introduces corrections to its working knowledge by changing the values of the weight coefficients on all its inputs on the basis of a set error value. In a single-layer network, the situation was simple and obvious. The output signal of each neuron was compared with the correct value given by the teacher and this step was sufficient to enable the neuron to correct the weights. The process is not quite as easy for a multilayer network. Neurons of the final (output) layer may have their errors estimated simply by a comparison of the signal produced by each neuron with a model signal from the teacher.

What about the neurons from the previous layers? Their errors must be estimated mathematically because they cannot be measured directly. We do not know what the values of the correct signals should be because the teacher does not define the intermediate values and focuses only on the final result.

A method commonly used to "guess" the errors of neurons in hidden layers is called backpropagation (short for backward propagation). This method is so popular that in most programs used to create networks and teaching networks, backpropagation is applied as default method. Other teaching methods, for example, involve an accelerated method of this algorithm called quick propagation and systems based on sophisticated mathematical methods such as conjugate gradient and Levenberg–Marquardt methods.

Backpropagation methods have the advantage of speed but the advantage is available only when a problem to be solved by a neural network (by finding a solution based on its learning)

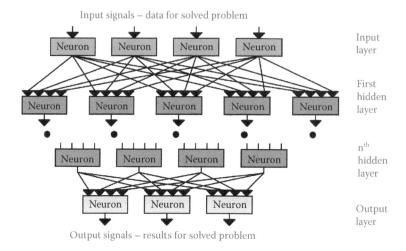

Figure 7.1 Hidden layers in multilayer nonlinear neural network.

meets all the sophisticated mathematical requirements. We may know the problem to be solved but have no idea whether it meets the complex requirements.

What does that mean in practice? Assume we have a difficult task to solve. We start teaching a neural network with a sophisticated modern method such as the Levenberg–Marquardt algorithm. If we had the type of problem for which the algorithm was designed, the network could be taught quickly. If the problem does not fit this specification, the algorithm will endlessly lead the network astray because the theoretical assumptions of the algorithm are not met.

The huge advantage of backpropagation is that unlike other techniques, it works independently of theoretical assumptions. While complex clever algorithms sometimes work, backpropagation always works. Its operation may be irritatingly slow but it will never let you down.

You should understand backpropagation because people who work with neural networks rely on it as a dependable partner.

The backpropagation method will be presented through the analysis of the behavior of another program. Before that, however, we must cover one new detail that is very important: the shapes of nonlinear characteristics used in testing neurons.

7.2 Changing Thresholds of Nonlinear Characteristics

Chapter 6 discussed neurons based on the all-or-nothing concept. They were based on logical categorization of input signals (true or false; 1 or 0) or on bipolar characteristics (approval or disapproval; +1 or −1). In both cases the transition between two states was sudden. If the summed output signals exceeded the threshold, the instant result was +1. If the output signals were so weak (a condition known as subliminal stimulation), the system indicated no reaction (0) or a totally negative (−1) reaction.

The rule of zero value of threshold was assumed, which meant that the positive sum of input signals was +1 and the negative value was 0 or −1, and this limited the possibilities of such networks. As we discuss the transitions of nonlinear neurons, keep in mind the value of threshold: it need not have zero value.

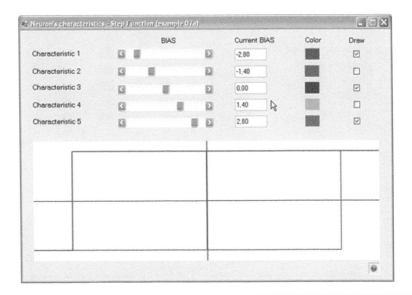

Figure 7.2 Family of threshold characteristics of neuron with changeable BIAS value (Example 07a).

In the nonlinear models of neurons analyzed in this chapter, the threshold will be released. This will lead to the appearance of moving characteristics chosen freely by a feature called BIAS included in programs for modeling networks. The Example 07a program will enable you to understand a family of threshold characteristics of neurons by changing BIAS values. The result will be a good overview of the role of BIAS in shaping the behaviors of single neurons and whole networks. This program demonstrates the behavior of a neuron with a freely shaped threshold (Figure 7.2).

7.3 Shapes of Nonlinear Characteristics

The characteristics of a biological neuron are very complex as noted in earlier chapters. Between the state of maximum stimulation (tetanus stage) and the subliminal state devoid of activity (diastole stage), several intermediate stages appear as impulses with changeable frequencies. In other words, the stronger the input stimulus a neuron receives from its dendrites (inputs), the greater the frequency of the impulses in the outputs. All information in the brain is transmitted by a method called pulse code modulation (PCM)[*] invented by Mother Nature a few billion years before engineers started using it in electronic devices.

A full discussion of coding the signals of neurons in a brain goes beyond the scope of this book, but if you are interested, review a book by one of the authors titled *Biocybernetics Problems.*[†] For purposes of this chapter, we simply need to know that it is possible (and practical) to use neural networks whose outputs consist of signals that change continuously in a range of 0 to 1 or –1 to 1. Such neurons with continuous nonlinear transfer functions differ from the linear neurons

---

[*] PCM is a method of impulse coding of signals used in electronics, automatics, robotics, and telecommunications.

[†] Tadeusiewicz, Ryszard. 1994. *Biocybernetics Problems* (Original Polish title: *Problembiocybernetyki*), Second edition. Warsaw: PWN.

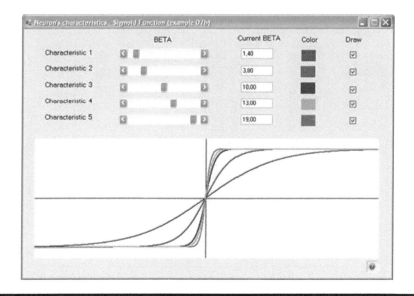

Figure 7.3   Various forms of logistic curves (Example 07b).

discussed at length in early chapters and also from nonlinear discontinuous neurons that are limited to two output signals covered in Chapter 6.

A full explanation of continuously changing operation requires the use of mathematical theorems and we promised not to use them in this book. However, we can certainly see that nonlinear neurons with continuous characteristics have huge potential. Because they are nonlinear, they can form multilayer networks and are far more flexible than linear neurons in handling inputs and outputs. The signals in such networks can take any values so they are useful in solving tasks that define values (e.g., stock market fluctuations). Their responses are not limited to the yes-or-no decisions of the networks we discussed earlier.

The second argument is less obvious but just as important and involves the abandonment of the simple "jumping" characteristics of primitive networks. For a multilayer neural network to teach, its neurons must have continuity and differential* characteristics. It is sufficient to understand that the transfer function of a neuron in a multilayer teaching network must be sufficiently "smooth" to ensure that teaching proceeds without interruptions.

We could find many uses for the transfer functions of neurons. The most popular is the logistic or sigmoid curve. A sigmoid has several advantages: (1) it provides a smooth transition between the 0 and 1 values; (2) it has smooth derivatives that can be calculated easily; (3) it has one parameter (usually called *beta*) whose value permits a user to choose the shape of the curve freely from very flat (almost linear) to very steep (transition from 0 to 1).

The Example 07b program will allow you to understand transition thoroughly. By building the nonlinear transition function of a neuron, the possibility of moving the "switch" point between the values of 0 and 1 with the use of BIAS is taken into account, but you may also choose the steepness of the curve and general degree of the nonlinear behavior of the neuron (Figure 7.3).

---

* *Continuity* and *differential* are of course mathematical notions. It would be helpful (but not critical) for you to understand them. The terms will not be used in subsequent chapters.

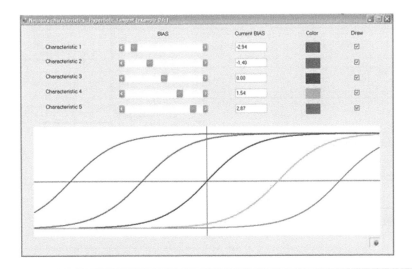

Figure 7.4 Various forms of hyperbolic tangent function (from Example 07c).

The logistic curve whose properties may be explored with Example 07b has many applications in natural sciences. Every development, whether it involves a start-up company or new technology, follows the logistic curve. At the beginning, growth is small and progress is slow. As experience and resources are gathered, development starts to accelerate and the curve rises more steeply. At the point of success (the steepest section of the ascending), the curve begins to bend toward the horizontal. The bend is almost unnoticeable but growth eventually stops—a state known as satiation. The end of each development involves stagnation (not visible on the logistic curve) and inevitable fall.

A variation of a sigmoid for bipolar signals (symmetrically arranged between –1 and +1) is a hyperbolic tangent (Figure 7.4). The best option is to examine it in the Example 07c program. After you understand the characteristics of nonlinear neurons, you are ready to build a network from them and start to teach it.

7.4 Functioning of Multilayer Network Constructed of Nonlinear Elements

Multilayer networks constructed from nonlinear elements are currently the basic tools for practical applications and many commercial and public domain programs are available to suit many needs. We will focus on two simple programs intended to demonstrate the functioning of a multilayer network (Example 08a) and a method for teaching such a network (Example 08b).

If you analyze the relevant sections carefully and conduct the experiments by using he programs, you will understand the uses and benefits of backpropagation because it serves a critical function in neural networks and is used universally. After you understand backpropagation, most network issues will be easy for you to recognize and correct in any area of practice.

Program Example 08a shows the functioning of complex network built of only four neurons (Figure 7.5) that form three layers: (1) input that cannot be taught (at top of screen); (2) output where the signals are copied, assessed, and taught (at bottom of screen); and (3) the

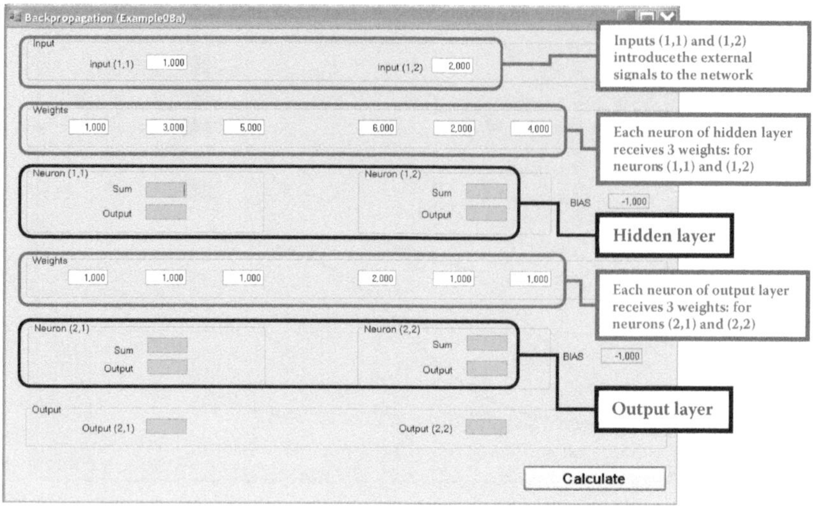

Figure 7.5 Setting parameters and input signals for network in Example 08a program.

vital hidden layer shown in the center of the screen. Neurons and signals in the network will be assigned two numbers: the number of the layer and the number of the neuron (or signal) in a layer.

Upon opening, the program asks you to give it the weight coefficients for all neurons in the network (Figure 7.5). You should input 12 coefficients. Our system has four neurons (two in the hidden layer and two in the output layer) to be taught and each of them has three inputs (two from the neurons of the previous layer plus one input also needing a weight coefficient and connected with the threshold that generates an artificial constant BIAS signal.

The advantage of this system is clear. In networks consisting of hundreds of neurons and thousands of weight coefficients, a user does not have to enter all the data because the neurons are designed to set them automatically during the teaching process. In the Example 08a program, you have the option of inputting the parameters to allow you to check whether the output results are what you intended. You will be able to shape the input signals to the network freely and observe both input and output signals of the neurons. Of course, the program includes default values. It is best to choose simple whole numbers as weight coefficients and input signals because they allow you to check easily whether the results produced are those you calculated.

After setting the coefficients, you must determine the values of both input signals (Figure 7.5). The program is now ready to work. Figure 7.6 depicts the beginning of the demonstration.

If you click the Calculate button, you will start the simulation process of sending and processing the signals in a modeled network. In each following layer the calculations are made and displayed (against a red background) as the sums of the values of signals multiplied by the correct weights of input signals (along with BIAS component).

Next, the calculated values of the output signals (answers) of particular neurons will be shown (also against a red background) after the added input signals passed through the transfer function. The paths of the signals are shown as arrows on Figure 7.7. The answers of neurons of the lower layer become the inputs for the neurons of the higher layer and the process repeats itself (Figure 7.8).

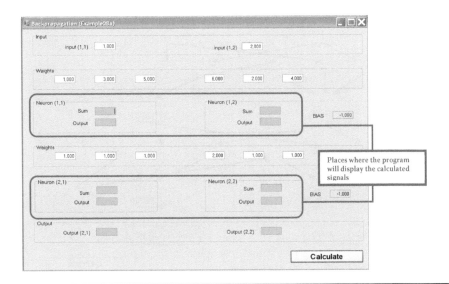

Figure 7.6   Beginning of network demonstration in Example 08a program.

If you press the Calculate button, you can observe the movements of the signals from the input to the output of the analyzed network model. You can change the values of the inputs and observe the outputs as many times as required to ensure that you understand the functioning of the network. We suggest you spend some time reviewing the analysis and the calculations. You can verify results on a calculator to be sure the numbers match those expected. This is the only way you can understand precisely how these networks function.

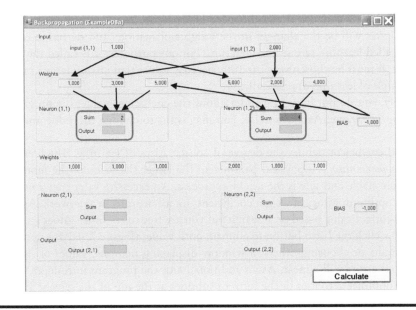

Figure 7.7   Direction of signal transmission in initial operation of network.

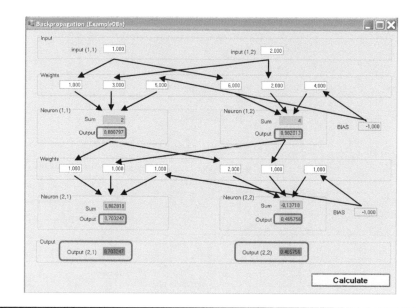

Figure 7.8 Final stage of functioning. All signals have been calculated.

7.5 Teaching Multilayer Networks

When a multilayer network utilizing your selected weight values and signals holds no more secrets for you, you may want to experiment with it as a learning entity. The Example 08b program is designed for teaching these networks.

After launching this program, you must set the values of two coefficients that determine the course of the teaching process. The first specifies the size of the corrections introduced after finding incoming mistakes and also marks the speed of learning. The larger the coefficient value, the stronger and faster will be the changes in the weights of neurons and detection of errors. This coefficient is called learning rate in the literature. For our purposes, it is called the simple learning coefficient. It must be chosen very carefully because values that are too large or too small will impact the course of learning dramatically.

Fortunately, you do not have to wonder about the coefficient value; the program will suggest an appropriate value. As an exercise, you may want to change the value and observe the effects.

The second coefficient defines the degree of conservatism of learning. The literature defines this quality as *momentum*—a physical parameter. The larger the value of the momentum coefficient, the more stable and safe is the teaching process. An excessive value may cause difficulties in finding the optimum values of weight coefficients for all neurons in a network. Again, the program uses the correct value based on research but you are free to try other values.

We can now click the Intro button to confirm both values (Figure 7.9). After setting the coefficients as defaults or choosing others, a window displaying neurons, values of signals, weight coefficients, and errors will appear. As an additional aid, the program introduces an additional element that simplifies activities in the form of subtitles at the top of the screen. The simplification is helpful because the tasks of this teaching program are more complex than those of the previous one.

Figure 7.9 Setting of parameters marking learning efficiency in Example 08b program.

7.6 Observations during Teaching

The task of the modeled network is to identify the input signals correctly. Ideal identification should display Signal 1 in the initial layer of the neuron assigned for a given class (left or right). The second neuron should of course give at the same time a value of 0. To assess the accuracy of network functioning, we can set some less strict conditions. It is sufficient if the error of any output is not greater than 0.5* because then the classification of the input signal of the network does not differ from the classification given by the teacher.

The notion of error measured as divergence between the real values of input signals and the values given by the teacher as models is not the same as the assessment of the correctness of solutions generated by the network because this assessment involves the general behavior of the network and not the values of single signals. We can often ignore small deviations as long as the network generates correct answers.

Teaching with backpropagation is not likely to be as tolerant as earlier methods as you will see in working with the programs. If an output should have been 1 and the neuron set it at 0.99, backpropagation considers the result an error. However, such perfectionism is an advantage in this situation. Perfect values determined by a teacher enable a network to operate more efficiently.

A school analogy comes to mind here. The concepts learned in geometry do not appear of practical value because we seldom encounter ideal geometric situations in real life. However, an understanding of basic geometry helps us solve practical tasks like determining the amount of fencing required for a building site. Likewise, some knowledge of physics and biology will help you understand the operations of neural networks and apply them as tools in various areas like medicine, economics, and environmental studies.

During teaching, your role will be limited to observation. You simply have to press buttons and review the results on the screen. The program generates the initial values of weights and input signals for identification. Some data such as initial weights and input signals are chosen at random but the models of correct identifications used to teach the network are not random. It may be of help to examine the way the program functions but the network will operate automatically and classify the signals correctly.

At the beginning the program shows only the structure of the network. Note the subtitles in red at the top of the screen (Figure 7.10). Notice that the sources of BIAS pseudo signals are marked on a yellow background so that they are not mistaken for the sources and values of the signals taking part in teaching.

---

* For example, for the input signals that appear during learning that equal −4.437 and 1.034, the network responses are 0.529 and 0.451, and they qualify as errors because the object with such coordinates should be treated as second class. In the meantime, the input of the second neuron is smaller than the first. The second object of the teaching array presented by the program with coordinates −3.720 and 4.937 causes responses of 0.399 and 0.593, and may be considered correct (they are also objects of the second class) although the values of mean squared errors in both cases are similar. Try to duplicate this situation during your experiments.

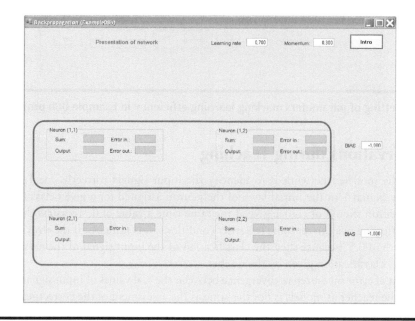

Figure 7.10 Network structure.

A second press of the Intro button will show you the values of weight coefficients chosen at random at the beginning for all inputs of all the neurons (Figure 7.11). Another click of the button will reveal the values of input signals of neurons [(1,1) and (1,2); Figure 7.12]. Teaching begins at this moment. Your role is limited to pressing the Next button as required to start and conduct a simulation of the network model (Figure 7.13).

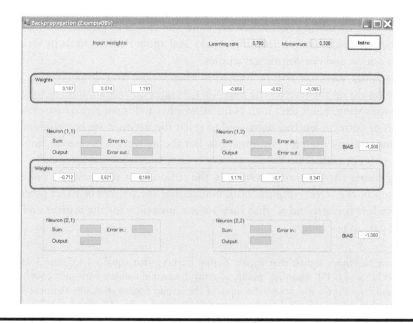

Figure 7.11 Network and its parameters.

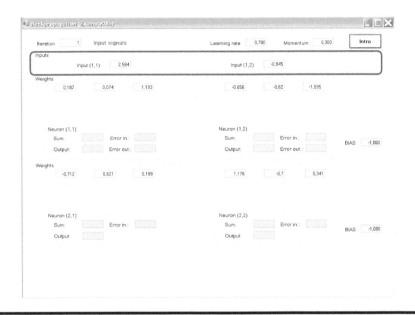

Figure 7.12   Appearance of input signals.

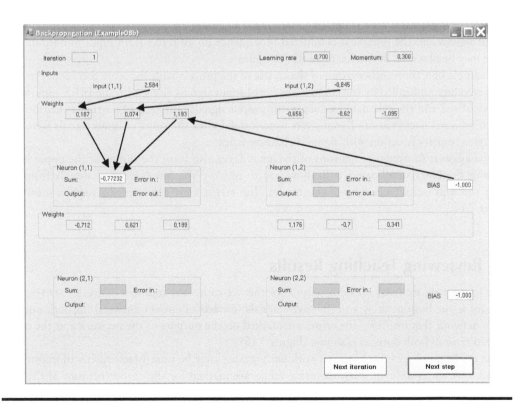

Figure 7.13   Screen view during initial stage of simulation of network functioning.

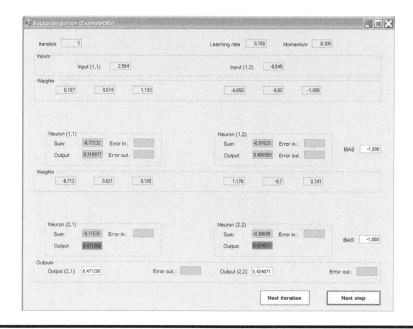

Figure 7.14   Network after finishing forward propagation.

First, the signals calculated to send signals from input to output will be shown for certain neurons. This process is forward propagation. Input signals are recalculated by the neurons on the output signals and the process is conducted in sequence on all layers from input to output. This phase may be observed in the Example 08a program.

Example 08b allows observation of the course of the process with the same precision. First the sums of values multiplied by the correct weights of input signals along with the BIAS component are calculated and the calculated values of the output signals (answers) of particular neurons are shown on a red background. The answers were formed after the sums of input signals were sent through a transfer function with sigmoid characteristics.

The answers (outputs) of neurons of the lower layer also form the inputs of the upper layer. Pressing the Next step button will allow you to observe the movements of signals from the input through output neurons of the model. The target view after several steps is shown in Figure 7.14.

7.7 Reviewing Teaching Results

After the signals are fixed on both outputs of the network, "the moment of truth" arrives. The subtitles at the bottom show you the given signals (models of correct answers) for both outputs of the network (Figure 7.15). The errors are marked on the outputs of the network and the mean squared error of both outputs is shown (Figure 7.16).

At the beginning of teaching, network performance may be unsatisfactory. It will improve as the network starts to learn. First the error values are marked for the output neurons of the network. Then the errors are recalculated into corresponding values on the inputs of neurons (that is

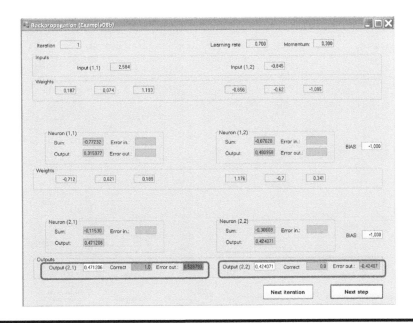

Figure 7.15 Comparison of results of network functioning with model given by teacher.

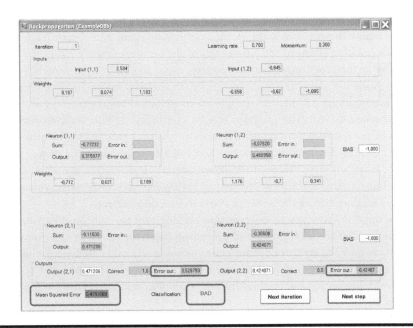

Figure 7.16 Marking errors of output layer neurons and mean error of entire network.

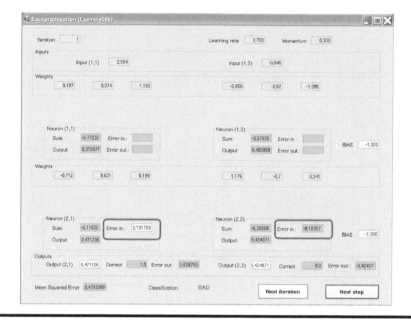

Figure 7.17   Transfer of errors on inputs of neurons.

why we need the differentiable transfer function of a neuron). The errors transferred to the input are marked in Figure 7.17.

We have now reached the most important stage—propagation of errors to the lower (hidden) layer. The right correct values of respective neurons are shown first as outputs and then by inputs (Figure 7.18). When all error values for all neurons are marked, the next step of the program leads them to setting new (corrected) values of weight coefficients for the entire network. New coefficients appear below the previous ones. A user can review them and determine how far and in which direction teaching changed the parameters of the network (Figure 7.19).

At this point in the program, the screen displays input signals, output signals, errors, and old and new weight values. Analyze the results carefully. The better your understanding of the process, the more chances you have for successful applications of neural networks.

Further experiments with the program can be continued. If you want to review the complete iteration of the teaching process (signal movements, backpropagation of errors, and weight changes), you can press the Next step button. You can also accelerate your review by "jumping" to the moment when the new values of the signals, errors, and weights are marked by using the Next iteration button. This is the most convenient review method. Otherwise, you will have to go through many iterations before the network starts to function correctly.

The review options allow you to observe the teaching process comfortably. You can view the changes of weights and the vital process of projecting the error values in the output layer backward. You will see how the errors of output neurons and errors calculated via backpropagation of hidden layers enable the system to find the needed corrections of values of weight coefficients for all neurons. You will also see the gradual introduction of corrections during teaching. The final result is shown in Figure 7.20.

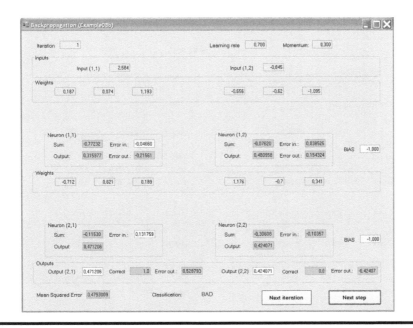

Figure 7.18 Result of backpropagation of errors.

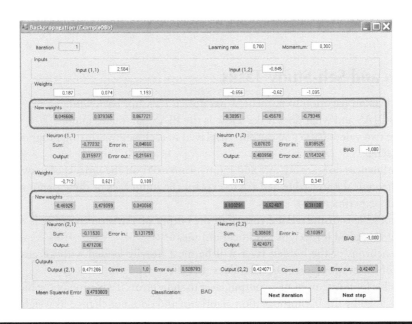

Figure 7.19 Change of weight coefficients.

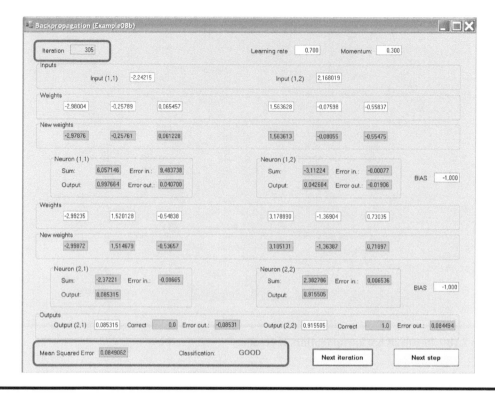

Figure 7.20 Final result of teaching.

Working with the Example 08b program required some effort because of its complexity. Observing the changing values and processes provided you a tool for understanding backpropagation—one of the most important methods of teaching modern neural networks.

Questions and Self-Study Tasks

1. Why is backpropagation so named? What does it transmit backward?

2. What is BIAS and what does it do? How is the BIAS parameter taught?

3. Why are two values (sum and output) displayed in each neuron during program work? How are they connected?

4. What influences do learning rate and momentum exert on the process of network teaching? Revise your theoretical knowledge and try to explain the influences of these parameters observed during program experiments.

5. What does the transmittal of errors from the output of a neuron (where it is marked) to its input (where it is applied for weight modification) mean?

6. Which neurons of the hidden layer will be most heavily loaded with an error made by a given neuron of the output layer? On what does this effect depend?

7. Is it possible for the neurons of an output layer to show errors if a neuron of the hidden layer has a zero error assigned by the backpropagation algorithm and does not change its weight coefficients?

8. How is the mean mark of the network functioning given? Can we assess the functioning of an entire network using a method that does not require analysis of single elements individually?

9. Advanced exercise: Add a module to the program that will show changes of error values of the neurons and entire network as graphs. Is it true that the functioning of an entire network improves if the errors made by single neurons of the network are minimized?

10. Advanced exercise: Try to expand the programs described in this chapter by using more input and output signals and more neurons arranged in more than one hidden layer.

11. Advanced exercise: Using a network that uses large numbers of inputs, try to observe the phenomenon of "throwing out" unnecessary information in the course of learning. To do so, assign unnecessary information (that has no connection with the required response of the network) to one of additional inputs. The other inputs should receive all data required to solve the required task. After a short period of learning, the weights of all connections leading to "parasitic" inputs to hidden neurons will take values near zero and the idle input will be almost eliminated.

12. Advanced exercise: The program described in this chapter demonstrated the functioning of networks displaying in all places the values of appropriate parameters and signals. This presentation made it possible to check (e.g., with the use of a calculator) what a network does and how it works. However, the program was not very helpful for observing the courses and qualities of the processes. Design and produce a version of the program that will present all values in an easy-to-interpret graphic form.

Chapter 8

Forms of Neural Network Learning

8.1 Using Multilayer Neural Networks for Recognition

Multilayer neural networks covered in detail in earlier chapters can handle many tasks. Nevertheless, if we want to analyze their properties and the way they work, the most appropriate area is probably image recognition in which a neural network (or other type of learning machine) classifies images into certain classes. The analyzed objects may vary widely, from digital camera images to scanned or grabbed analog images. We present a comparison of digital and analog images in Figure 8.1 to help explain this point. Each neuron of the hidden layer receives three weights for neurons 1.1 and 1.2; each neuron of the output layer receives three weights for neurons 2.1 and 2.2.

This book is about neural networks and not about images. Hence, we will not delve deeply into the theories of image recognition. However, the challenge of having a machine recognize images started a new field of computer science. The first neural network built by Frank Rosenblatt (Figure 8.2) was used to recognize images and was thus called a perceptron. While of poor quality, the figure is a relic of an early and outstanding achievement in the area of computer outputs.

The meaning of image has become so general that neural networks are used now for recognizing samples of sound signals (spoken commands), seismic or other geophysical signals, symptoms of patients to be diagnosed, scores of loan applicants, and other tasks. All these tasks involve image recognition although the images in the areas cited are in fact acoustic, geophysical, diagnostic, and economic.

A neural network used for image recognition usually needs several inputs supplied with signals representing features of the objects to be recognized. These may, for example, be coefficients describing the shape of a machine part or liver tissue texture. We often use many inputs to show a neural network all the features of an object so that the network learns how to recognize the object correctly. However, the number of image features is far fewer than the number of image elements (pixels). If you supply a network with a raw digital image, the number of its inputs can reach millions. That is why we rarely use neural networks to analyze raw images. The networks usually "see"

Figure 8.1   Left: analog image. Right: poor digital image.

the features of an image extracted by other programs outside the network. This image preparation is sometimes called "preprocessing."

A neural network used for recognition usually generates several outputs as well. Generally speaking, each output is assigned to a specific class. For example an optical character recognition (OCR) system may use over 60 outputs, each assigned to a certain character (e.g., the first output neuron indicates A, the second neuron denotes B, etc.). We discussed this in Chapter 2. Figures 2.30, 2.31, and 2.33 depict the possible output signals of a network used for recognition.

At least one hidden layer or neurons is generally sited between the input and output layers of a network. We will now study the hidden layer in more detail. A hidden layer may contain a few or many neurons. After analyzing briefly the functioning of neural networks, we usually think that more neurons in a hidden layer constitute a smarter network. However, we will see that a network with great intelligence may also be disobedient.

8.2 Implementing a Simple Neural Network for Recognition

We are now going to build a sample network with two inputs. In reality, it is not possible to recognize an object based on only two features. For this reason neural networks are most commonly used to analyze multidimensional data whose outputs require more than two inputs. However,

Figure 8.2   Rosenblatt's perceptron—the first neural network to recognize images.

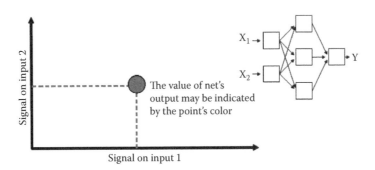

Figure 8.3 Presenting signals to a neural network.

using two inputs in our example has a significant advantage: each recognized object may be represented as a point on a plane. The first and the second coordinates of the point indicate the values of the first and second features, respectively.

We encountered a similar situation in Chapter 6 (Section 6.4) where we imagined a brain of a hypothetical animal as a two-dimensional input space with two primitive receptors—eyes and ears. The stronger the signal captured by the eyes, the more to the right is the point on the plane; the stronger the sound, the higher the point is on the plane. Figure 6.8 will be useful for explaining this material.

Every image shown to the network (each environment of the animal) may be shown as a point on an axis or as a pixel on a screen. The coordinates correspond to the features of the environment (Figure 8.3). We will use a screen of a fixed size so we should start by limiting the values of our features. In the example considered here, both features of the analyzed image will take values from –5 to +5. You will have to remember that scale when formulating tasks for the network.

Each network has an output we will use to observe its behavior. Our example will always generate one output. We have already interpreted its meaning in Figure 6.8.

To review, the animal may react to a presented situation with a positive or negative attitude indicated by the intense red or blue color, respectively. We will place our animal in various environments by supplying the network with sets of input signals that correspond to positions of the animal as it senses different features. You will be able to prepare a map of places where the animal is comfortable and where it is not. The map should be built of separate points because it will be created by the program we are going to run (Figure 8.4). To improve the appearance of our maps, we will "smooth" them (Figure 8.5).

As the network grows, we will more often observe intermediate states: partial disgust (light blue), neutrality (light green), and partial applause (yellow turning to light red); see Figure 8.6. The fact that the network has only one output will make its workings easy to understand. By switching on a pixel corresponding to a certain input vector, you will see whether the point is accepted (red) or rejected (blue) by the network. Of course, the data describing these points will have to be prepared by the program; this will be covered later.

You will see maps like these during network training. They will change as the network dislikes an item it approved earlier or accepts something it already rejected. It is interesting to watch how initial confusion turns into a working hypothesis and then crystallizes into absolute certainty. It is not easy to illustrate these phenomena so clearly for a multiple-output network, but the exercise is necessary because real-world systems usually generate many outputs.

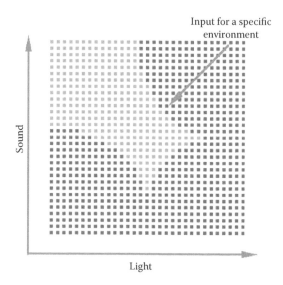

Figure 8.4 Example map showing conditions the hypothetical animal should accept and reject.

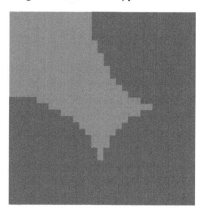

Figure 8.5 Figure 8.4 map after smoothing.

Figure 8.6 Sample map of animal at some stage of training.

Using only one output in our example has another advantage: you don't have to decide whether the better network is one that classifies a signal into several classes at a time with the same confidence or a network that generates all weak responses among which the strongest is the correct one. Multiple-output networks may create other problems and thus it is difficult to judge performance of a network based on its reaction to unseen situations (ability to generalize its knowledge). The result from a single-output network is always clear.

8.3 Selecting Network Structure for Experiments

The Example 09 program allows you to experiment with network structures. At opening, the program shows a panel for defining the structure of the network to be tested (Figure 8.7). The program will suggest default parameters that may be changed and we will do that as an exercise.

The network you are going to teach and analyze will have a **2 - xxx - 1** structure. The successive numbers stand for two inputs, a number to be modified in the course of teaching (xxx) and one output. To define a specific network, you will only have to specify the number and the order of hidden neurons (how many hidden layers to create).

You will be able to define the number of neurons in each layer of the network, depending on how many layers you choose in the Layers field. When specifying numbers of layers, remember that the only layers that count contain neurons that can learn. That is why the output layer counts, although it contains only one neuron and the two input neurons that accept only input signals do not count. Thus if you choose a one-layer network, you will get **2 - 1** and be unable to specify the number of hidden neurons as this number is fixed by the network architecture.

If you choose a two-layer network, the structure will be **2 - x - 1** and the Neurons field will appear in the hidden layer in which you can specify the number of hidden neurons (Figure 8.8). Finally, if you choose a three-layer network (or leave the default settings unchanged), the resulting architecture will be **2 - x - y - 1** and will have to set the number of neurons in both hidden layers (the Neurons field in the first hidden layer and also in the second hidden layer).

Our program cannot simulate networks of more than three layers. You may try to change this limitation by "playing" with the source code. We chose to limit the number of layers because the

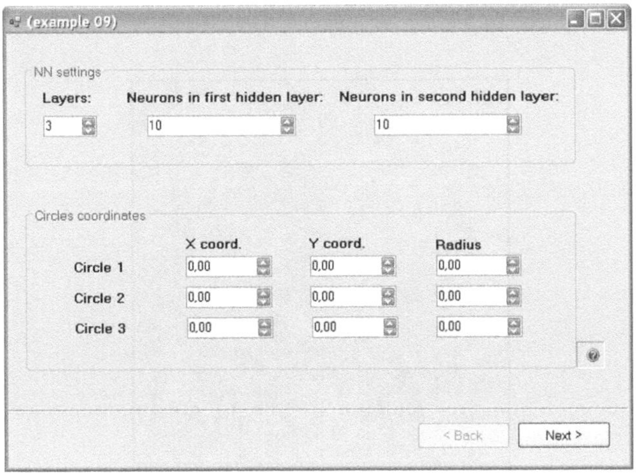

Figure 8.7 Defining network structure in Example 09.

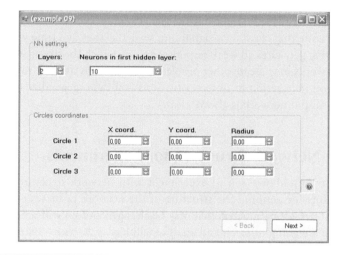

Figure 8.8 Defining network structure in Example 09 as two-layer network.

program works slowly for large networks. You will see that a few hundred training steps (not many for a learning process) will take time even with a fast computer.

8.4 Preparing Recognition Tasks

After choosing the size of the network, and if necessary, the numbers of neurons in all its layers, we may proceed to the most interesting step: preparing the task to be solved. As you know, the concept of recognition is that a network should react positively to ("recognize") certain combinations of input signals (images) and react negatively ("reject") other combinations. The training set for the Example 09 program is shown in Figure 8.9. It consists of a certain number of points on a plane, each of which has two coordinates so that we know where to put a point on the screen and we know the network will produce a positive (red [darker]) or negative (blue [lighter]) response.

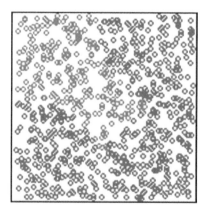

Figure 8.9 Sample training set generated by Example 09.

The user decides where to put blue and red points indicating acceptance and rejection. You could attempt this experiment manually using sets of three numbers (two inputs and one output) but the final image or preference map would be difficult to generate and interpret. For that reason, we designed Example 09 to generate examples automatically. The user's task is simply to show the network the positive and negative areas. Again, the system made the decisions. You could certainly specify the shapes of these areas but that would require including a complex graphical editor in the program that would be hard to use.

We sought a middle-of-the-road solution. The areas of positive decision (fragments of input space to which the network should respond positively by red points on the plot) will belong to three circles. This is a large constraint, but also a fast and comfortable way of preparing tasks. You will be able to devise interesting problems for the network, by combining the three circles of any size at any position.

You may set the coordinates of these three circles in the same window (the first one that appears after the program starts) in which you defined the architecture (Figure 8.10a) of the network. First coordinates (x and y) define the center of the circle and the third coordinate defines its radius. You may set values for the three circles independently. You are free to choose these parameters, but as noted earlier, only the part of the plane for which both coordinates are in the range –5 to 5 is used in the recognition process. A circle with parameters 0, 0, 3 positively would be a reasonable area for placing the points; however, a circle with parameters 10, 10, 3 may not be so, and hence, not useful in our experiments.

After setting the parameters of the task to be solved by the network, you may see the results of your choice in the next panel where the network is simulated. You reach this panel by pressing the Next button at the bottom of the window (Figure 8.10a). The results of your decisions are shown as a map of positive and negative response areas. This allows you to check easily whether your expectations of learning were met. If you choose not to specify a task, you may always return to the previous panel by pressing the Back button. This will allow you to modify the center coordinates and sizes of the circles.

Training will start when a random point for which the class will be decided according to your map is chosen, then a set of two input coordinates and the desired class will be supplied to the network as an example from the training set. This procedure will be repeated many times.

We must note one detail that is easy to miss. If you define the decision areas so that most of the decision plane is positive (red), the network will usually chose these examples during training and will rarely utilize the points generating negative answers. Thus it will learn negative reactions

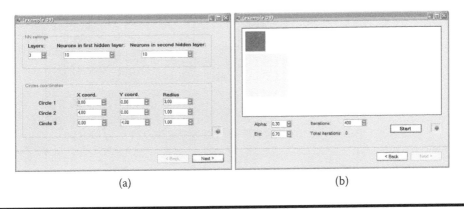

(a)   (b)

Figure 8.10   (a) Defining network structure and regions for recognition. (b) Map of regions to which the network should react with a positive or negative answer after training.

slowly. The impact on positive reactions will occur if a network is trained with excessive negative (blue) examples. Approximately the same numbers of red and blue training points were included in our training set to maintain a network's ability to handle both negative and positive signals efficiently.

After specifying the task as a map that is well balanced and meets your needs, you can start training the network by pressing the Start button (Figure 8.10b). You will see the network's assignments of random weights to all its neurons. Usually this initial distribution has no relation to the task you defined. How can a network possibly know what result you want before it is trained? It is helpful to compare this initial map with the map of the task.

Training success depends on how similar these two maps are at the beginning. If they look alike, the network will learn quickly and effectively. If the maps differ significantly, the network will learn slowly. Little progress will be seen initially because the network will have to utilize its inborn intelligence to start improving its functioning (Figure 8.11).

The structure of the figure displayed requires some explanation. The small rectangles filled with color spots that appear during the simulation represent the "consciousness" of the network during each training state. As you know, each point inside the rectangle represents two features (corresponding to coordinates of the point) that serve as input signals. The color of each point indicates the network's answer to the input.

Consider the first two rectangles in the upper left corner of the figure. The first one shows what you want to teach the network. Following the steps described in the preceding section, you set conditions to be accepted or rejected by your "animal" and they are shown on the map of desired reactions. The second rectangle in the upper row shows the network's natural predispositions. Each experiment may involve different initial parameters set randomly. Thus, the network's behavior is unpredictable.

The remaining diagrams correspond to the subsequent stages of training. They are drawn as rectangles in Figure 8.11 and may be shown as different time steps. The user determines (using the Iterations field) the number of steps of training before showing the results. The Iterations field includes an additional read-only feature called Total Iterations that shows the total number of training steps already performed.

Before performing the number of steps set at the preceding state or specified by you, you may change the values of the training coefficient (alpha) and momentum coefficient (eta) parameters in

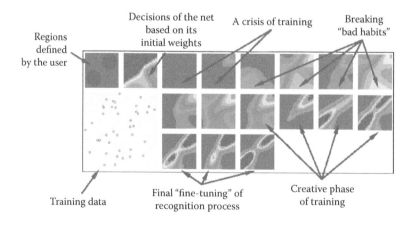

Figure 8.11 Example 09 presentation of subsequent phases of training.

the corresponding fields shown on the screen. You may set them to any values, but we advise you to retain the defaults during training. After you learn the components of the training process, you may want to experiment with the parameters to see how they affect the results.

8.5 Observation of Learning

The Example 09 program allows you to investigate many aspects of learning by neural networks. We spent many hours devising tasks for networks and analyzing combinations of training parameters to make the program experiments interesting and enlightening.

Learning processes in living organisms, particularly neural mechanisms that determine and control learning, have always been key interests of biological scientists. Through the years they studied learning in humans and animals to learn the basic components of the process. Their findings based on behavior have revolutionized education and training methods but we still do not understand fully the mechanisms behind the processes.

Thousands of neurophysiological and biochemical experiments conducted to dissect learning processes yielded less than satisfactory results. Fortunately, new methods have revealed some aspects of neural system functioning. Many of these methods use artificial neural networks to simulate learning processes and utilize programs like Example 09.

As you remember, training a neural network involves submitting examples of input signals (chosen randomly from the training dataset) to its inputs and motivating the network to produce an output according to the map of preferred behaviors. This scenario may be adapted to the earlier example of an animal with two senses (sight and hearing).

We place the animal in various conditions that allow it to sense random (but known) signals. The animal (or neural network) reacts according to its current knowledge. It accepts some conditions and rejects others. The teacher (training computer) that has a map of preferred reactions supplies the network with the desired output signal, in essence telling the network to "like this and dislike that."

You may watch the training process on your screen. The large square in the lower left corner of the example screen illustrates points corresponding to the input signals presented to the network. As you can see, they are randomly chosen from the entire area of the square. Each point is marked in red or blue based on the teacher's suggestions. The network uses these instructions and corrects its errors by adjusting its parameters (synaptic weights). The adjustment is performed according to the backpropagation algorithm presented earlier.

The training pauses periodically and the network is examined. The network should generate answers for all the input points. The results are presented as maps of color points arranged as consecutive squares from left to right and from the upper to lower rows of the image produced by Example 09. After each such pause, the user determines the number of steps until the next examination.

We will begin by demonstrating the ways neural networks learn using an example of a one-layer network denoted 2, 1. The network's task is simple: divide all possible input data into approved and rejected regions using an almost straight line. To define this problem, the following coordinates of three circles were defined in the program:

```
100, 100, 140
0, 0, 0
0, 0, 0
```

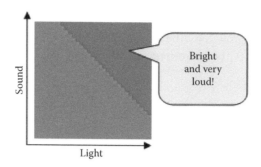

Figure 8.12   Model of environment and preferences defined by the teacher.

We defined a map of preferred behaviors that is simple and easy to interpret (Figure 8.12). It indicates our animal should seek a bright and loud environment.

As you know, the Example 09 program examines the natural (inborn) preferences of the network at the start. The second square on the screen (Figure 8.13) should be regarded as a complete result of testing the animal before it starts to learn. The program places the animal in every possible environment (checks all points inside the square) and waits for a reaction. Each point is drawn red if a reaction was positive or blue if negative. The color scale is continuous to illustrate all the reactions between the two extreme stages. As we can see, our animal initially likes dark and silent places but it tolerates some light. Generally the more sound it hears, the more light it accepts.

The network you will train on your computer will have a different map of initial preferences because they are random. Because the network's state desired by the teacher and the actual state are very different, as occurs in most experiments, intensive training must take place. You proceed by specifying the number of training steps to perform before the program pauses to show the decision map. We suggest you watch the training effects in small networks fairly often, say, every 10 steps. For larger networks of several layers and many hidden neurons, much more training is needed to yield results. For now it is sufficient to specify the lengths of subsequent training epochs, then watch, compare, and learn. That is the best way to analyze the workings of neural networks; it is more effective than studying loads of scientific books and articles.

We now suggest you analyze some training stages that we observed while preparing examples for this book, although your computer may generate somewhat different images. The rectangle we obtained after the first stage of training (Figure 8.14) shows an image similar to that of a "newborn" network. This means that despite intensive training, the network is holding onto its original beliefs. This attachment is typical for neural networks. The same dynamic appears when people and animals learn.

Figure 8.13   Presentation by teacher of desired and built-in properties of network.

Figure 8.14   State of network after first stage of training.

Figure 8.15   State of network after second stage of training.

The next stage of training adds another square to the figure and shows intermediate training. The network starts to change its behavior but it is far from the final solution. The boundary between the positive and negative areas is almost horizontal (Figure 8.15). The network "thinks" it knows the teacher's intentions but more adjustments are needed. After another segment of training, the network's behavior more closely resembles the desired one, but the position of the decision boundary is not ideal yet (Figure 8.16).

You may consider this performance outstanding, especially based on the short time it took to achieve such a result. Generally we should stop training at this stage. However, for exploration purposes, we continued training the network, assuming that our strict teacher aims for absolute perfection and compels the network to adjust even very minor mistakes. The only effect of the next stage of training is a sudden crisis. The network performance deteriorates and the decision boundary position is worse than it was earlier (Figure 8.17).

Figure 8.16   After three steps of training, network approaches success.

Figure 8.17   Training crisis caused by overly strict teacher.

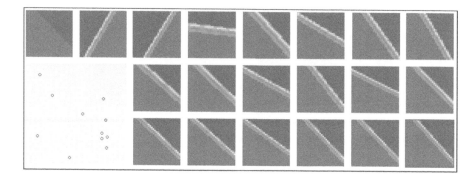

Figure 8.18   Final result of training.

A long time and many training steps were required for the network to recover and achieve the accuracy level imposed by the teacher. This effect is worth noticing. At this training stage, the network's knowledge is not yet stable. Excessive teaching rigor at this state is usually damaging and in extreme cases can lead to a complete breakdown of the learning network. The process of learning this simple task after 12 training steps is presented in Figure 8.18.

We will interrupt the training sequence and return to the screen on which we set new parameters for the problem to be solved. After specifying the same network structure (one-layer network), we will formulate a more difficult task. We want our animal to be enthusiastic about "the golden mean" which is an Aristotelian philosophy that is a desirable mean between two extremes: excess and deficiency. Thus, it needs to discard all the extremes and feel comfortable only in a specific environment. It is easy to do this by defining only one circle to be learned, as follows:

```
0, 0, 3, 5
```

We shrink the other two circles to zeros:

```
0, 0, 0
0, 0, 0
```

The scheme of ideal network behavior is presented in Figure 8.19.

Observe the learning process in Figure 8.20 (prepared in the same way as Figure 8.18). We can see that the network struggles and continuously changes its behavior in attempts to avoid the

Figure 8.19   New task for network.

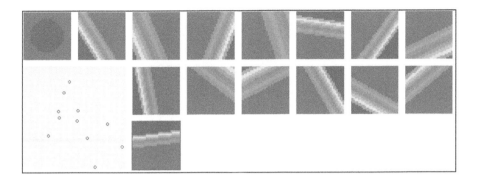

Figure 8.20   Training failure caused by overly simple network structure.

penalties imposed by the teacher—without success. Whatever parameters are chosen for a network and however the decision boundary between positive and negative reactions is set, the network will always fall into the trap of accepting a region of extreme conditions.

Subsequent figures show that the animal tries to hide in the darkness, accepting the examples with small amounts of light. This behavior will be punished by the teacher in the next steps of training. Before we interrupted the experiment, the animal formulated another incorrect hypothesis. It started to avoid the regions of silence, thinking that the clue to success was noise. This action was also incorrect.

The reason for these failures is simple: the modeled neural network was too primitive to learn a complex behavior such as choosing the golden mean. The network we used in our experiment was capable of understanding only one method of input signal selection—linear discrimination—which was too simple and primitive for the second problem.

Therefore, the next experiment will engage a larger and more complex network for the same task. When setting the structure, we may specify the parameters as shown in Figure 8.21. After we set more than one layer in a network, the program asked for the number of neurons. In brief,

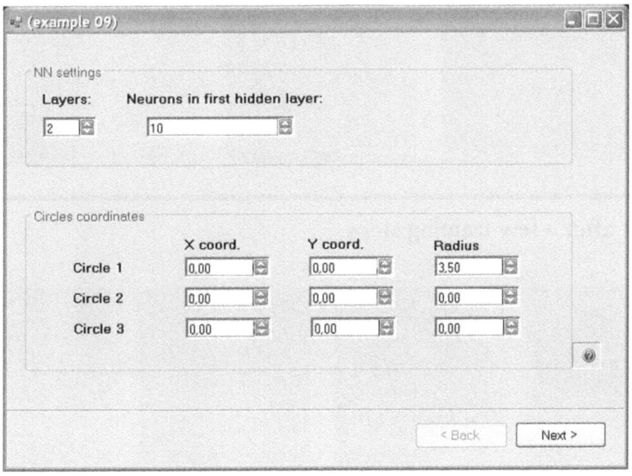

Figure 8.21   Setup of a "more intelligent" network.

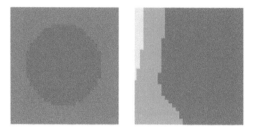

Figure 8.22   Initial state of more complex network.

more layers require more answers and provide greater intellectual potential. Such a network can better use its inborn intelligence.

We can see how it learns. Its initial distribution of color areas shown in Figure 8.22 indicates that the network is initially enthusiastic about all values. The modeled animal feels comfortable in most situations although it prefers dark and quiet corners.

The first training steps show the network that the world is not always perfect. The network reacts in a typical way. At the start, it cultivates its initial prejudices. It is less positive about dark places after the first stage of training, but still far from the final result (Figure 8.23). Further training leads our animal through a series of disappointments. It receives punishment for being too trusting and enthusiastic. It formulates a more suspicious attitude toward the untrustworthy world. Its initial enthusiasm and favorable view diminishes to a slight fondness for quiet and sunny places (small yellow dot at the bottom right of the last square on Figure 8.24).

However, this attitude also meets the teacher's disapproval. After the next training stage, the animal (network) becomes completely stagnant and rejects everything (Figure 8.25). This state of discouragement and breakdown is typical for neural networks in training and usually precedes attempts to construct a positive representation of the knowledge desired by the teacher.

Figure 8.23   Result after a few training steps.

Figure 8.24   Result after more training steps.

Figure 8.25 Total negation during training.

Figure 8.26 Wave of optimism.

In fact our network tries to create an image like Figure 8.26. Only a few positive examples shown by the teacher are enough for the network to revert to a phase of enthusiasm and optimism in which it approves all the environments except those that are very loud and dark. Total darkness and intensive light reduce its tolerance for loudness. Of course, the next training stage must suppress this enthusiasm so the network returns to the states of rejection and frustration, retaining only traces of positive memories that did not lead to punishment. In the next stage, the small positive reaction will become the seed of a correct hypothesis (red [dark] spot near the middle of the volatility region in Figure 8.27).

After that, training is only about controlling another rush of enthusiasm and reducing the area of positive reactions to a reasonable size. When we interrupted training after 15 stages, the network appropriately followed the teacher in this signal classification task so that further improvement of its performance was not necessary (Figure 8.28). As we can see, the system with larger and more efficient "brain" (more than ten times more neurons and more powerful connections between them) was capable of learning behaviors the smaller system could not manage to learn.

Another interesting experiment is presented in Figure 8.29. It illustrates how the same ability (of reasoning that the teacher wants acceptance of medium light and sound conditions and rejection of the extremes) is learned by another network with the same structure as the one analyzed in Figure 8.28. In the training process depicted in Figure 8.29, the network is somewhat melancholic at the start of training even though it has the same structure as the network in Figure 8.28. The figure is dominated by cool green and blue colors indicating apathy or dislike.

Initial training makes it a little more interested in "disco" conditions (yellow spot in the rectangle illustrating the first training stage). Several consecutive failures throw the network into an area of rejection. At the fourth training stage, the network tries to put forward a hypothesis that

Figure 8.27 Formation of proper hypothesis.

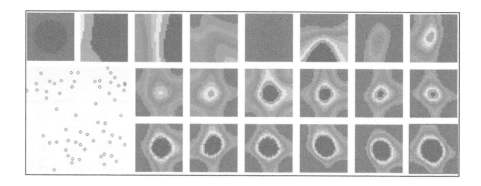

Figure 8.28 Learning more complex task.

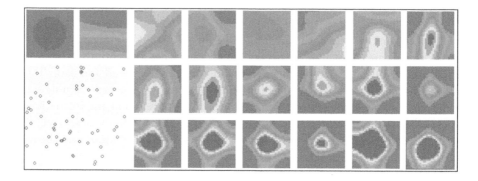

Figure 8.29 Training another network.

the teacher wants it to approve bright and medium loud places. At the next stage, the network guesses the average conditions to be accepted. As training continues, the hypothesis grows stronger and clearer as shown by the red (dark) dot indicating complete acceptance.

With each training step, the dot's shape matches more exactly the acceptance area set by the teacher. Green and yellow areas of confusion and uncertainty are replaced by more exact divisions into like and dislike conditions. Finally the melancholic network learns to act exactly the same way as the enthusiastic network. This proves that built-in predispositions are not controlling. Strong and focused training always achieves its goal but methods of reaching it vary based on starting points.

You may perform many different experiments using our program. Figures 8.30, 8.31, and 8.32 show a few of them. You will benefit from analyzing these figures, reconstructing them on your computer, and conducting your own experiments to study training variations and results.

Compare Figures 8.30 through 8.32 with Figure 8.20. You can see how the behavior of an intellectually well-equipped network differs from the behavior of a simple network that cannot learn more sophisticated rules. Note that the neural "simpleton" could not learn simple behaviors but its reactions were very strong and categorical. The world is only black or white for this network. An object is absolutely good or definitely wrong. If the network's experience failed to conform to these extremes, it generated another opinion—far more rigid and usually incorrect.

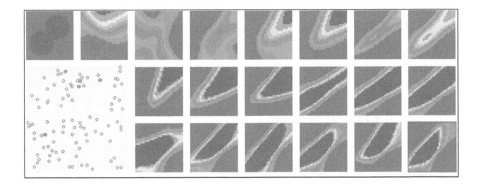

Figure 8.30   Problem for two-layer network.

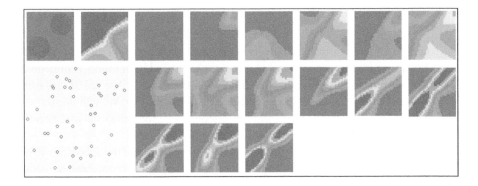

Figure 8.31   Problem some two-layer networks cannot solve.

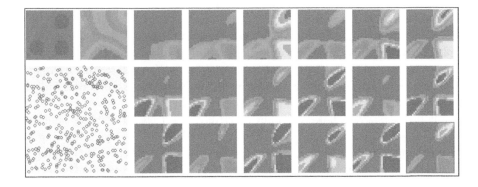

Figure 8.32   Very difficult problem for three-layer network.

The networks with more intellectual power were able to model more subtle divisions. However, they took more time to reach their goals and remained in inactive states (hesitation, breakdown, and indecision) longer. Despite these downsides, these neurotic, hesitating, excessively intelligent individuals reached the goal of understanding the teacher's rules and adjusting to them, while the tough moron circled and failed to reach a rational conclusion.

Notice how many interesting and diverse behaviors of neural networks we observed with one simple program. The computer running it did not resemble a dull and limited machine or perform monotonously and repeatedly. On the contrary, it demonstrated some individual characteristics, mood changes, and a variety of talents. Does that remind you of anything?

8.6 Additional Observations

We could end this now, leaving you to use the program to discover more interesting aspects of training, but we will suggest some sample shapes worth investigating before you pursue real-life projects. Our experiments showed that interesting training results may arise from using a snowman made of three circles:

```
0, 0, 3
4, 0, 1
0, 4, 1
```

The task is complicated enough so that the network must work hard to discover the actual rule of recognition. The network for this task should have three layers and high numbers of neurons in its hidden layers (17 neurons in the first hidden layer and 5 in the second). The task is also sufficiently compact to be displayed on the screen so the results are easy to observe. We will not show you the results for these examples because you may want to discover the properties of neural networks and their sensitivities to some parameters that affect training.

As you know, you may specify training parameters that influence the speed of the program before it executes the number of training steps you select. The first (alpha) parameter is the learning rate. The greater the learning rate, the more intense the training process. Alpha sometimes yields good results or it may lessen them. This is another area for program exploration. The second parameter (eta) is momentum. It makes learning conservative: the network does not forget the previous directions of weight changes while performing a current training step. Again, higher eta values may help learning or impede it.

The learning rate and momentum coefficients are always accessible in the program window of Example 09 and they may be changed during training to allow a user to observe interesting results. They may be modified only once before learning starts. You will see that training accelerates with higher alpha values. Figure 8.33 presents the training process for a task with standard values and Figure 8.34 shows training at higher alpha level.

An overly high alpha rate, however, is not effective. It can trigger instability as illustrated in Figure 8.35. The way to suppress the oscillations that result from too high a learning rate is to increase the eta (momentum) coefficient. You may wish to analyze the effect of changing momentum on training and demonstrate its stabilizing power when training goes out of control.

Another possible area of interesting research is the dependence of behavior on network structure. To analyze that, you must choose a very difficult problem to be learned. A good one is presented in Figure 8.4 and Figure 8.5. The difficulty is the need to fit the blue area defining negative into tight bays (Figure 8.36). Very precise parameters must be chosen to fit the slots; this is a large challenge for a network.

A three-layer network can distinguish all the subtle parts of a problem (Figure 8.37), although it is sometimes difficult to maintain training stability. This type of network, even when it is close to a solution, may abandon it due to backpropagation of errors and search for a solution in an area

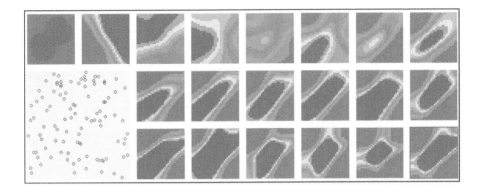

Figure 8.33 Default value of learning rate leads to quiet, steady, but slow training.

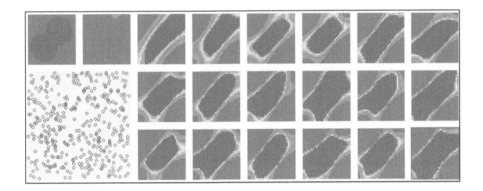

Figure 8.34 Higher value of learning rate may achieve faster training.

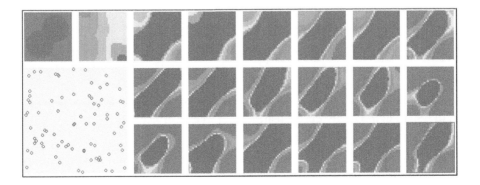

Figure 8.35 Excessive learning rate produces oscillations. Network approaches desired solution, then changes direction.

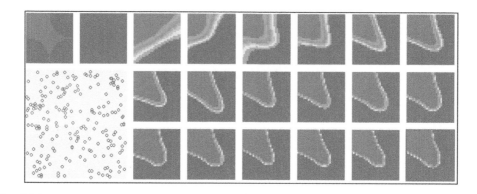

Figure 8.36 **Regions learned do not match desired ones with two-layer network.**

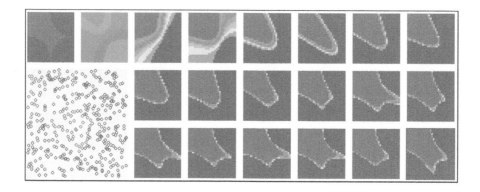

Figure 8.37 **Good solution found quickly by three-layer network.**

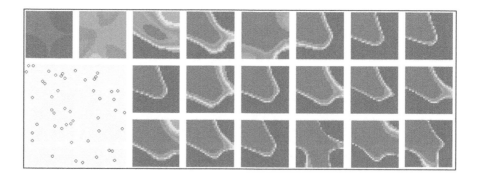

Figure 8.38 **Signs of instability during learning of three-layer network.**

where a correct solution cannot be found (Figure 8.38). You may use your imagination and freely define the regions where a network should react positively and negatively. You may run tens of experiments and obtain hundreds of observations. Just remember that training a large network may take long time, especially in the initial stages. You will need a very fast computer or a lot of patience. We suggest that patience is cheaper.

Questions and Self-Study Tasks

1. Does image recognition refer only to visual images (e.g., from a digital camera) or does the phrase have a wider meaning?

2. How do we input image data (and information about objects to be recognized) into a classifying neural network?

3. How do neural classifiers usually present the outcomes of their work. How do they demonstrate what they recognized? What consequences does the presentation method have on the usual structure of the output layer?

4. Use the observations from this chapter for training networks for several problems with theoretical information from Chapter 6 explaining how multilayer networks with different numbers of layers work. Notice the greater capabilities of the networks presented in this chapter resulting from the use of neurons that can produce continuous output signals instead of only 0 and 1 values.

5. Think about the relationship of the number of hidden neurons in a complex multilayer network and the number of separate areas in the input space that allow a network to learn to make 0-or-1 decisions.

6. Figure 8.39 illustrates the relation between numbers of hidden neurons and network efficiency in performing learned tasks. The left side of the plot is easy to interpret: a network with a small number of neurons is not "intelligent" enough to solve the problem and adding neurons improves its performance. How should we interpret the concept (proven many times in neural networks) that too many hidden neurons will deteriorate the performance of a network?

7. Learning rate measures the intensity of weight adjustments applied to a network after detecting a faulty operation. The informal interpretation of learning rate is that high values represent a strict and demanding teacher and small values correspond to a gentle and tolerant one. Explain why the best training results are observed for moderate values of learning rate (neither too small nor too high). Try to confirm your explanation by experimenting with our program. Plot learning rate versus training performance after a set number of epochs (after 500, 1000, and 5000 steps).

8. Many training methods in which the learning rate is not constant throughout the process are known. Under what conditions should the learning rate be increased and when should it be reduced?

9. Some training theories suggest that the learning rate should be small at the beginning when network makes a lot of mistakes. If we apply strong weight changes in response to the errors, the

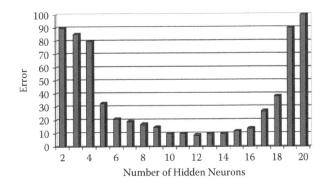

Figure 8.39 Plot of numbers of hidden neurons versus efficiency.

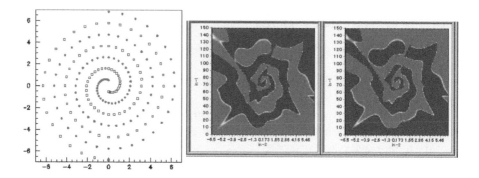

Figure 8.40 **"Two spirals" problem. Training set (left) and two possible solutions (right).**

network would experience "convulsions," avoiding some mistakes and making new ones. Early in training, a network needs a gentle and mild teacher. As it gains more knowledge, the learning rate can be increased because the network will make fewer and less serious mistakes. At the end of training after the network acquires a lot of knowledge, a slower learning rate is advisable, so that incidental mistakes (caused by a few challenges in the training set) do not spoil the result since improvement of one area produces weakening in other areas. Design experiments to confirm or negate this theory.

10. We can compensate for the effects of a too-large learning rate value that can risk the stability of training by increasing the momentum coefficient that measures the conservatism of training. Design and conduct some experiments to generate a plot showing what minimal values of momentum are needed for different values of learning rate to guarantee fast and stable training.

11. Advanced exercise: Modify our program so that it can define the regions for different classes (areas where the animal should feel comfortable and uncomfortable) with the use of a graphical editor. Use this tool to build a network that will learn a very difficult problem, in which these regions are defined as two spirals (Figure 8.40).

12. Advanced exercise: Design and make a model of an animal with more receptors (senses to observe features of the environment) and capable of more complex actions (moving through the environment to seek conditions it likes or search for food. Designing and observing a neural network as the brain of an animal may be a fascinating intellectual adventure.

Chapter 9

Self-Learning Neural Networks

9.1 Basic Concepts

We have explained the structures and utilized programs to demonstrate how a neural network utilizes a teacher's guidelines for pattern recognition and comparison to complete its tasks. This chapter will detail network learning without a teacher. We discussed self-learning networks briefly in Section 3.2 in Chapter 3. We will now discuss these networks in some depth.

We will not examine the common self-learning algorithms devised by Hebb, Oji, Kohonen, and others in great detail or discuss their mathematical bases. We will explain their operations and uses, and utilize examples to demonstrate their workings. We suggest you start by running the Example 10a program.

The program deals with a single-layer network of neurons (Figure 9.1). All neurons are given the same input signals, and each one determines independently of the others the value of its degree of excitation and multiplies its input signals (the same for all neurons) by its individual weighting factors (Figure 9.2).

The self-learning principle requires that all neurons at the beginning obtain random weighting factor values that appear in the figure produced by the Example 10a program as a "cloud" of randomly scattered points. Each point represents a single neuron and the point locations are determined by the weighting factor values as shown on the right side of Figure 9.3. The window on the left side of the figure, as in previous programs, appears soon after start and serves to modify network parameters.

Set-up requires two parameters: the number of neurons in the network and a parameter named *etha* that represents the intensity of learning (higher values yield faster and more energetic learning). You may change these parameters at any time. However, at this stage we suggest you accept the default settings we selected after studying program behavior. We will return later in this chapter to descriptions of individual parameters and experimenting with their values.

After starting the program you will have a network composed of 30 neurons characterized by a moderate enthusiasm for learning. All the weights of all neurons in the network will have random values. To begin, we enter input signals that are examples of sample objects the network will analyze. Remember the Martian example in Chapter 3? Entering these objects in the Example 10a program will produce an impact. This contradicts the idea of self-learning that requires the user to

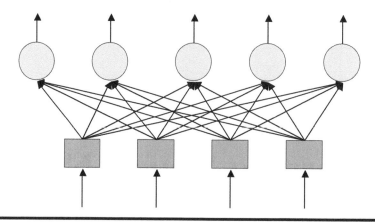

Figure 9.1 Structure of a single-layer network that may be amenable to self-learning.

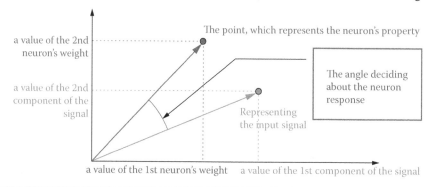

Figure 9.2 Interpretation of relationship between weight and input vectors.

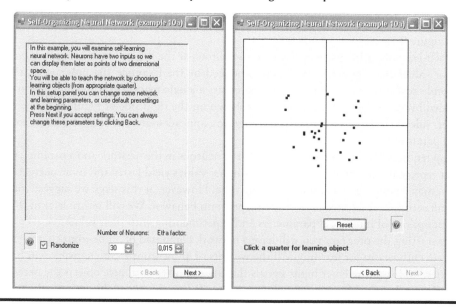

Figure 9.3 Initial window showing parameters (at left) and locations of points representing neurons after Example 10a program is run.

do nothing. While the process of learning can proceed independently of user actions, we devised Example 10 intentionally to deviate from the ideal to demonstrate how the presentation of learning objects affects independent knowledge acquisition by a network.

However, some explanation is needed. All the knowledge the network can gain during self-learning comes from the objects presented to it at the input and also from the similarities among classes of objects. Thus, some objects are similar to each other (Martian men) and belong to another class (Martian women) because they are different. Therefore, neither you nor the automatic generator can prevent the network from showing objects that are distributed randomly in the input signal space. Presented objects should form explicit clusters around certain detectable centers that can be named and interpreted (typical Martian man, typical Martian women, etc.).

While working with Example 10a, you may decide each time what to show to the network, but your choice will not be fine-tuned because the details will be determined by the system. You will be able to indicate the quadrant* within which the next presented object should be located. All you have to do is to click the mouse on the right quadrant to control what the network will "see." For example, the objects in the first quadrant belong to the Martian men; the second quadrant is for Martian women, the third to Martian children, and the fourth to Martianamors.† With a little imagination, you can see the window displayed by Example 10a in a manner (Figure 9.4) that shows Martians in sketch form instead of points representing their measured features.

As you can see, every Martian is a little different but they have certain similarities and therefore their data are represented in the same area of the input signal space (this will help a neural network learn how a typical Martian looks). However, since each Martian has individual characteristics that distinguish him, her, or it from other Martians, the points representing them during self-learning will differ little bit. They will be located in slightly different places within the coordinate system. However, since more features distinguish Martians generally than features that distinguish each of Martian individually, the points representing them will concentrate in certain subareas of input signal space.

Generating objects used in the learning process will enable you to decide whether to be shown the Martian man, Martian woman, Martian child, or Martianamor. You will not need to provide details such as eye color because the program will find them automatically. At each learning step, the program will ask you about Martian type—the quadrant to which the object belongs. After you choose one quadrant, the program will generate an object of a specific class and show it to the network.

Each Martian shown will differ from others, but you will easily notice that their features (associated with locations of corresponding points in the input signal space) will be clearly concentrated around certain prototypes. Perhaps this process of object generation and presentation

---

* The *quadrant* term for a space defined on the basis of a two-dimensional coordinate system is derived from mathematics. Although we promised that no mathematics details would be discussed, a little knowledge of coordinate systems is required for mastery of the material in this chapter. The signal space of a coordinate system is divided into quadrants (four sections). Assume the quadrants are numbered starting from upper right corner or quadrant (where variables on both axes are of positive value only) is numbered 1. The numbering proceeds counter-clockwise for consecutive quadrants. Quadrant 2 is at upper left; quadrant 3 is under 2 and so on. The lower right corner of Figure 9.13 further on in this section shows four buttons corresponding to quadrant numbers. You will learn how to apply the buttons later.

† Martianamors are representatives of a third gender on Mars. The inhabitants of Mars merge into triangles to produce offspring. Their complex sex lives have prevented them from developing a highly technological civilization and constructing large structures. Therefore we cannot detect them.

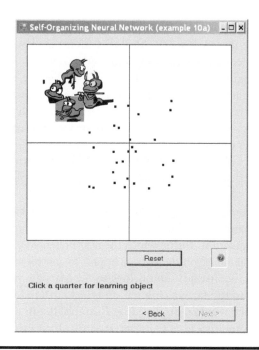

Figure 9.4 Representation of points of input signal space as Martians.

to the network seems complicated now, but after a short time of working with the Example 10a, you will understand it. The program includes screen tips to help you understand the process.

At the time of the emergence of a specific input signal of the learning set, it will appear on the screen as a green square much larger than the point of identifying the location of a neuron (Figure 9.5). After receiving the signal at input, all the neurons of a self-learning network define their output signals (based on the components of the input and its weights). These signals can be positive (red points indicating the neuron "likes" the object) or negative (blue points indicating the neuron "dislikes" the object). If the output signals of some neurons (both positive and negative) have low values, relevant points exhibit gray color (corresponding to indifference to the subject).

All the neurons of self-learning networks correct their weights based on the input signals and established output values. The behavior of each neuron during correction of its weights depends on the value of its output (response to stimulation). If the output neuron was strongly positive (red on the screen), the neuron weights will change toward the "likes" point. If the same point is presented again, the neuron will react even more enthusiastically; the output signal will have a larger positive value.

Neurons that show negative reaction to a pattern (blue points on the screen) will be repelled from it. Their weights will motivate them to even more negative responses to the pattern in the future. In Example 10a, you can see the "escape" of negatively oriented neurons outside the viewing points that represent them. In this case, the neuron is no longer displayed. This is a natural result if we consider that self-learning neural networks typically exhibit equally strong attractions and repulsions.

You can see clearly the moving of points showing the positions of the weight vectors of neurons because the program presents an image at each step to show the previous and new locations of

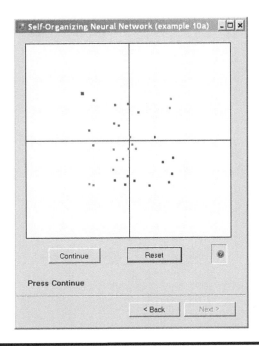

Figure 9.5   Situation after appearance of Martian input learning object.

points representing the neurons (Figure 9.6). Furthermore, the old location is combined with a new one by a dotted line so you can follow the paths of neurons during learning.

In the next step, the new neuron weights become old. After the system displays the next point step the cycle begins again (Figure 9.7) and a new object is presented to the network, perhaps belonging to a new class (Figure 9.8). If you repeat this process long enough, a cluster of neurons specialized in the recognition of typical objects belonging to a group will appear in each quadrant (Figure 9.9). In this way, the network specializes its recognition capabilities.

After you observe the processes of self-learning, you will certainly see that this learning strengthens the innate tendencies of neural networks expressed in the initial (random) spread of weighs vectors. These initial differences cause some neurons to respond positively to an input object while others react negatively. The correction of all neurons is made in such a way that they learn to recognize common elements appearing at the inputs and effectively improve their recognition abilities without interference from a teacher who may not even know how many objects should be recognized and what their characteristics are.

To ensure that self-learning proceeds efficiently, we must provide initial diversity in the neuron population. If the weight values are randomized in a way that ensures the needed diversity in the population, self-learning will proceed relatively easily and smoothly. If, however, all neurons will have similar "innate tendencies," they will find it difficult to handle all emerging classes of objects and exhibit the phenomenon of "collective fascination," which causes it to reactive positively to a selected object and ignore others.

The diversity in Example 10a was intentional. Because the initial random distribution of neurons is of primary importance we prepared a variant of the program called Example 10ax that allows a user to request random spreading of the features or draw the initial positions of the neurons from a narrow range. The field (checkbox) called Density must be set properly in the initial

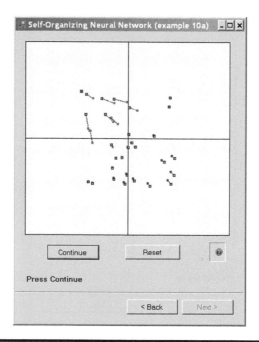

Figure 9.6 Weight correction achieved by self-learning process.

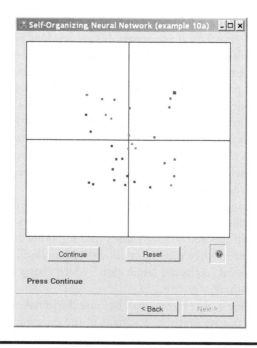

Figure 9.7 Another iteration of self-learning process.

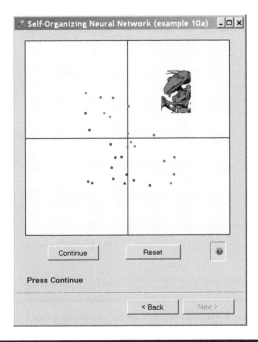

Figure 9.8   Interpretation of next iteration of self-learning process.

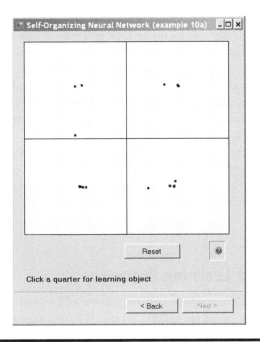

Figure 9.9   Final phase of self-learning process.

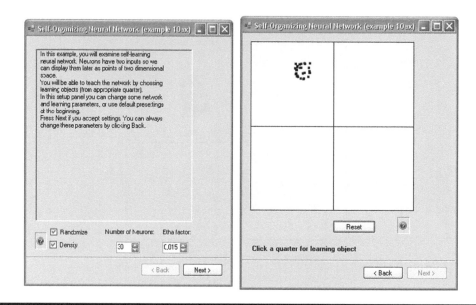

Figure 9.10 Initial window with parameters (left) showing effect of drawing initial values of weight vectors in Example 10ax program.

panel (left screen in Figure 9.10). Initially, it is better to choose widely spread neurons and not set a density value. After you are familiar with basic pattern of the network self-learning process and ready to see a new reaction, check the Density box.

You can see how important the initial random scattering of neuron weights is. Figure 9.10, Figure 9.11, and Figure 9.12 show the results of insufficiently differentiating neuron weights.

You can use the Example 10a and Example 10ax programs to carry out a series of studies, for example, to examine the effects of a more "energetic" self-learning process by increasing the value of the learning rate (etha).

Other interesting phenomena can be observed by unchecking the Randomize default parameter. The network will always start with the same initial weight distribution and you can observe the effects of the order and frequency of presenting of objects from different quadrants on the final neuron distribution.

Another parameter for experimentation is changing the number of neurons (number of plotted points). This value can be reset by going back to the first window appearing after program launch (Figure 9.3 and Figure 9.10) and the results are interesting. The initial distribution of certain neurons can be considered by analogy to the innate process by which a human learns from his or her experiences.

9.2 Observation of Learning Processes

Example 10a demonstrated the machine learning process of a neural network. It required many presses of the Continue button to see results. To eliminate the repetitive use of the button, we devised Example 10b to implement the machine learning process almost automatically. As with previous programs, Example 10b starts by allowing a user to accept or change default values. You

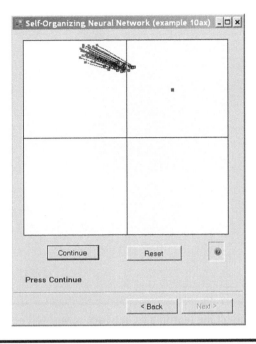

Figure 9.11   Self-learning process in Example 10ax. All neurons are attracted by same attractor.

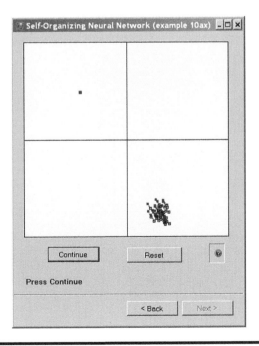

Figure 9.12   Self-learning process in Example 10ax. All neurons are repelled by same attractor.

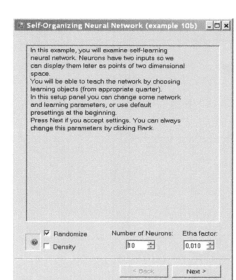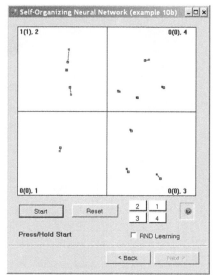

Figure 9.13   Beginning of machine learning of network composed of ten neurons.

can then watch the process in the windows. The learning is "almost" automatic because you have an option via the Start button to observe the steps as learning proceeds. You can halt the operation to observe progress.

One issue to consider before starting the program in the mode described above is the network size. The program lets us simulate a network composed of freely chosen neurons, starting with a network that contains only a few neurons (Figure 9.13 and Figure 9.14). Because the network

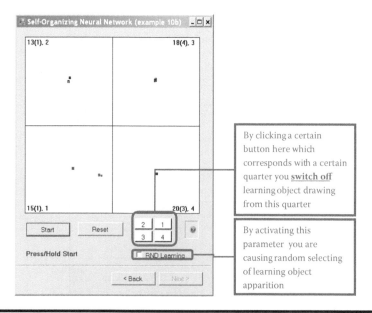

Figure 9.14   Final stage of machine learning of network composed of ten neurons.

builds four clusters in four quadrants, there is no point in analyzing a network composed of fewer than four neurons, but you can see how a single neuron behaves. The simulation follows the program; the user monitors the process and draws conclusions.

To make the observation of the ongoing processes easier, each quadrant displays additional information that indicates (1) how many times the object of a learning sequence was shown in the quadrant (this demonstrates the crucial role of initial presentations); (2) the results of the first nine presentations (in brackets); and (3) how many neurons are currently located in the quadrant. For example, the 10 (3), 1 notation in a quadrant means that the learning object appeared ten times, three times in the first nine presentations, and one neuron is now located in the quadrant.

This information is especially useful for a system containing many neurons. It allows a user to the track the number of neurons and where they are, and interpret situations such as neurons that overlap near the repetitive point of a learning sequence object and make judgment difficult. Observing randomly appearing asymmetric effects caused when objects from a certain quadrant are presented more often than others is also an interesting exercise.

This program helps you understand how large networks, composed of thousands of neurons behave. Figure 9.15 and Figure 9.16 demonstrate how 700 neurons learn simultaneously. The program generates initial weight distributions for all the neurons and then shows input signal patterns as points in the centers of certain randomly chosen quadrants. Each input is followed by a vector weight change caused by the machine learning process. The next input object is shown and the next step of machine learning follows.

At first, when you click and release the Start button, machine learning proceeds step by step. It stops after every presentation of inputs so that you can view what happens in the network. The interruptions are eliminated later, and machine learning continues automatically and continuously. To simplify your view of more of the more complex operations of the system, subsequent figures in this chapter will display only the main parts of windows depicting point distributions for specific experiments.

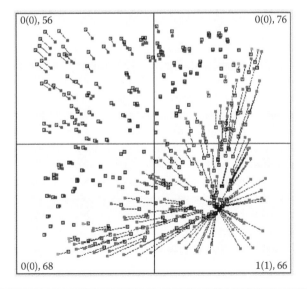

Figure 9.15   Learning initial stage of network composed of 300 neurons.

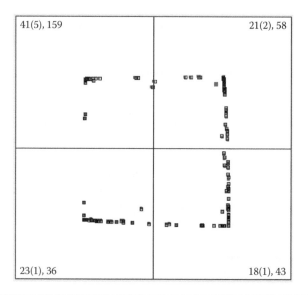

Figure 9.16   Learning final stage of network composed of 300 neurons.

Machine learning processes and supervised learning can be achieved with different values of learning coefficients. Figure 9.15 shows how a network with a very high learning coefficient behaves. It displays an exceptionally enthusiastic attitude; every new idea attracts its attention entirely. The attracting object interests an enormous number of neurons that want to recognize and locate the object as quickly as possible. The attractor tactic enables a network to learn quickly but also causes immediate saturation of its cognitive potential. A minor number of attractors (in comparison with the number of neurons) can completely involve all the neurons in attempts to recognize them. As a result, the neurons will have no adaptation capabilities left for recognizing new patterns and thus the network becomes unable to accept and assimilate new ideas.

A network with small consolidation coefficients behaves differently. When a new object appears, the network reaction is calm and balanced (Figure 9.17). This is why learning is not a fast process. Compare Figure 9.18 depicting a similar learning level of a "calm" network and Figure 9.16 that displays an "enthusiastic" network. The network retains a reservoir of neurons that are not yet specialized and are thus able to accept and assimilate new signal patterns.

The acceptance of new ideas by some humans is similar. Some people accept an idea uncritically at first (e.g., a political issue). They learn about it, identify with it, and then become fanatic to the point where they cannot accept other ideas or views, almost as if their brains have no space left. In extreme cases, their religious or political ideas possess them to the point where they are capable of murdering and torturing those who oppose their views.

Researching a highly excitable neural network may produce an interesting phenomenon. If a "fanatic" network receives no signals from its attractor for a long enough time, it will rapidly change its focus. All the points previously associated with a certain pattern (or fanatic idea) will suddenly migrate toward (and fixate on) a completely different pattern (Figure 9.19). Humans behave similarly. The literature is full of examples of people who suddenly changed their beliefs or lurched from one extreme to another.

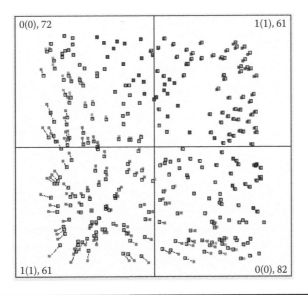

Figure 9.17 Slow and deliberate beginning of machine learning process in system with low value of learning coefficient (etha).

The phenomena described above occur only in networks with high learning coefficient values. Shifts that can be seen in Figures 9.18 and 9.19 arise when the learning sequence objects belonging to the same class are not identical and a network learns continuously.

A network model with a low learning coefficient (Figure 9.17) resembles a reluctant human who has to examine every new idea completely before assimilating it on a limited basis. However, once this human adopts a preference, he or she generally does not change it easily.

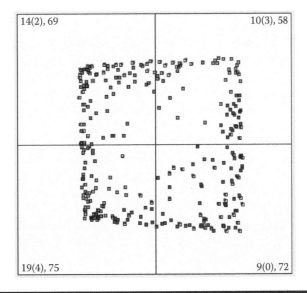

Figure 9.18 Similar stage of machine learning process shown in Figure 9.14. We see numerous "vacant" neurons with low values of learning coefficients.

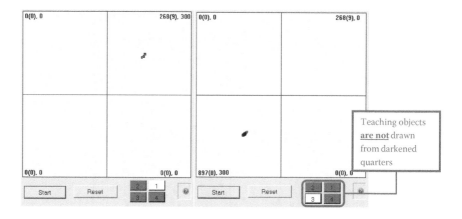

Figure 9.19 Left: Attraction of all neurons to objects coming from one class only. Right: Abandonment of attractor and transfer of recognition of all neurons to second attractor.

9.3 Evaluating Progress of Self-Teaching

We will now present some simple experiments you can conduct to analyze the features of the program described above. These experiments will help you to learn more about the characteristics of the self-teaching processes in neural networks and the impacts of changes on learning progress. We will describe the use of the Example 10b program which is designed so that you can work with it and discover the various features it presents.

After activating learning with a given number of neurons, we can observe how the neurons detect repetitive presentations of certain characteristic objects within the input data. You will notice immediately that the initially chaotic set of points representing the locations of neuron weights display an inclination to divide the population of neurons into as many subgroups as the number of object classes appearing at the input.

This is easy to check. During a simulation, when you click on the picture with a number of a quadrant (1 to 4), the objects appearing during teaching will only come from three or fewer quadrants, not all four. Objects from the chosen quadrant will be omitted and the quadrant will be marked with a darker color. This option of the program allows you to assess the efficiency of detection performed by the network and the number and types of object classes it should recognize (Figure 9.20 and Figure 9.21).

At the beginning of the teaching process, the network partially organizes neurons that potentially may recognize the objects of the missing class (Figure 9.21), leading to increased focus of the network on these objects. However, even at the final stage of the self-teaching process, when the network already achieved a high level of recognition and identification of objects through self-teaching (three clusters in Figure 9.21), the area with no attractors still contains spare neurons. They are dispersed randomly and they will disappear as the self-teaching process continues.

Sometimes, even after basic learning has ended and a new object appears, the neurons take over the learning process rapidly and attempt to identify the new object. Even after a long period of systematic self-teaching and considerable experience, a network may deploy all its neurons into a certain orbit of an attractor. If a new object appears after this type of network petrification, it will have no free neurons capable of accepting the new object and learning to

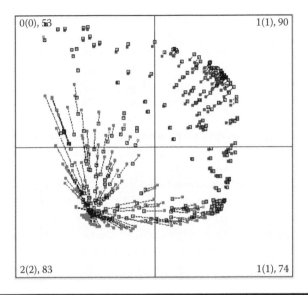

Figure 9.20   Beginning of self-teaching process during which objects from second quadrant are omitted.

identify it. Thus, a long process of self-teaching leads to the network's inability to accept and adapt to new inputs.

Humans are subject to the same phenomenon. Young people adapt to new conditions and acquire new skills (e.g., using computers) easily. Older people who have experience performing certain functions and recognizing situations may take a skeptical view of new ideas and resist learning new tasks.

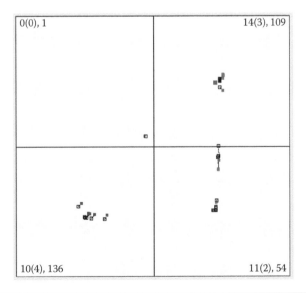

Figure 9.21   Final stage of self-teaching process during which objects from second quadrant are omitted.

The detailed course of self-learning depends on the initial set of the values of neural weights—the innate qualities of individuals. Learning also depends on the sequence in which the learning series objects (life experiences) are presented. Some people retain their youthful curiosity and sense of amazement, and approach new situations enthusiastically. Others remain rigid and cling to their biases. You can track this process in a network.

Example 10b is constructed so that pressing the Reset button will restart the self-teaching process with the same number of neurons, randomly chosen initial weight vector values, and a new and random set of learning objects assigned to chosen quadrants. By clicking on the buttons that mark the quadrants, you can freely switch presentations of objects on and off. In essence, this allows the user full control of the experiment.

If you repeat the learning process, you will see that the tendency for self-organization—the spontaneous tendencies of individual neurons to identify certain classes of input signals—is a constant feature of a self-teaching neural network. It does not depend on the number of classes, the number of neurons, or the arrangement of their initial values of weights. You will also notice that "more talented" networks consisting of more neurons can accept new types of inputs and maintain new skills for longer times.

9.4 Neuron Responses to Self-Teaching

You can perform various analyses using Example 10b. We suggest you begin with an analysis of the influence of object presentation on self-teaching. The program has no built-in mechanisms that present the relevant facts "on a plate." However, if you watch the simulated self-teaching process several times, you will notice that the classes whose objects are shown more often attract far more neurons than the classes whose objects appear less frequently (see Figure 9.22 results for first and second quadrants). This may lead to a lack of willing neurons' recognition of some classes of inputs, especially in networks with small numbers of neurons (compare third quadrant in Figure 9.22).

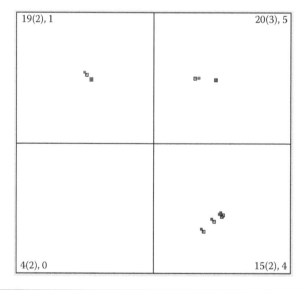

Figure 9.22   Representations of classes created via self-teaching process.

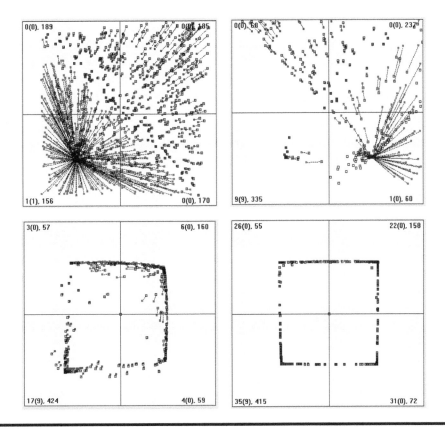

Figure 9.23   Self-teaching course showing initial preference for third class.

This is a big problem that was mentioned briefly in an earlier chapter. As a result of this tendency of neurons to focus on certain inputs, self-teaching networks must contain many more neurons than networks that carry out the same tasks after training by a teacher.

Examining the self-teaching process on many samples will demonstrate that the first reaction of a network is particularly relevant. This can be seen in Figure 9.23. The reproduced images of the first (top left) and final (bottom right) self-teaching steps accidentally draws only objects of the third quadrant in the first nine steps of the algorithm. Notice how it strongly affected the final distribution of the number of neurons in different quadrants.

Note that the overwhelming influence of experiences on later development of preferences and habits can also be seen in humans. If certain reactions (quadrants) are initially disabled (e.g., by an unhappy childhood experience), the representation of the initial experiences (represented in the model by a quadrant containing signals) remain visible in the network as limited or absent signals. This observation explains why successes in eliminating the effects of a difficult childhood are so rare.

Observing the attraction processes of some neurons and repulsion reactions of others allows you to imagine what happens when your brain encounters new situations and must analyze them. Consider a neural network with a large number of neurons. Figure 9.23 shows the self-teaching process of a network containing 700 neurons. You will see the mass movement of the "states of consciousness" as many neurons converge toward the points corresponding to the observed input stimuli and thus become detectors of these classes of input signals.

You can also view the "revolution" that takes place in the first steps of the self-teaching process. This is best done by conducting an experiment in steps. Information about which objects are often and rarely shown in the initial stages of learning is shown as numbers in the relevant quadrants, so you can easily observe and analyze the basic relationship between the frequency of presentation of the specified object in the training data and the number of neurons ready to recognize them. You can observe the effect especially clearly when you compare the results of many simulations. Recall that the results of all the individual simulations strongly influence the initial distribution of the weighting factors of individual neurons and the order of presentation of the training set objects. Both these factors are randomly drawn in the experimental programs.

9.5 Imagination and Improvisation

After you observe how networks form and classify ideas, you can move on to more subtle network activities. You may have noticed when practicing examples with large number of neurons the process of formation of neuron clusters recognizing main objects introduced to the system. We can also view tracks of neurons. These neurons are spontaneously aspiring to detect and recognize inputs and related objects (Figure 9.24). During self-learning, these neurons act as detectors focused on signaling the presence of real-life objects but "fantasize" about non-existing entities with astounding regularity.

How does this impact results? A network that is shown a fish and a woman repeatedly will learn to recognize both images but this requires explanation. At appropriate points, some neurons will correctly recognize a woman and a fish; some will be ready to recognize entities displaying the features of the fish (tail) and the woman (the head and shoulders). Although the creatures were not shown during the self-learning process, the network prepared neurons to detect them. In a certain sense, the network may have "imagined" them.

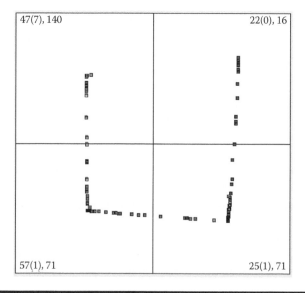

Figure 9.24 Parameter localization for neurons (detectors of hybrids) ready to detect objects having properties shared by real objects.

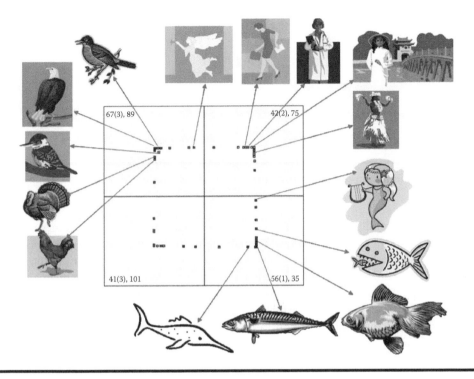

Figure 9.25 **Representatives of real and imaginary objects in self-learning neural network.**

Following a similar principle, the same network that developed an ability to recognize bird species can associate bird features with the characteristics of a woman (head, hands, dress) and thus create an image of an angel (Figure 9.25).

After repeating many experiments, we are convinced that every young (not fully taught) neural network will have a tendency to invent objects that do not exist. If experiments regularly prove that women and fish both exist and no creatures share the properties of women and fish (e.g., mermaids), the neurons will change their specialization to accommodate the hybrid combination.

These neurons will proceed to recognize real-life creatures instead of fantasies. They exhibit this tendency during experiments. If a hybrid creature (e.g., a bat that is in essence a mouse with wings) is presented, a network's previous experience with combination objects will facilitate the detection and classification tasks.

It appears that this ability to invent non-existent objects by combining elements of impressions and experiences is displayed by networks only during the early stage of self-learning. The analogous human behavior is a child's enjoyment of fairy tales and legends that are boring to adults. When you observe feeble chains of neurons emerging during self-learning, as shown in Figure 9.26, then you may be watching the formation of associations, analogies, and metaphors.

During some experiments, certain (usually single) neurons remain outside the areas concentrated near the spots where input objects appear. Actually, these are of little practical significance because most neurons are taught easily and are subject to precise specialization. The majority of them aim toward perfection in handling detection and signaling of real-world objects. The neurons that are out of touch with reality will stay and retain (Figure 9.27) their images of non-existent entities.

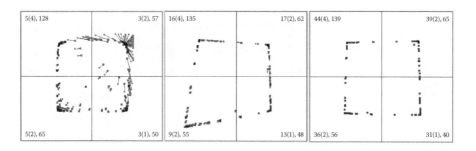

Figure 9.26 Voluntary appearance and destruction of associations during self-learning.

If you watch carefully the initial stages of self-learning, you may notice another interesting phenomenon. After an object is shown at a certain point in the space of the input signals, a few neurons will change their original positions. When they reach a new location distant from the original one, they remain in the same direction as the input object even though they are far from the origins of the coordinate system. This is a rare event because it depends on the initial distribution of weight coefficients. If you patiently repeat your experiments, you will notice this change (Figure 9.28). As a rule, rebellious neurons land outside the borders of the limiting frame and they can be seen because lines with no empty squares at the ends will appear.

Neurons that wander far at the start of self-learning will be pulled back in consecutive stages of teaching to the area associated with the presented standard and they will find their way back to where they should be. We are concerned with them because they illustrate a well-known psychological effect known as grandiosity (Figure 9.29). Indeed, a neural Gulliver escaping the display area becomes the standard of an object that displays roughly the same features as the model object perceived at the start of teaching—with all its features magnified.

If a lion is shown, the image produced after enlarging its perceivable features depicts a real monster that has huge fangs and claws, ruffled mane, and dangerous roar. The image contains all

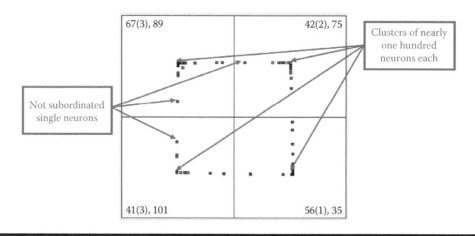

Figure 9.27 Appearance of single neurons outside global centers during advanced self-learning (after 200 steps).

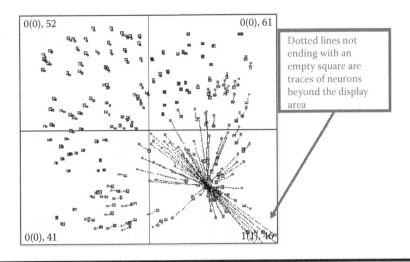

Figure 9.28 Effect of neuron escape in initial stage of self-learning.

the features of a lion, only larger, as in Figure 9.30. Such exaggerated ideas of a neural network are usually short lived and the system behaves as programmed.

At the end of self-learning, most neurons form tight clusters near the spots where input objects will signal (they have already chosen a master and are ready to serve). Sometimes, rebellious points appear beyond the display area. Despite their resistance, they are pulled back to the areas where real objects are recognizable (Figure 9.31). These neurons pursue different paths and the results may be incorrect reactions. As time passes, the rebel neurons are forced to join the conforming majority on the correct path. On occasion, an unexpected input gives these non-conformists a chance to win, but such occasions are rare.

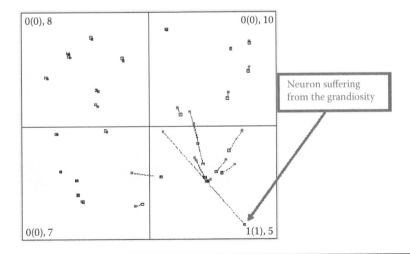

Figure 9.29 Effect of grandiosity at lower scale than in Figure 9.28, but still noticeable.

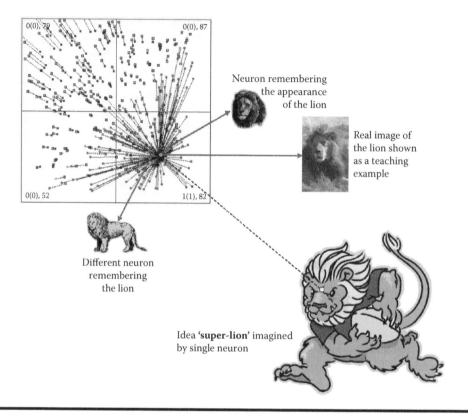

Figure 9.30 Interpretation of effect of grandiosity.

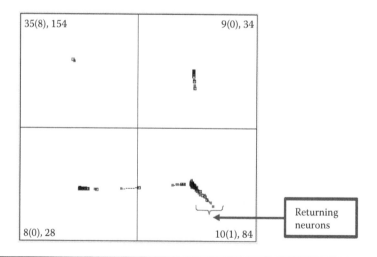

Figure 9.31 Pulling back neurons that escape in the initial stage of teaching and create fictional representations of data—effect known as grandiosity.

9.6 Remembering and Forgetting

This chapter concentrates on the activities of self-learning networks such as storing information and gaining knowledge, and explains how they accomplish these tasks. Networks are also subject to another event that occurs daily in human life: forgetting. This phenomenon is burdensome in some situations, but it is an essential biological function. Our living environments change constantly. Actions we mastered at some stage of life may become outdated or even harmful, and we are compelled to gain new skills and forget earlier ones. Forgetting unneeded information prevents conflict and confusion.

We can use neural network simulation to observe and analyze this process. New objects appearing during simulation of self-learning networks may divert neurons from tasks they already learned. In extreme cases, new objects can "kidnap" neurons that recognize earlier patterns that are obsolete (Figure 9.32). In this situation, the neural network recognizes quite well all four patterns that were presented to it. Please note that pattern number 1 has the strongest representation in the 1st quarter.

The network in the figure recognizes all four patterns presented to it. The first pattern in the first quadrant displays the strongest representation. At this point, self-learning is interrupted intentionally and the experiment proceeds to "kidnapping." A class is a collection of objects that are similar to each other within a class and different from the objects belonging to other classes—each object is an instance of its class. Classes can be named (e.g., "dogs," "cats," "horses," "cows"), but in our considerations the names are not important. Therefore, we use numbers instead of names. Our discussion is concentrated on classes 1 and 4, because class 1 loses neurons and class 4 gets them. Classes 2 and 3 are stable, and therefore not interesting. Neurons recognizing objects of class 1 change their specializations immediately. They quickly focus on recognizing other classes of objects (class 4; Figure 9.33 left). The earlier familiar class is forgotten but not completely. Even

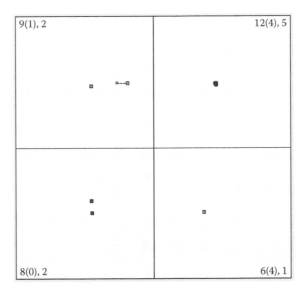

Figure 9.32 First stage of forgetting process during self-learning. Network still possesses earlier (class 1) knowledge.

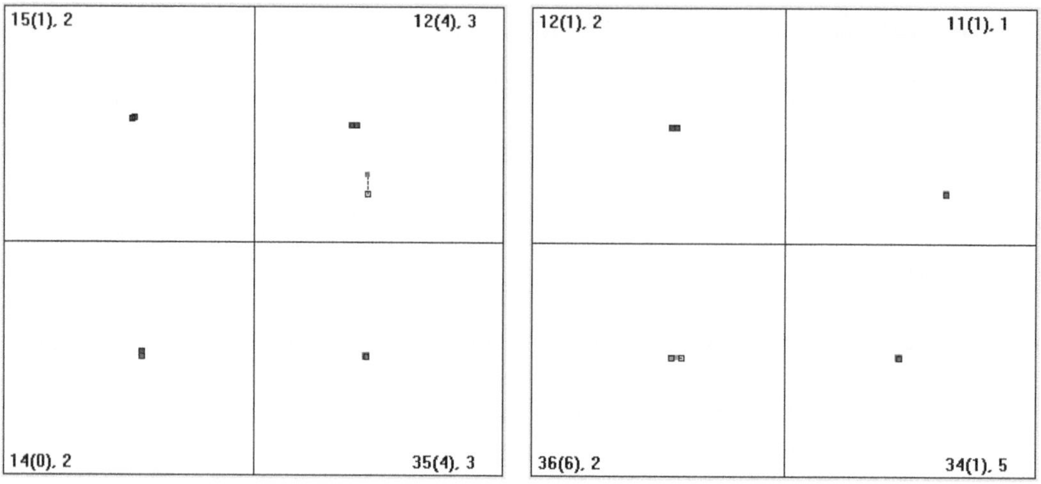

Figure 9.33 Forgetting of class 1 when trace in memory is not enforced systematically during self-learning.

extended learning courses leave traces of earlier learning in neuron memories (Figure 9.33 right). Although the trace in the figure is very weak (involving only one neuron), it significantly altered the position of the neuron.

Humans have similar experiences. You may be interested in botany and learn the names of and characteristics of new plants. If you fail to revise and solidify your knowledge quickly, you will forget what you learned. The old information will be blurred by new knowledge and plant identification will be difficult.

9.7 Self-Learning Triggers

During experiments with Example 10b, we saw that the impulsive nature of self-learning caused some classes of objects to be stronger (better recognized) and other classes to be weak or absent. This is an important shortcoming of self-learning methods and we will describe it in detail in Section 9.8.

We should demonstrate that self-organization and self-learning occur only when a network is based on patterns in the input data sequence. The situation in Example 10b was simple. The objects shown to the network belonged to a specific number (usually four) of well-defined classes. Furthermore, the classes occupied distinct areas, namely the central parts of four quadrants of the system.

The objects appeared in a random sequence but were not located in random places. Each time a point presented to the network was located (with some deviation) in the central area of a given quadrant, it represented an example of an object. A completely typical (ideal) object would have appeared exactly in the center of the quadrant. This type of object representation may reveal a familiar result. The self-learning process caused neurons to form groups specialized to recognize specific patterns: combinations of slightly varied object representations from one class—variations of the same perfect pattern.

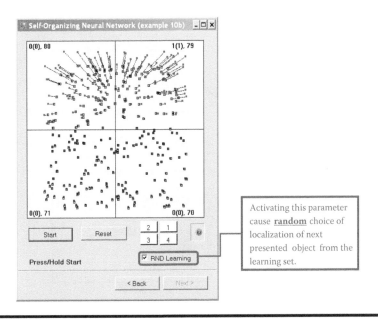

Figure 9.34   Beginning of self-learning with random input objects.

We now consider how a network behaves when points used during learning are located completely randomly. In an example from an earlier chapter, we discussed a space probe sent to Mars. In this example, no Martians are found. The landing vehicle sensors receive images only of random shapes of Martian dust formed by winds.

A feature of Example 10b allows easy observation of this situation during learning by activating the RND learning option. You must check the box because this option is disabled by default. From this point, you will *not* see the quadrant in which the learning sample is located (Figure 9.34). It is not important if you enable random point selection from all quadrants as in the figure. The sample object will appear randomly anywhere in the coordinate system.

Because of the lack of order, no information will be generated in the input data sequence. Neurons may be attracted to the center of the area on one occasion and at other times will be pushed outside (Figure 9.35). In this case, the self-learning process will not lead to the creation of visible groups of neurons. Instead the neurons will form a large circle within which the mean signal pattern will appear. When you watch this aspect of self-learning for a time, you will see that the size and location of the circle change with every presentation of the learning sample (Figure 9.36). However, no groups of neurons will emerge because the input data contain no such groupings.

The conclusion is both optimistic and pessimistic. The optimistic view is that the self-learning of a neural network may help it find unknown patterns present in the input data; users do not have to know what and how many patterns are present. Sometimes, self-learning networks appear to answer unasked questions. In general, they accumulate knowledge during learning and also discover it. This is an awesome development because computer science has many good tools (Internet and databases) that yield good answers to good questions. We can even obtain good answers to stupid questions but no commonly available tools can find answers to unasked questions.

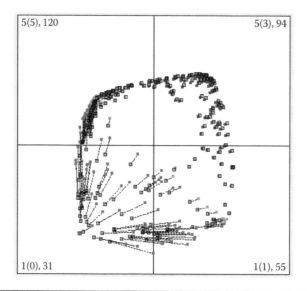

Figure 9.35   Chaotic neuron movements when random objects are shown.

Self-learning neural networks have such abilities. Finding answers to unasked questions is called data mining. It is used, for example, to determine customer behaviors and preferences of mobile phone users. The marketing specialists can make use of even the smallest piece of data about repeatable and common customer behaviors. The result is a huge demand for systems that provide such information.

The (slightly) pessimistic part relates to a self-learning network that generates data devoid of useful information. For example, if input values are completely random (without explicit or

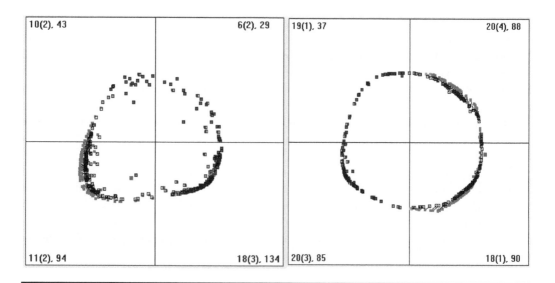

Figure 9.36   Advanced stage of chaotic learning.

implicit meaning) even the longest learning process will not provide meaningful results. This characteristic has a positive side. Neural networks will never replace humans by generating new ideas suddenly and spontaneously.

9.8 Benefits from Competition

Any type of neural network can be self-learned. The most interesting results arise by enriching self-learning with competition. The competition between neurons is not a new concept; it was described in Section 4.8. Example 02 demonstrated the operations of networks in which neurons compete.

All neurons in competitive network receive input signals (generally the same signals because the networks are usually single-layer types). The neurons then calculate the sums of those signals (multiplied by weights that vary with each neuron). All values calculated by neurons are compared and the "winner"—the neuron that generated the strongest output for the input—is determined.

The higher the output value, the better the agreement between the input signal and the internal pattern of a neuron. Therefore, if you know the weights of the neurons, you can predict which ones will win by presenting samples that lie in particular areas of the input signal space. The prediction is easy to make because only the neuron whose internal knowledge is in accord with the current input signal will win the competition and only its output signal will be sent to the network output. Outputs of all the other neurons will be ignored.

Of course, the success of the neuron is short-lived. The arrival of new input data means another neuron will win the competition. This is not surprising there. The map showing the arrangement of the weight values determines which neuron will be the winner for any given input signal—the neuron whose weight value vector is the most similar to the vector representing the input signal.

A few consequences surround the winning of a competition by a neuron. First, in most networks of this type, only one neuron has a non-zero output signal (usually its value is 1). The output signals of all other neurons are zeroed. This is the winner-takes-all (WTA) rule. Furthermore, the self-learning process usually concerns only the winner. Its (and only its) weight values are altered so that presentation of the same input signal will cause the same winning neuron to produce even output. Why is that?

To answer, let us examine carefully what exactly happens in a self-learning network with competition. At the start, we present an object represented by its input signals. The signals are propagated to all neurons and form a combined stimulation. In the simplest case, combined stimulation is a sum of input signal multiplied by the weight values. We can apply the same rule to neurons with nonlinear characteristics. The more weight values of the neuron are similar to the input signal, the stronger the combined stimulation of neuron's output.

We already know that the sets of weight values can be treated as input signal patterns to which each neuron is particularly sensitive. Therefore, the more the input signal is similar to the pattern stored in the neuron, the stronger the output when this signal is used as an input. Thus, when one of the neurons becomes the winner, its internal pattern is the most similar to the input signal among signals of all the other neurons. But why is it similar?

In the beginning, this result may arise from random weight value initialization. The initial values of these are random in all networks. The randomly assigned values are more or less similar to the input signals used during learning process. Some neurons accidentally acquire an innate bias toward recognition of some objects and aversion to others. The learning process later forces internal patterns to become more similar to some kinds of objects at each step. The randomness disappears and neurons specialize in the recognition of particular classes of objects.

At this stage, a neuron that won by recognizing the letter A will probably win again when another A is presented on an input even if it is slightly different from the previous sample. We always start with randomness. Neurons decide which of them should recognize A, which should recognize B, and which should signal that a character is a fingerprint and not a letter. Self-learning process only reinforces and polishes a neuron's natural bias (again randomly assigned during initial value generation).

This happens in every self-learning network, so what does competition mean? Competition makes self-learning more effective and efficient. Because initial values of weights are random, a few neurons may be biased toward a single class of object. Without competition, the bias will be strengthened simultaneously in all the affected neurons. Eventually there will be no variety in behaviors of neurons. Neuron behaviors will become more similar as shown in experiments with Example 10b.

When we introduce competition, the situation changes completely. Some neurons will operate more suitably for recognizing the input object than their competitors will. The natural consequence is that a neuron whose weight values are (accidentally) most similar to the presented object will become the winner. If this neuron (and only this one) is learning during this step, its inborn bias will develop further. The competition will stay behind and compete only for recognizing other classes of objects.

You can observe self-learning with competition using the Example 10c. We designed competitive learning in a task similar to the Martian family examples from Section 9.1. This time, the learning principle is different because the system will process completely new behaviors.

After starting, the application will display a parameter window. You can specify the number of neurons in the network. We suggest you manipulate only this parameter at first. It will be too easy to stray from the goal if you change several parameters.

The rule to determine the number of neurons is simple: the fewer neurons (e.g., 30), the more spectacular the results of self-learning with competition. You can observe easily that all neurons except the winner remain still; only the winner is learning. The exercise allows a user to trace changes of locations of learning neurons to reveal their trajectories. In Example 10c, a neuron that reaches its final location appears as a big red square that indicates completion of learning process for the particular class (Figure 9.37).

When self-learning starts, you will see that only one neuron will be attracted to each point where objects belonging to a particular class appear. This neuron will eventually become a perfect detector for objects that belong to this class. You will see a big red square in a place where objects of that class typically appear during learning. If you click the Start button again, you will activate a step-by-step feature (if you hold the Start button down, the self-learning process will become automatic).

You can observe trajectories of moving weight vectors of specific neurons and read messages shown in each quadrant to see which neuron wins in each step. One neuron in each quadrant is chosen to win every time samples from the quadrant are presented. Moreover, only this neuron changes its location and moves toward a presented pattern. Eventually it reaches its final location and stops moving (Figure 9.38).

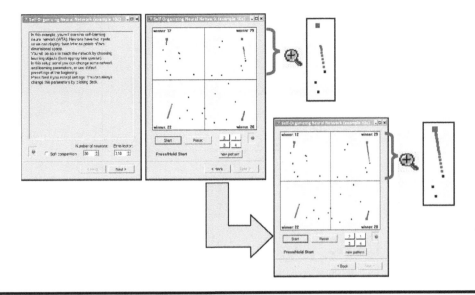

Figure 9.37   Example 10c parameter window and self-learning visualization in network with competition before and after eventual success.

Self-learning with competition is more difficult to observe in systems with huge numbers of neurons. Unlike the classic self-learning process in large complex networks, learning with competition has a very local character (Figure 9.39). With many neurons, the distance from the nearest neighbor to the winning one is very short and therefore the trajectory of the winner is barely visible.

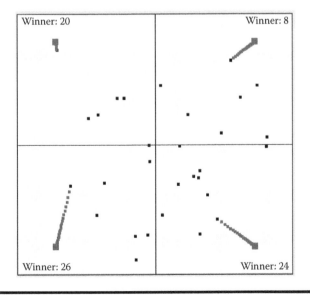

Figure 9.38   Self-learning in a network with competition.

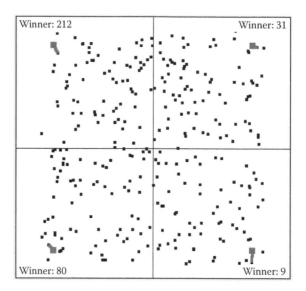

Figure 9.39   Self-learning with competition in a large network.

Conversely, with a small number of neurons (e.g., five), trajectories are long and spectacular. Moreover, the competition feature allows detection of even very weak initial biases toward recognizing some classes of objects can be detected. The biases will be strengthened during learning provided that competitors have even weaker biases toward recognizing objects of a particular class (Figure 9.40). The visibility of the sequence of changing locations will allow you to notice another interesting characteristic of neural networks: the fastest learning and greatest location changes occur at the beginning of the learning process.

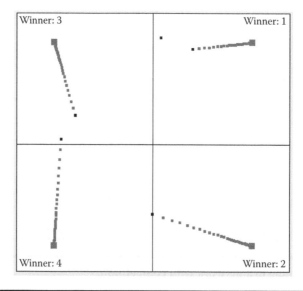

Figure 9.40   Self-learning with competition in network with few neurons.

9.9 Results of Self-Learning with Competition

Example 10c permits you to active the soft competition parameter (Figure 9.37 left). We suggest you use the default setting at first. We will experiment with soft competition after you understand the benefits and disadvantages of hard competition.

The hard competition displayed in Example 10c allows us to avoid cliques of neurons that have exactly the same preferences as those formed during our work with Examples 10a and 10b. If you are lucky, especially when working with networks consisting of many more neurons than classes of recognized objects, you may also avoid holes and dead fields in representations of input objects. Holes and dead fields denote the objects that no neurons could recognize. There is a high probability that when competition is used in a network, no neuron will be able to recognize multiple classes of objects. Conversely, no class of objects will not be recognized by any neuron, as noted in the old proverb that says, "Every Jack has his Jill."

When learning with competition, the neurons other than the winner do not change their locations so they are ready to learn and accept other patterns. If objects from a completely new class suddenly appear during learning, some free neurons will be ready to learn from and identify this new class. Example 10c includes an option that allows you to order a new class of objects to appear.

To do that during simulation, click the New Pattern button. By clicking the button a few times, you can lead your network to recognize many more classes of objects than only four types of Martians. Learning with competition assigns each of those classes of input objects a private guardian neuron that from that moment will identify with this class (Figure 9.41). Usually some free neurons are available to learn new patterns that may appear in the future.

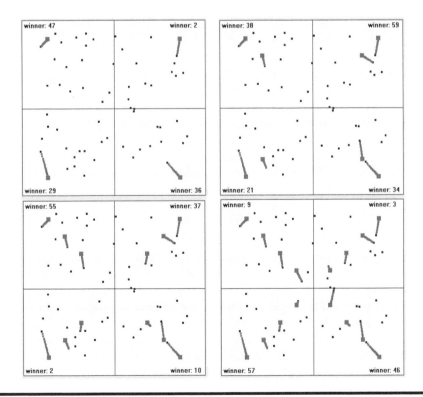

Figure 9.41   Opportunity to teach recognition of multiple patterns in network with competition.

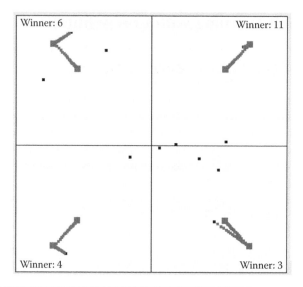

Figure 9.42 Replacing previously learned skills with new information.

Unfortunately, the pure self-learning process combined with hard competition may cause abnormalities. When you initiate self-learning with a low number of neurons (four in the example application), one neuron will identify with and recognize one class of object. If new classes of objects are introduced when you click the New Pattern button, the "winner" may be a neuron that already specialized in recognizing some other class. Some class of input objects that gained a strong representation among neurons suddenly loses it. This is similar to the human reaction when new information replaces old information.

Figure 9.42 shows such an effect, in this case very strong. All trained neurons recognizing some objects re-learned after being shown new objects and started recognizing the new ones. This situation is not typical. Usually more neurons are available than recognized classes of objects are presented so the "kidnapping effect" is somewhat rare—it happens in one or two classes out of a dozen (Figure 9.43). That explains why some details disappear from our memories and are replaced by more intense memories. Unfortunately, memories that are "lost" may be important.

During experiments with Example 10c, you will notice other "kidnap-related" phenomena. New objects may kidnap neurons that already were in stable relationships with some class of objects and many neurons may still be free if they are distant. In the sample application, the phenomenon intensifies after one class of objects is shown and only when neurons start identifying with this group are new classes of objects shown. The new objects sometimes "steal" neurons from established classes. If all objects are shown at the same time, a competition can be observed when neurons are attracted to the first group and then to the second. You can see this in Example 10c when you start the self-learning process with a very low number of neurons; see Figure 9.44.

In this case, it is possible that a network will learn nothing despite a very long self-learning process. That will sound familiar to students who are not prepared to take a battery of examinations in mathematics, physics, geography, and history in a single day.

The solution may be "softening" the competition by clicking the Back button to return to the parameter window (Figure 9.37 left). Activate Soft competition by checking the box. From this moment, the application will apply softer limited competition. This means the winning neuron

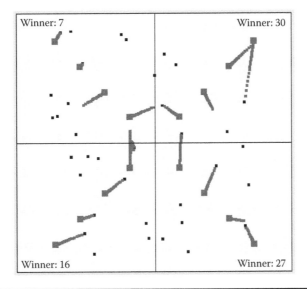

Figure 9.43   Few learned patterns are lost in a network with "hard" competition.

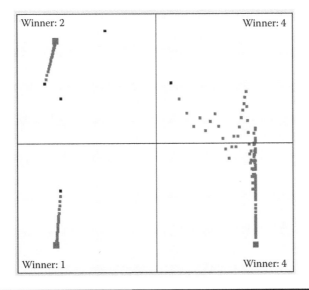

Figure 9.44   Attracting a neuron between objects of classes 1 and 4.

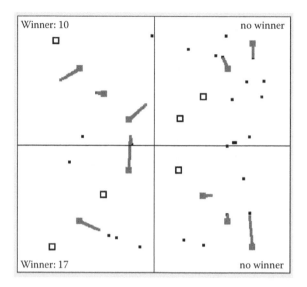

Figure 9.45 Omission of some classes in network with soft competition.

will be chosen only if the value of the output signal is exceptionally high.* Thus those neurons will be evenly divided between classes of recognized objects and no kidnapping of neurons that already belong to some other class will occur.

Unfortunately, you may see another worrying phenomenon. Under some circumstances (especially in networks with low numbers of neurons), no winner may appear among the neurons when an image is shown[†] (Figure 9.45). Use Example 10c with soft competition to examine this phenomenon carefully. It will be easy, because the application uses special markers that show the locations of patterns of classes that are omitted (for which there is no winner among neurons).

In the absence of strong competition, such omissions happen often, especially in networks with small numbers of neurons. In such cases for most classes in the network, voluntarily patterns will be created to allow automatic recognition of signals that belong to the specific classes. However, the "unlucky" class of signals no neuron wants to detect will have no specialized detectors. Such a neuron is like a person who has a flair for history, geography, and languages but cannot master mathematics.

Questions and Self-Study Tasks

1. Explain for whom, when, and why a self-learning neural network might be useful?
2. What determines whether points representing neurons in Example 10a will be blue or red?

---

* Soft competition is like partners who love each other and get married. Short and strong fascination does not lead to long-lived relationships such as marriages.
† Another analogy applies to this situation. Unmarried people sometimes engage in hard competition in attempts to achieve monogamy.

3. Taking into consideration experiments described in this book and your own observations, formulate your own hypothesis on the influence that the inborn talents (represented by initial randomly organized weight vectors) exert on the gained knowledge represented by the self-learning process. Do you think that systems of small numbers neurons (such as primitive animals) are strongly influenced by their instincts and inborn qualities and more complex systems of many neurons (such as human brains) are more strongly influenced by external factors such as personal experiences and education? Find arguments for both views using self-learning networks of various sizes.

4. Describe the features of self-learning networks with very low and very high learning factor (etha) values. Do we observe similar phenomena in animal brains? When answering this question, remember that learning is easier for younger brains and it becomes more difficult with age (diminishing etha values in a neural network). For example, a young puppy has a brain that can be modeled by a network with a very high etha value. Its brain is different from the brain of an older dog (whose etha value may approach zero). Present the positive and negative views of this concept.

5. Do you think that a self-learning network that has "imagination" capabilities and can devise a new idea that has no similarity to known input signals used during self-learning?

6. Can you imagine a real-life situation that represents the experience described in Section 9.7? Explain what influence the situation would have for an animal brain or the brain of a young human.

7. Do you think that the forgetting mechanism triggered by over-learning described in Section 9.6 explains all the issues related to over-learning? Is the forgetting of information that is not constantly updated beneficial from a biological view or not?

8. Which adverse phenomena that occur during self-learning of a neural network can be eliminated by introducing competition? Which phenomena will remain?

9. In networks with competition, the winner-takes-all rule is sometimes replaced by the winner-takes-most rule. The Internet has information about this concept. What does the replacement indicate? What do you think?

10. Assume you want to design a self-learning network that can create patterns for eight classes. Prepare an experiment to determine how many more neurons (more than eight) the network should have at the start of self-learning, so no class will be omitted and the number of free neurons will be as low as possible.

11. Advanced exercise: Modify Example 10b to demonstrate how the etha parameter changes over time. Allow for the planned appearances of some objects during the network's lifetime (e.g., early during learning or after training and experience). Run a series of experiments with such a real-life application. Describe your observations and develop conclusions. What observed phenomena have their representations in real-life situations? Which ones result from simplifying real neural networks (brains)?

12. Advanced exercise: Modify Example 10c to enable competition with a "conscience" (a neuron keeps winning but gradually lets other neurons win). Compare such a behavior with serious competition. What conclusions can you derive? Do those conclusions apply only to neural networks or could they also apply to real-life processes, for example in economics?

Chapter 10

Self-Organizing
Neural Networks

10.1 Structure of Neural Network to Create
Mappings Resulting from Self-Organizing

To this point, we demonstrated that neural networks can be taught by teachers or learned independently. We will now talk about networks that teach themselves without teachers and agree based on the interactions to handle the functioning of all neurons so that their cumulative results take on some new quality. These systems automatically generate complex mapping by transforming a set of input signals into output signals. This mapping generally cannot be predicted or controlled. Thus these networks are far more self-reliant and independent than the networks described earlier in this book.

The creator of such a network can impose only slight control over the properties. The essence of their operation and the final mapping depends on the results of their functioning. The actions of such networks are determined mostly by a process of self-organization. Details of the process will be illustrated later in this chapter. Before that, we will briefly explain various applications of self-organizing neural networks because they serve as serious tools for serious purposes.

Mapping is a rich and complex mathematical concept that exhibits several specific properties. We intend to discuss important ideas without burdening you with theory. Some important details are admittedly complex, but they will prepare you to build and work with self-organizing networks and take advantage of their unique properties. We assume that you are an eager adventurer willing to explore difficult issues if you have read this far.

We often must convert signals from input to output according to certain rules. When building a robot to perform certain tasks, we must ensure that it can convert the input signals received by sensors (video cameras, microphones, touch replacement contact switches, ultrasonic sensors, approximation sensors, etc.) correctly to control the signals for actuator devices driving the mechanisms that operate legs, graspers, arms, and so on (Figure 10.1). The conversion of input signals into correct output signals is called mapping (Figure 10.2).

Figure 10.1   Functioning of robot based on mapping X signals to Y signals.

Of course, a simple random mapping would be useless. Mapping is crucial because it ensures that a robot moves correctly, performs meaningful tasks, and responds properly to commands. The mapping binds stimuli recorded by sensors to concrete moves performed by actuators. Thus mapping must be properly designed and programmed correctly. Engineers who design robots and other sophisticated devices work hard on mapping because mapping is an essential component of the "brain" that controls a robot. Mapping is simple if a system has only one input signal and one output signal.

However, even the simplest robot involves many sensors and actions, and mapping becomes a difficult and demanding task. Attempting to program the mappings for complex tasks manually would require more time than an average human life span.

This is where self-organizing neural networks prove useful. Figure 10.3 illustrates such a network structure. Self-organizing networks usually have several inputs. Figure 10.3 shows only three so we can keep the illustration simple. A tangle of connections of 30 inputs would be impossible to trace in a diagram. However, self-organizing networks in practice usually involve more than a dozen inputs. This number is usually more efficient in various applications than networks utilizing far more signals.

A more important issue is that these networks tend to generate more outputs because of vast numbers of neurons that form the so-called topological layer. "Vast numbers" means at tens to thousands of neurons. These networks are far larger and more flexible than all the networks discussed to this point and we should understand the topological layer and what it does. We described the concepts of rivalry and "winner" neurons in an earlier chapter. Because they are also useful for this discussion, a brief review is in order. After providing specific input signals to the network, all the topological layer neurons calculate their output signals in response to the input signals. One signal in the group is the largest and the neuron that produced it becomes the winner (Figure 10.4).

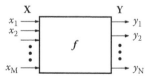

Figure 10.2   General representation of mapping.

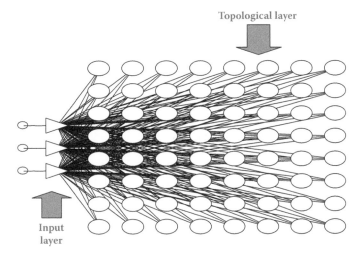

Topological layer

Input layer

By activating this parameter you are causing random selecting of learning object apparition

Figure 10.3   Structure of self-organizing neural network.

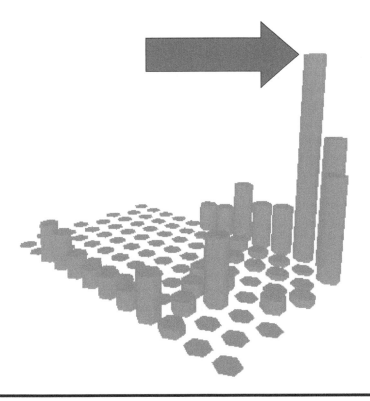

Figure 10.4   Example distribution of output signal values presented on topological layer of network with selected signal from "winner" neuron.

Self-organization identifies one and only one winning neuron. Thus the predominance of the winner among the competitors is clear. In exceptional cases, a network may generate a completely abnormal input signal (not included in teaching set) after self-organization. Determining the winner in such cases is difficult because all the topological layer neurons produce very weak but consistent signals.

10.2 Uses of Self-Organization

Self-organizing networks form certain representations of a set of input signals into a set of output signals based on certain general criteria. The networks perform this task independently, solely on the basis of observations of input data. The representation is no way determined in advance by the network's creator or user. The structure and properties arise spontaneously in a coordinated self-learning process involving all the elements of the network.

This spontaneous creation of signal projection is called self-organization. It is another form of self-learning from a different view. The effects from the program used in this chapter will be interesting. Self-organization involves an obviously higher level of network adaptation of a network by optimizing the parameters of each neuron separately. The coordination of activities of neurons contributes produces highly desirable grouping effects.

The grouping effect results when a network in the process of self-organization tries to divide the input data based on certain classes of similarities. The groups are detected automatically among the input objects (described by the input signals) and the system places similar signals in an appropriate group. The signals for each group are distinctly different from the signals assigned to other groups.

Such data clustering is very useful in many applications. A number of specialized mathematical techniques involving the analysis and the creation of such groups were developed and they constitute the specialty of cluster analysis. These analysis methods are useful in various business applications, for example, comparing similar companies in an effort to predict their returns on investments. The methods can be used in medicine for studying disease symptoms to determine whether they are indicative of a known or unknown disease.

Figure 10.5 depicts an example of a neural network that can group input signals (color image pixels coded as the usual red, blue, or green components) according to similarities of their colors. Figure 10.6 shows the effect of the network before self-organization (left) and afterward (right). The figure was created in such a way that in every place where there is a topological layer neuron, was drawn a box filled with such color of the pixel input, which makes this particular neuron able to become a "winner."

Figure 10.6 (left) shows the activity projection of the network before self-organization. The figure at right shows the process. Grouping image pixels of similar color is not a task that yields special benefits. You may view Figure 10.6 and ask why such a feature is needed. The answer is in Figure 10.7 depicting topological layer of a self-organizing network programmed to compare data of different companies.

Network inputs cover type of business, capital owned, number of employees, accounting data reflecting profits and losses, and other parameters. The network grouped these companies and so placed the parameters that each neuron wanted to become the winner when information about its company was shown. A year later, the companies were analyzed again. Some produced losses or were threatened with bankruptcy. Those neurons are shown in red on Figure 10.7. Other companies suffered economic stagnation. The neurons assigned to them via

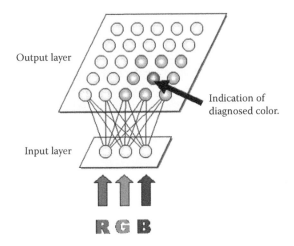

Figure 10.5 **Network grouping input signals (components corresponding to typical coding of digital image) in collections indicated by different colors.**

Figure 10.6 **Activity projection of network from Figure 10.5.**

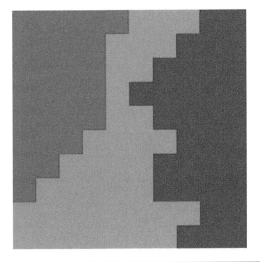

Figure 10.7 **Effect of clustering in self-organizing neural network.**

self-organization are indicated in blue in the figure. Finally, companies that yielded optimistic results are shown in green.

You may find plenty of impressive examples of self-organization like this on the Internet. You can input "self-organizing network" or "SOM" (self-organizing map) on Google and you will find a lot of information about grouping input data into similar classes and practical applications.

Neural networks engaged in self-organization are very attractive tools for grouping input data and creating similarity classes among them. The attractiveness of the neural approach is mainly that self-organization can proceed automatically and spontaneously. The network creator does not have to provide clues. The necessary information is contained in the same input data from which the network will extract the observation that some inputs are similar and some are not.

After a network learns how to cluster input data, it produces useful results. Winning neurons that specialize in identifying specific classes of input signals act both as detectors and indicators. Now that we understand the effect of clustering in self-organizing neural networks, we will briefly consider the collectivity of network activity.

The networks in which the self-organization takes place are organized so that an image a neuron identifies depends to a large extent on what other neurons located in its vicinity identify. In this way, a community (or collective) of neurons can process information more fully than any one of the individual neurons could (Figure 10.8).

The figure shows the results of our research related to the recognition by a self-organizing neural network of simple geometrical figures shown to it as images. It indicates places where the network independently placed the neurons indicating the various shapes of figures shown to it. A brief tour of this map will reveal that this distribution of neurons is not accidental.

We start with red arrows from the neuron that becomes the winner whenever a square is shown to the network. Nearby are the neurons indicating pentagons; a little farther away are those signaling octagons. This is correct because a pentagon is more similar to a square than an octagon. The neurons recognizing circles are placed near those recognizing octagons and a short path leads to neurons signaling an ellipse, not far from the neuron that understands a semicircle. This neuron has a clear affinity for a segment of a circle (sector) whose shape is similar to that of a triangle.

The workings of collective self-organized networks are interesting and lead us to broader considerations. A community of appropriately linked and cooperative elements makes it possible to

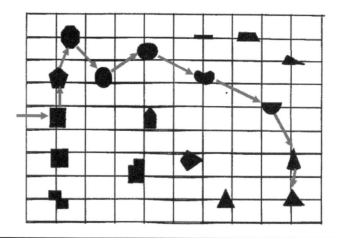

Figure 10.8 **Effect of recognition of geometric figures of self-organizing neural network.**

discover new forms of behaviors and actions that reveal far more information than individual elements. The same dynamic appears in entomology. A single insect is intellectually primitive and tiny. However, communities of insects are capable of complex, deliberate, and intelligent actions, for example, constructing bee colonies, complex nests, and termite mounds.

Self-organizing networks are convenient and valuable tools and also interesting research subjects. You can master the details of the self-organization processes of neural networks by studying the material in this chapter and performing experiments with the program devised for this purpose. The key concept for understanding and using self-organized networks is the formation of neuron neighborhoods.

10.3 Implementing Neighborhood in Networks

To understand the structure and function of a self-organizing network completely, we had to analyze its functioning and compare its performance with those of simple self-learning networks described in Chapter 9. We learned that the overwhelming influence of random initial values on the course of simple self-learning means that the creator of the network does not control what the neurons will learn.

After completing self-learning, the distributions of neurons may signal events that may not conform to the user's wishes. Applying manual intervention to influence self-organizing network behavior is difficult and also contradicts the principle on which such networks are based. The introduction of competition into a network may cause some neurons with adequate inborn abilities to be amenable to the teaching process; the others will resist it. This dynamic can be seen in Example 10c.

The program outputs results that include identification of "winner" neurons for each class that later advance to become detectors. The numbers appear chaotic and seem to have no relation to the locations of detected objects. Thus, the assignment of specific object detection functions to specific neurons may increase or decrease the utility of a network. If, for example, some of the input signals are similar, you may want their appearance signaled by neighboring neurons in the network. A self-organizing network works as shown in Figure 10.8. Pure self-learning networks do not require interference; users can simply accept what will happen.

A solution to these issues is to introduce a new mechanism: neighborhood. Teuvo Kohonen of Finland first applied the neighborhood concept to neurons in networks in the 1970s. Subsequently, networks utilizing neuron neighborhoods and competition became known as Kohonen neural networks.

We will now demonstrate how neighborhood works and what benefits it provides. To date, we have considered neurons in networks as largely independent units. Although they were linked together and transferred signals to each other, their relative positions in the layers did not matter. The numbering of neurons was introduced solely for ordering purposes for organizing calculations in programs simulating networks.

The self-organizing network described in this section is important. The adjacent nature of neurons in the topological layer significantly influences the behavior of the entire network. We usually associate neurons of a topological layer with points of some map displayed on a computer screen—typically a two-dimensional neighborhood. Neurons are depicted as if they were placed in nodes of a regular grid composed of rows and columns. Each neuron in such a grid has at least four neighbors [two horizontal (left and right) and two vertical (top and bottom)] as illustrated in Figure 10.9.

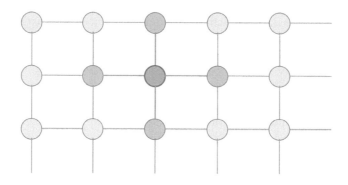

Figure 10.9   Simplest case of a neuron neighborhood.

If required, a neighborhood can be considered more broadly by admitting neurons on the diagonal (Figure 10.10) or neurons located in more distant rows or columns (Figure 10.11). The choice of type of neighborhood is entirely up to the user. For example, you can describe a network of one-dimensional neurons that will form a long chain. As shown in Figure 10.12, each neuron will have the neighbors preceding and following it along a chain.

Specialized applications of self-organizing networks may even involve three-dimensional neighborhoods. Neighboring neurons look like atoms in the crystal lattices frequently appearing in textbooks. A neighborhood can include four, five, or more dimensions but the two-dimension type is definitely the most practical and for that reason we will limit our discussion to that type.

A neighborhood consists of all the neurons in a network. Each neuron has a set of neighbors, and in turn it acts as a neighbor to other neurons. Only neurons located at the edge of the network do not have full sets of neighbors. However, sometimes this can be remedied by a special arrangement, for example, a network may be "closed" in such a way that the neurons of the upper edge are treated as neighbors to neurons from the lower edge. Similarly, closings can be applied using the left and right edges.

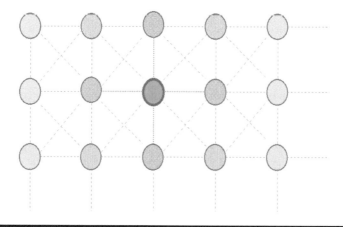

Figure 10.10   Richer neighborhood.

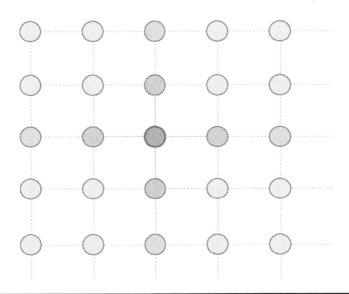

Figure 10.11   Neighborhood reaching longer distance.

Figure 10.12   One-dimensional neighborhood.

10.4 Neighbor Neurons

Adjacent neurons (neighbors) play an important role in network learning. When a neuron becomes a winner and undergoes teaching, its neighbors are also taught as we will explain later. Figure 10.13 depicts the self-learning process for a single neuron in a self-learning network.

Now let us compare this with self-learning of the winning neuron illustrated in Figure 10.14. Notice that a winner neuron (navy blue point) is subject to teaching because its initial weighting factors were similar to the components of the signal shown during the teaching process (green point). Therefore, amplification and substantiation of only natural ("innate") neurons occur. The preferences of such neurons were noted in other self-learning networks. The "winner" in the figure was attracted strongly by an input point. Its vector of weights (and a point representing this vector on a figure) will move strongly toward the point representing the input signal.

Neighbors of a winner neuron (yellow points lightly toned in red) are not so lucky. However, regardless of their initial weights and output signals, they are taught to have tendency to recognize this input signal even though another neuron became the winner. The neighbors are taught slightly less intensively than the winner (arrows indicating magnitudes of their displacements are visibly shorter).

One important parameter defining a network is the coefficient specifying how much less the neighbors should be taught. The neighbors (yellow points) often have much better parameters and tendency to learn (they were much closer to the input point) because they did not undergo initial teaching as the winner did.

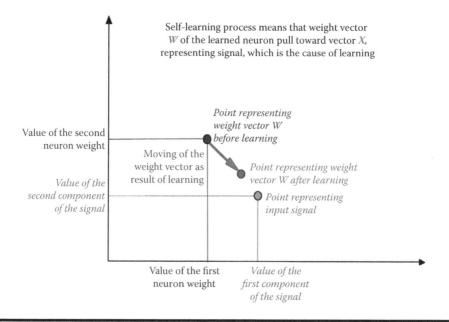

Figure 10.13   Self-learning of single neuron.

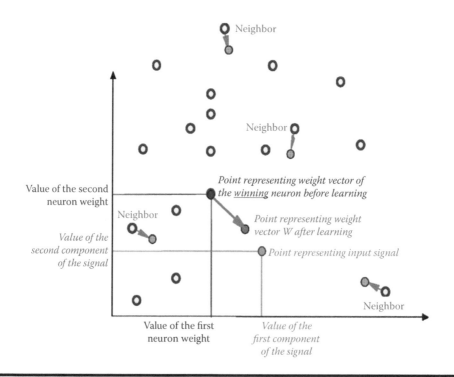

Figure 10.14   Self-learning of winning neuron and its neighbors.

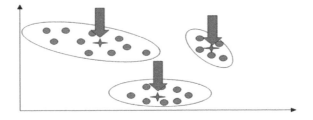

Figure 10.15   Result of self-learning: clustering of input data.

What will be the outcome of this strange teaching method? If the input signals arrive in a manner such that clear clusters are formed, the individual neurons will try to occupy (by their vectors of weights) the positions at the centers of the clusters. The adjacent neurons will "cover" the neighbor clusters as illustrated in Figure 10.15. The green dots in the figure represent input signals; red stars correspond with the locations in the same coordinate system of vectors of weights of the individual neurons.

A less desirable situation will occur when input signals are equally distributed in an area of the input signal space as shown in Figure 10.16. In this case, the neurons of the network will have a tendency to share the function of recognizing these signals and each sub-set of signals will have its "guardian angel" neuron. Each such neuron will detect and recognize all signals from only one sub-area (Figure 10.17). Clearly after input of a set of randomly appearing points and systematic teaching, the location of the point representing the winning neuron's weights will be the central location in the set (Figure 10.18).

As seen in Figure 10.18, when a neuron (represented as usual by its vector of weights) occupies a location in the center of the "nebula" of points it is meant to recognize, further teaching cannot move it from this location permanently. This is because different points that appear in the teaching sequence cause displacements that compensate each other. To reduce "yawing" of a neuron around its final location, a decreasing teaching coefficient is often applied. Therefore, the essential movements that allow a neuron to find its proper location occur early in the process when the teaching

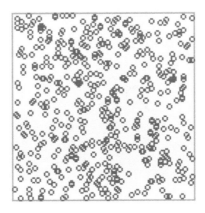

Figure 10.16   Self-learning using uniform distribution of input data presents a difficult task for a neural network.

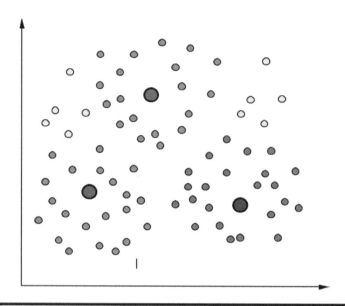

Figure 10.17 Localization of weight vectors of self-learning neurons (larger circles) in points of input space. Neurons may represent sub-sets of input signals (small circles) of the same color.

coefficient is still large. The points shown at the end of teaching exert weak influences on the positions of neurons. After a time, a neuron fixes its location and never changes it.

Another process occurs during the teaching of a network. The range of neighborhood systematically decreases. After the start of teaching, the neighborhood restricts and tightens at every step. In the end, each neuron is alone and devoid of neighbors (Figure 10.19).

Notice that when teaching is complete, the neurons of the topological layer will portion the input signal space among themselves so that each area of this space is signaled by a neuron. As a consequence of the influence of neighborhood, these neurons will demonstrate the ability to

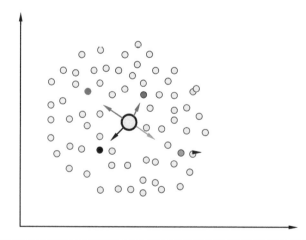

Figure 10.18 Mutual compensation of pulling from input vectors reacting with weight vector of self-learning neuron located in the center of a data cluster.

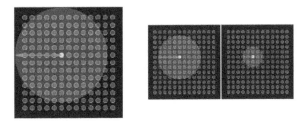

Figure 10.19　Decreasing neighborhood area during self-learning.

recognize input objects that are close (i.e., similar to the neurons). This feature is convenient and useful because this kind of self-organization is the key to remarkably intelligent applications of networks as self-organizing representations. We discussed examples of this in the early sections of this chapter.

When presenting the results of teaching a Kohonen network, you will encounter one more difficulty. This is worth discussing before you must deal with simulations in practice. When presenting results (changes in locations of points corresponding to specific neurons during learning), you must also watch the adjacent neurons. In Figure 10.14, it was easy to correlate the movements of the winner neuron and its neighbors. The system had only a few points, and identifying neighbors on the basis of the changed color was easy and convenient. During simulations, sometimes you may have to deal with hundreds of neurons, so the dynamic depicted in Figure 10.14 is impossible to expand to a large network. When presenting the activity of a Kohonen network, mapping of neuron positions is often used. The relation of neighborhood is shown in Figure 10.20.

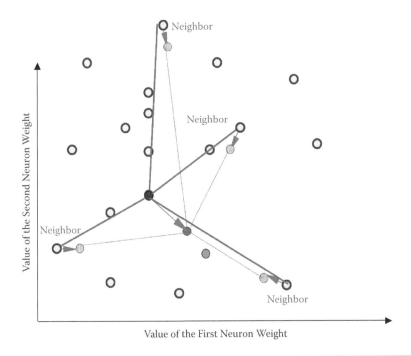

Figure 10.20　One step of Kohonen network learning.

You can see in Figure 10.20 that points corresponding to adjacent neurons are connected by lines. If the points shift as a result of teaching, the corresponding lines shift too. Of course, this should involve all the neurons and relationships of a neighborhood. For maximum clarity in the figure, we show only lines referring to the winner neuron and its neighbors and omitted all other connections. We will demonstrate this in detail for the full network in the Example 11 program.

10.5 Uses of Kohonen Networks

The program for Example 11 depicts the working of a Kohonen network. Before we attempt to use it, a few comments are in order. At the start, the window will allow you to set the network dimensions in both horizontal and vertical directions (Figure 10.21). The network size is your choice. However, to obtain clear results, start with a small network, perhaps 5 × 5 neurons. Such a network is primitive and it will not be useful for dealing with more complex tasks. However, it will learn quickly and allow you to progress to analyzing networks of greater sizes.

The program code imposes no specific limitations for network size. However, the range of inputs for these parameters is restricted from 1 to 100. During the teaching of big networks on a less efficient computer, you must be patient because finalizing teaching of a large network may require performance of several thousand steps.

Besides setting both the network dimensions in the initial window (Figure 10.21), you can also determine the range of numbers from which the initial values of the weight coefficients (range of initial random weights) will be drawn. We propose that you start by accepting the defaults. You can experiment with various values in further experiments to analyze how the "inborn" abilities of neurons forming a network affect its activity.

After determining the network dimensions and range of initial values, we can proceed to the next screen (Figure 10.22) by using the Next button. We can now follow the progress of teaching. In this window, the location of each neuron in the input signal space will be marked with a

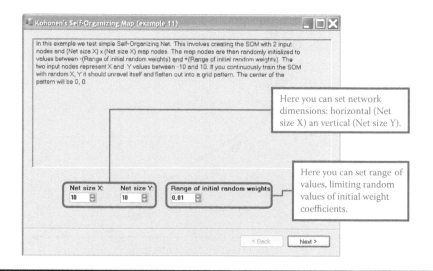

Figure 10.21 Initial interaction with Example 11 program.

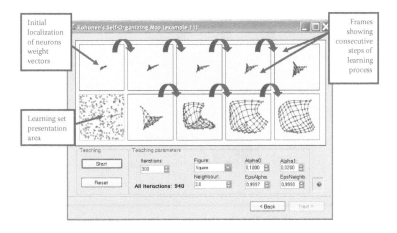

Figure 10.22   Example 11 working screen.

blue circle. The red lines connecting circles indicate that the neurons are neighbors based on the assumed rules of binding them (Figure 10.20).

In the input signal space, where the circles are, one neuron recognizes and indicates the appearance of a signal from this point and its close neighborhood (because neural networks always generalize acquired knowledge). The experiments with Kohonen networks usually involve randomly shown points from a certain sub-area of an input signal space. As a result, the blue circles will consequently disperse over the entire input signal space. To be more precise, the teaching signals will be generated from these neurons during teachings. However, these points of input signal space that will not be shown during teaching will not attract neurons.

To demonstrate this effect in the Example program, we prepared three options of presenting the training series. Points that teach a network may come from the entire visible area of the input space (this is the "square" option). However, the points may be taken also from the sub-area in the shape of a cross or a triangle. Keep in mind that a network finds representations of only the input signals that are shown in the areas that do not undergo teaching. Generally, not even a single circle representing a neuron "lying in wait" would appear in the area.

After determining the number of steps (iterations) the program must perform, you can use the Figure combination among a group of training parameters to determine the shape of an area. The points recruited to be shown to a network in consecutive phases of teaching will be in this area. The Training Parameters group lists other selections for the self-teaching process.

Pressing the Start button will initialize the network teaching process. The networks of points will appear gradually in the window in the lower left corner (marked by a green frame in the figure) after the count is fixed in the Iterations parameter. All the points have the same color because no teacher has classified them yet. You may notice the sub-space of the input signal space that emits the signals and compare the image with the result of teaching displayed at the end.

After pursuing the number of steps selected, the program will display a new map showing the distribution of points symbolizing neurons (and their neighborhood relations according to network topology) on the background of the input signal space. The previous map is also visible; the program displays the results of the last few teaching steps. You can monitor the progress of teaching the network. The result of the last training step can be identified easily by the red color of the frame. This is necessary when all the frames will be occupied after many steps of teaching and the screen spaces will be used rotationally.

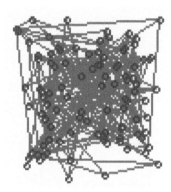

Figure 10.23   Initial neuron weight distribution.

At the beginning, before the teaching process establishes some order, the neurons occupy somewhat accidental positions in the input signal space. Hence, the blue circles are scattered with no order and the lines connecting the neighbors appear to have no rhyme or reason (Figure 10.23).

As noted earlier, the initial random values are set within the range the user selects. We recommended the use of small initial values of weight coefficients in experiments (e.g., the program suggests 0.01). Usually the unordered cluster of blue circles symbolizing neurons will occupy the densely filled central area of the input signal space.

Although the details will be difficult to see (as in the example in Figure 10.22), we wanted you to see the initial network state before the start of the simulation of teaching. This initial state is shown in Figure 10.23. We set a value of 7 for a scope of random initial weights. We wanted to demonstrate the chaotic initial state of a network, particularly the lines representing the neighborhood.

After every display of neuron location, you may change the number of steps that must be completed before a new point map is generated. It is advisable to use the default values initially. When you understand the workings of the program, you can experiment by changing the number of steps between the consecutive presentations of teaching results. You will note that teaching consisting of dozens or hundreds of steps will produce major changes in the display. If the progress after a segment of teaching is minimal, you may want to use larger jumps (100 or 300 steps) to improve the process, but keep in mind that larger networks mean longer waits to see results.

The intent of this section is to examine the self-organization capability of Kohonen network. We will first investigate the process with simple cases. When teaching starts, a modeling program will activate and show the network points originating from various parts of an input signal space. You can follow the process. The lower left corner of the window will show an area where points shown to the network are displayed (Figure 10.22). You will see the formation of blue circles representing the weights of neurons. These circles at first appear completely chaotic but they will move gradually and distribute equally throughout the input signal space.

You can also view the impact on their locations exerted by neighborhood relations. The red lines indicating which neurons are neighbors will form a systematic mesh and the mesh is subject to expansion. As a result, the vectors of weights of neurons from a topological layer will move so that each of them takes a position that is a centroid (pattern) for some fragment of the input signal space. This process is described as the Voronoi mosaic.

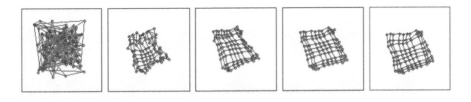

Figure 10.24 Initial stages of self-organizing process of Kohonen network.

For purposes of this book, we can assume that neurons forming a network step by step specialize in detecting and signalizing different groups of input signals. As a result, after every input signal appears often enough, one neuron in the network will specialize in detecting, signalizing, and recognizing it. In the initial stage (Figure 10.24), the random distribution of points and lines is superseded by an initial ordering of points. The learning process then becomes more subtle and tends to regularize the point distribution.

The important issue is that the network creates inner representations in the form of adequate distributions of the values of weight coefficients only for the sub-area of the input signal space where the points were presented originally. Thus, if the input signals come from a limited area (square form in the figure), the Kohonen network tries to cover only this square with the neurons. This occurs with networks having few neurons (Figure 10.25), networks that operate slowly with large numbers of neurons (Figure 10.26), and cases when the initial distribution of neurons takes place in a large area of weight space (Figure 10.27).

Remember that the goal of self-organization always is to have an individual neuron in the network that detects the appearance of a specific point of the input signal space even if the point was not presented during teaching (Figure 10.28).

10.6 Kohonen Network Handling of Difficult Data

The program in Example 11 has superb capability that will enable you to use your imagination to perform several interesting experiments. For example, you can study how a network's behavior and self-organization are influenced by the method of showing input data. By using the program options, you can demonstrate how the sub-area of the input signal space from which values are taken in a network will be limited even more than the case of squares.

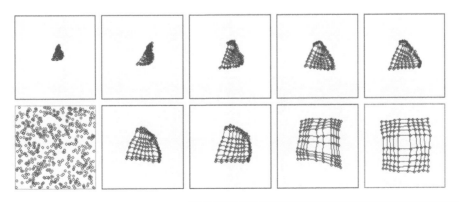

Figure 10.25 Consecutive steps of self-organization in relatively small network.

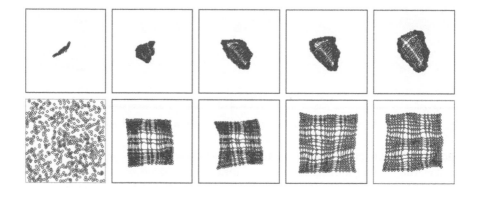

Figure 10.26   Self-organizing in large Kohonen network.

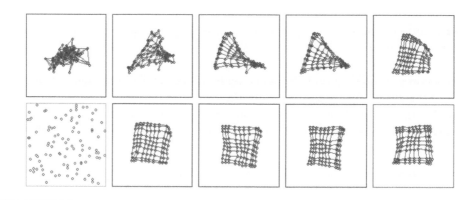

Figure 10.27   Self-organizing in case of wide distribution of initial neuron weight values.

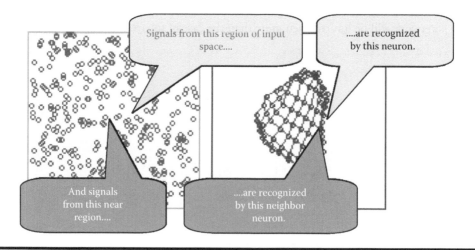

Figure 10.28   Effect of self-organization.

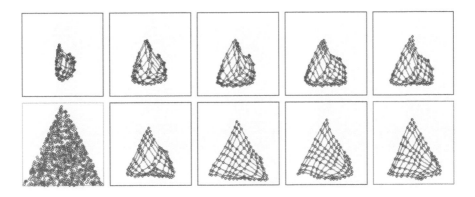

Figure 10.29 Self-organization where data presented during learning are taken from sub-area (triangle) of input space.

In such a scenario, self-organization tends not to create useless representations of input data. You can observe this phenomenon by providing appropriate input signals to the network. The signals must be chosen from some sub-area of input signal space (e.g., the shape of a triangle). The program will show how all neurons position themselves to recognize all the points inside the triangle (Figure 10.29). No neuron will specialize in recognizing input signals from the space beyond the triangle. Such points were not shown during teaching, so the neurons assume they do not exist and do not have to be recognized.

A little more difficult task for a network to fulfill is a more complex form (e.g., a cross) chosen as a sub-area of input signal space. At the start of teaching, the network will be unable to find the proper distribution of neurons (Figure 10.30). Usually tenacious teaching can lead to success in such cases (Figure 10.31). However, success is easier to achieve when teaching a network with a larger number of neurons (Figure 10.32).

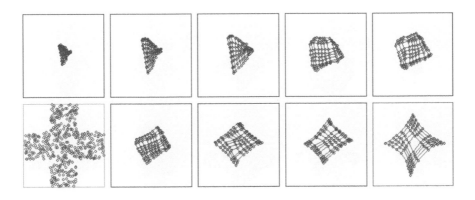

Figure 10.30 Unsatisfactory result of self-organizing where input data are randomly taken from input sub-space in the form of a cross.

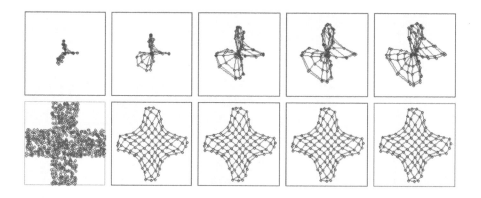

Figure 10.31   Better results of self-organization than those depicted in Figure 10.30.

10.7 Networks with Excessively Wide Ranges of Initial Weights

A large initial spread of weight coefficients of modeled neurons is not a favorable factor for achieving success from self-organization (Figure 10.33). In such cases, omissions can occur despite a long teaching process. A self-organizing network may ignore certain fragments of active areas of input signal space (bottom right corner of the triangle in Figure 10.34).

After you experiment with the correct functioning of a network, we encourage you to initiate teaching by using very large values of initial random weights (e.g., 5) for a small simple network (e.g., 5 × 5 neurons) to generate results very quickly. You will probably see the common twisting and collapsing (Figure 10.35 and Figure 10.36) that result from initially overloading a Kohonen network. You may want to experiment by producing such phenomena and determining self-learning cannot lead networks from such "dead ends."

10.8 Changing Self-Organization via Self-Learning

Kohonen networks learn to map their internal memories without intervention from a teacher. They use weight coefficients typically shown as patterns of external (input) signals. You may perform interesting experiments with the Example 11 program. You can change the shape of a sub-area of

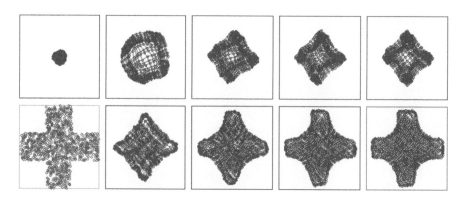

Figure 10.32   Successful self-organization of a network having many neurons.

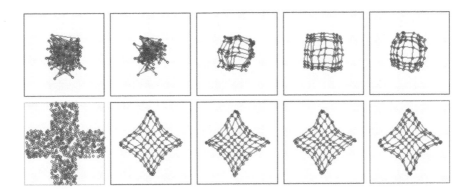

Figure 10.33   Network ignores input data (right lower part of input space) when spread of initial values of neuron weights is too large.

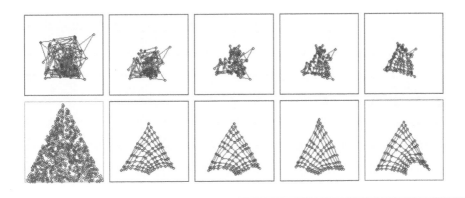

Figure 10.34   Failure during self-organization.

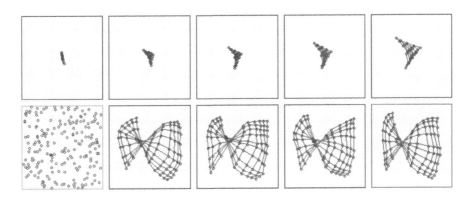

Figure 10.35   "Twisted" Kohonen network.

Figure 10.36 Rare case of "twisted" network learning of data in cross form recruited from sub-area.

an input signal space for selecting input data "on the fly." For example, you can start teaching with a rectangular shape of a sub-area and when the network approaches the desired state, you may change the sub-area shape to a triangle. Figure 10.37 illustrates the results.

You will not always be able to perform such experiments so predictably. Sometimes the final arrangement of a network will contain visible relics of a previously taught figure. Figure 10.38 illustrates the result of abnormal teaching. At first, the network adjusted to the triangular sub-area, then was forced to recognize a rectangular arrangement, and eventually revert to recognizing the triangular shape again.

10.9 Practical Uses of Kohonen Networks

We assume by now that you have a notion of the capabilities of Kohonen networks but what are their real-life practical uses? At the start of this chapter, we described mappings, for example, in robotics that created Kohonen networks spontaneously. If you know how a network works, you will understand this next example. Imagine a robot that has two sensors (because we studied networks that had only two input signals). Let one sensor provide information about the

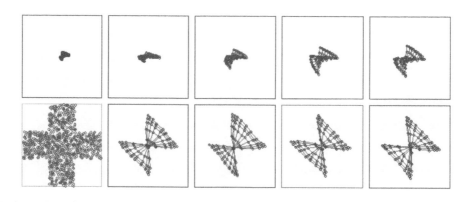

Figure 10.37 Change of goal during self-learning.

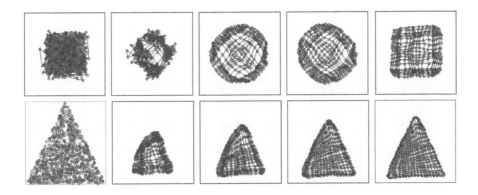

Figure 10.38 Result of self-learning showing relic created by change of goals during learning.

brightness of illumination and the other sense sound volume. This way every point of the input signal space will correspond to a certain environment with specific characteristics (bright and quiet, dark and loud, etc.).

A robot equipped with a Kohonen network starts functioning by observing its surroundings. They may be bright, dark, loud, or quiet. Some combinations of input signals will occur in the robot's surroundings and others will not. The robot classifies and learns incoming data, specializes its neurons, and after a time has trained its Kohonen network so that every relevant situation corresponds to a neuron that identifies and detects it.

A Kohonen network functions like a robot's "brain" that reacts to the external world. Humans model such behaviors also. The human brain has neurons that recognize faces, find appropriate routes to various places, select favorite cookies, and avoid a neighbor's biting dog. The human brain has a model that detects and recognizes every sensory perception and known situation that it encounters. Jerzy Konorski, an outstanding Polish neurophysiologist, associated these internal models of fragments of the outside world with distinct parts of the human brain he called gnostic units.[*]

Most human perception and ability to recognize conditions of surroundings are based on patterns the brain creates after years of experience in different situations. The patterns are stored in "grandmother cells." Signals from your eyes, ears, and other senses active these cells (Figure 10.39). Activation considers thousands of models stored in the brain and selects the one that best corresponds to a situation. The capabilities of these cells enable your senses to respond quickly, efficiently, and reliably. However, if your brain fails to develop such models early enough, perception via the senses becomes difficult, slow, and unreliable.

Much research supports that conclusion. Most evidence demonstrating the impacts of the external world on internal mechanisms was gathered from animal experiments, for example, studies of sensory deprivation of young cats. Kittens do not develop sight until several days after birth. A group of researchers allowed sighted kittens to see only geometric patterns. Whenever the kittens could have seen other objects, for example, during feeding, the researchers turned off the light.

After a month of such training, the kittens were returned to their normal environment. Kittens who had no sight problems acted like blind animals. They could not see obstacles, food, or even

---

[*] Konorski J. 1948. *Conditioned Reflexes and Neuron Organization*. Cambridge, UK: Cambridge University Press.

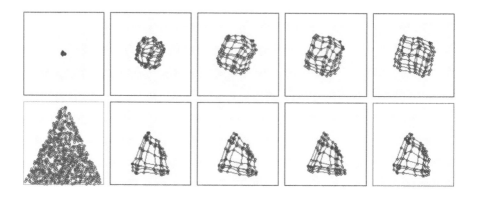

Figure 10.39   Representation of brain somatosensory stimulus and motion control regions (Source: http://ionphysiology.com/homunculus1.jpg)

humans because their brains retained only models of geometric figures. Their perception of common objects such as chairs, bowls, and other cats was completely disrupted and long periods of learning were required to enable these cats to regain the ability to see normally.

A similar phenomenon occurs in humans based on studies of anthropologists who observed small-statured Pygmy tribes in Africa. Their natural habitat is dense jungle. The thick vegetation prevented them from seeing long distances. When they were led to open spaces, they completely lost their senses of direction. The simple activity of looking at a distant object left them confused. They reacted to a change of environment such as the approach of an animal as a magical event because their brains lacked models for perceiving events and activities in open spaces.

You may understand how the human brain utilizes internal models of objects by observing daily activities. You can read a newspaper in your native language very easily. If you know the language well, you can scan an article and your brain will turn individual letters into words, words into concepts, and concepts into knowledge. This is possible because many years of learning made your brain adept at reading, developing information, and recalling information later if needed.

A different dynamic occurs when you encounter an unknown word in a text or try to read a message in another language. You may split words into syllables in an effort to understand the meaning but this type of reading is neither easy nor rapid. The reason is that your brain has no ready patterns (models) to relate to the unknown material. This is why archeologists puzzle over inscriptions in unknown ancient languages. If your model of the outside world has no patterns for unfamiliar letters or symbols, you will not understand or remember the material simply because your brain has no gnostic units trained to handle it.

The human brain is capable of creating a map of the body on the surface of the cerebral cortex in the area called the gyrus postcentralis (Figure 10.40). Interestingly, the map does not resemble exactly the shape and proportions of the body. On the surface of a brain, for example, the area mapping the hands and face occupies much more space than the trunk and limbs. This arrangement is analogous to the self-organizing capability of an artificial neural network. Controlling the movements of hands and face and reception of sensory stimuli involves more brain cells because these actions are repeated constantly. In summary, many patterns similar to those in the human brain are created spontaneously in neural networks during the process of self-organizing.

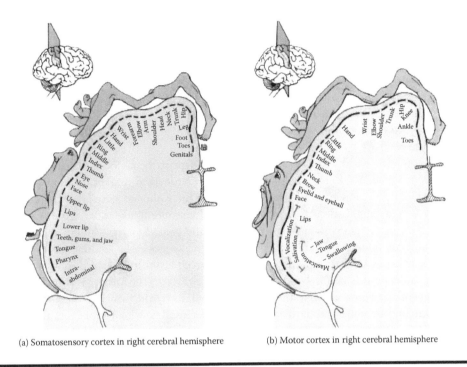

(a) Somatosensory cortex in right cerebral hemisphere   (b) Motor cortex in right cerebral hemisphere

Figure 10.40   Each area of the body is assigned a proportionate sensory neural area. (Source: http://www.basefields.com/T560/homunculus.htm)

Let us return to the robot example discussed earlier in this section. Every neuron in the robot's Kohonen network recognizes recurring states of an external world, much like the functioning of gnostic units in the human brain described above. The self-learning process of a Kohonen network creates a specific set of gnostic units (models) within the robot's controller that are designed to handle every situation the robot may meet. Models are vital because they allow robots and humans to classify every input situation based on signals provided by sensors. After classification of an input into a defined class, a robot may adjust its behavior.

The designer determines what a robot will do in certain situations. For example, in a normal situation, the robot will continue moving forward. It may be programmed to stop if lights are turned off or it hears a noise. The important issue is that the robot does not need constant direction. Its learning is based on the detection of similar situations by a neighborhood of neurons. A trained Kohonen network in a robot brain will figure out what to do.

If a neural network fails to find a ready procedure for a perceived situation, it will determine the closest one based on the neighborhood structure among a set of different states for which proper behaviors have been defined. For example, if a learned action involves forward movement, neighboring situations that are undefined by the user may be applied at reduced speed. If a designer clearly defines actions for a few model situations, a robot will be able to function in most simulation situations, even those not covered by self-learning because of the Kohonen network's ability to apply averaging and generalization processes.

During teaching, a network may be shown objects (environments) that differ slightly from one another. The objects will be characterized by certain dispersion but the network will remember a certain averaged pattern of input signals in the forms of weight coefficients for certain neurons.

The network will involve many typical sample signals and their related environments. The number may be the same as the number of neurons in the network. However, in reality, the system will have fewer neurons than possible environments because the freely changing parameters that characterize a robot's operations make the number of possible environments infinite.

Through generalization, when a network encounters an environment characterized by parameters not presented during teaching, it will try to fit the environment into a learned pattern. Knowledge gained by a network during learning is generalized automatically, usually producing perfect results.

A robot equipped with a Kohonen network will adapt its behavior to the environment for which it was designed. We know there is a very small commercial market for intelligent mobile robots and thus may wonder about the practical uses for Kohonen networks. In reality, these networks have many applications. For example, banks commonly use these networks to protect against thefts—not thefts involving masked bandits and getaway cars. Modern thefts are more likely to result from fraudulent credit practices. Banks make money by lending money but not all borrowers repay loans. Losses from unpaid loans far exceed losses from armed robberies.

How do banks protect themselves by lending money safely? The answer is simply: building a Kohonen network based on an honest borrower who will repay the principal borrowed and a fair rate of interest, and serve as a standard against which potential new loan applicants are compared.

10.10 Tool for Transformation of Input Space Dimensions

A unique characteristic of a Kohonen network is that it contains a topological representation of an input signal space that applies to neuron neighborhoods. In the illustrations of network actions, blue dots represented neurons and red dots were used to connect adjacent neurons. At the start of example programs, the lines and dots were distributed randomly. During teaching, the network formed orderly arrangements that could be interpreted. Neurons within a network tend to signal and detect adjacent points from an input signal space. As a result, points representing input signals are close together and will be transposed to a network area where adjacent points will be signaled only by adjacent neurons.

In all the figures seen earlier in this chapter, it was easy to associate the notion of similarity of input signals and adjacency (neighborhood) of neurons in a network because input signal space and weight space were two-dimensional (Figure 10.13 and Figure 10.16). The network topology also was two-dimensional (Figure 10.9 and Figure 10.11), thus allowing us to understand such notions as "an input signal lying higher than the previous signal" (higher value of second component) and "an input neuron lying higher than the previous neuron" (in the previous row); see Figure 10.41.

Other situations are possible. We can easily imagine a one-dimensional network that will learn to recognize two-dimensional signals (Figure 10.42). Our program helps you to study the network behavior that makes possible the conversion of a two-dimensional input signal space to a one-dimensional structure using chains of neurons (Figure 10.43).

This unconventional structure may be achieved by giving one dimension of a network (the best is the first one) a value equal to 1. The second dimension should have far greater value (e.g., 100) to ensure it behaves in an interesting way. However, such networks learn quickly so dimensions need not be limited. Figure 10.44 and Figure 10.45 show more examples of such mappings. The figures indicate that one-dimensional networks reasonably fit into the highlighted areas of input signal spaces. This configuration provides two important advantages.

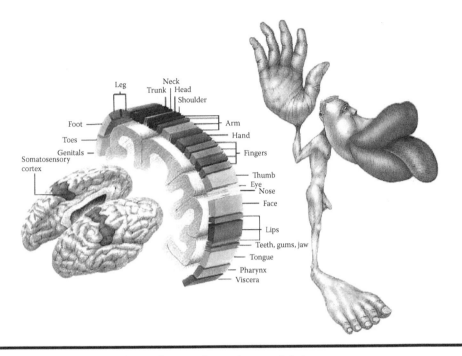

Figure 10.41   Same dimensions of network topology and data space.

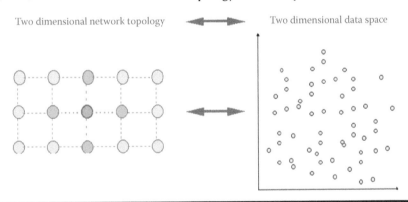

Figure 10.42   Different dimensions of network topology and data space.

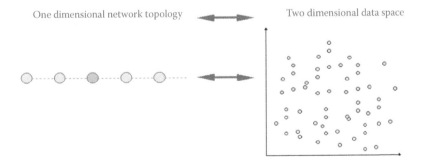

Figure 10.43   Mapping of two-dimensional input space into one-dimensional neural topology.

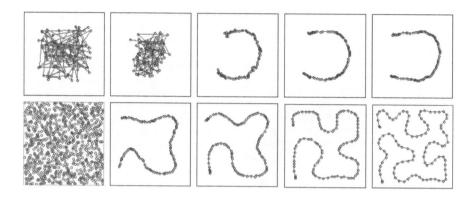

Figure 10.44   More examples of mapping of two-dimensional input space into one-dimensional neural topology.

First, a chain of neurons arranged as a one-dimensional network fills the entire selected area of an input signal space. Thus, for every point of two-dimensional input signal space, a representative in a one-dimensional neural network will indicate its occurrence. There are no "orphaned" points or areas in the multidimensional input space.

Second, for objects in an input signal space that lie close (are similar) to each other, the adjacent neurons correspond in the one-dimensional chain of neurons. Unfortunately, although this is likely, it is not guaranteed and you should expect errors (Figure 10.46). However, in most cases, the fact that some states of an input signal space are represented by two adjacent neurons implies that they are similar.

Let us consider the semantics behind this concept. We encounter similar and very difficult problems in many tasks related to informatics. For example, consider the enormous quantities of data required to indicate the complex operations of a nuclear power generating plant. Many hundreds of parameters must be measured and evaluated continuously. Blast furnaces in steelworks, multi-engine aircraft, and manufacturing plants also require effective management of huge amounts of data generated by measurements of thousands of parameters.

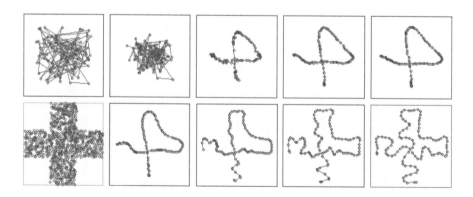

Figure 10.45   Another example of mapping two-dimensional input space into one-dimensional neural topology.

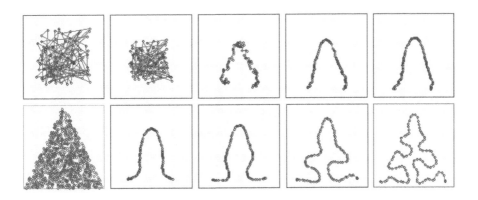

Figure 10.46 Proper and improper representations of similarities of input signals in neural network topology.

We may picture a complex operation as a space involving a great number of dimensions. The result of each measurement (signaling device) should be shown on a separate axis. As certain processes evolve, values of every parameter change and a point corresponding to a state of the considered system changes its position.

Therefore, to estimate the condition of an aircraft, the stability of a reactor, the efficiency of a blast furnace, or company profitability, we need only evaluate the position of a point in a multi-dimensional space. Specifically, the point represents the state of a parameter and it has a specific meaning, for example, stability of a nuclear reaction or excessive product defects.

To control and inspect a process or product, an engineer or other specialist must have updated and specific information about the process or product including trends of change. To solve such problems in modern engineering, all relevant data are compiled in giant control rooms full of gauges and blinking lights and passed to a person who can make decisions. This procedure is ineffective in practice simply because one individual cannot inspect, control, analyze, and make split-second decisions based on thousands of input data items. In reality, the decision maker does not need such detailed data. He or she needs integrated and well-abstracted global information such as that produced by a Kohonen network.

Imagine that you have built a network in which every neuron gathers thousands of signals. Such a network is more difficult to program than a network with two inputs and also requires more computer memory and more computer time for simulation. Imagine that this network predicts two-dimensional proximities of neurons and the input signal of every neuron will appear at some predetermined point on a screen. Signals of neighbors will be displayed in neighboring rows and columns to indicate their relationships. After teaching a network via Kohonen's method, you will obtain a tool capable of specific mapping of multidimensional, difficult-to-evaluate data on one screen that may be reviewed and interpreted easily.

Every combination of input signals will be represented by exactly one neuron (winner) that will detect and signal occurrence of this exact situation. If you depict on a screen only an input signal of a specific neuron, you will obtain an image of a moving luminous point. Based on previous experiments, you know which areas of a screen correspond to correct states of a supervised process and which ones indicate unsatisfactory states. By observing the path of the luminous point, you can evaluate system performance.

You can also display output signals of neurons on a screen after introducing competition. You can arrange to have values of output signals displayed in different colors and change parameters

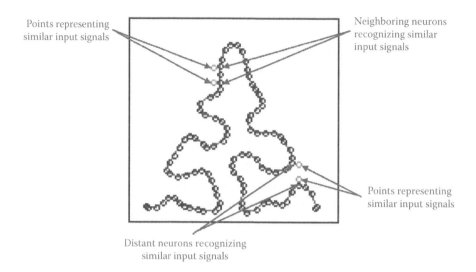

Points representing similar input signals

Neighboring neurons recognizing similar input signals

Points representing similar input signals

Distant neurons recognizing similar input signals

Figure 10.47 Example of proper and improper representation of similarity of input signal in neural network topology.

to create a colorful mosaic after some practice. What may at first appear as a collection of illegible signals will eventually form an interpretable image.

Other ways exist for depicting results of Kohonen network functioning. However, their one common feature is the use of two-dimensional images because they are relatively easy to interpret. These images do not convey detailed values of data. However, they exhibit synthetic overall images that are valuable to a person who evaluates the results and makes decisions. These images present fairly low levels of data but averaging and generalization techniques described above allow very good results to be obtained. Examples of proper and improper representations of similarity of input signal in neuron network topology are illustrated in Figure 10.47

Questions and Self-Study Tasks

1. What is the difference between self-learning and self-organization?

2. Kohonen networks are known as tools that let us look into multidimensional spaces of data. Can you explain this description?

3. One possible application of Kohonen networks is using them as novelty detectors. A network used for this application should signal a set of input signals that never occurred earlier in identical or similar form. Automatic signaling of such situation may have essential meaning (e.g. for detecting a credit card theft or a thief's use of a cell phone that differs from the way its owner used it). How does a Kohonen network indicate an encounter with a signal with novel characteristics?

4. Study the course of a self-organization process after a change of sub-area of an input signal space from which random input signals come. The space contains a grid created by the network. The program lets you choose one of three shapes (square, triangle, or cross) of a sub-area. Analyze consequences of the choice. If you have advanced programming knowledge, you may devise a program and add more shapes.

5. Study the impact of a coefficient of learning named Apha0 on a neuron. Increases of this coefficient cause acceleration of learning and decreases cause "calming." If the coefficient is decreased gradually, a learning process that is fast and dynamic at the beginning becomes more stable as time elapses. Change the coefficient and analyze observed results.

6. Study the impact of the changes of a coefficient of learning on neuron neighbors of a winner neuron in a self-organization process. The coefficient is called Alpha1. The higher the Alpha1 value, the more visible the effect when the winner neuron "pulls" its neighbors along. Analyze and describe results of changes of the coefficient value, the Alpha0:Alpha1 ratio, and their impacts on network behavior.

7. Study the impacts of different values of neighborhood range on a network's behavior and self-organization. This number indicates how many neurons constitute a neighborhood (i.e., how many undergo forced teaching when a winner neuron is self-learning). This number should depend on network size and the default setting. However, we suggest as an exercise a careful examination of its impact on network behavior. Note that larger neighborhood range numbers visibly slow the learning process.

8. Study the impact of changing the EpsAlpha coefficient on self-organization. The EpsAlpha coefficient controls the decreases of Alpha0 and Alpha1 coefficients in every iteration. Note that the smaller the coefficient, the faster the decrease of learning coefficients and the faster learning stabilizes. You can set a value 1 to this coefficient and the learning coefficients will not decrease or set a value slightly more than 1, which will result in more "brutal" learning at every step. Describe the results.

9. Study the impact of changing the range of a neighborhood on network behavior and learning. You can change the EpsNeighb coefficient that controls narrowing (in consecutive iterations) of neighborhood range. Compare the effects of this change to those seen with the EpsAlpha coefficient.

10. Study the effects of over-teaching a network that at first learns to fill a cross-shaped sub-area of an input signal space, then forms a rectangle or triangle. Remember that in over-teaching experiments, you must increase the values of Alpha0 and Alpha1 coefficients and neighborhood range after you change a sub-area.

11. Advanced exercise: Modify the program to model tasks in which a Kohonen network deals with a highly irregular probability of points coming from different regions of an input signal space. Conduct self-learning and you will see that in a taught network, many more neurons will specialize in recognizing signals coming from regions more often represented in a teaching set. Compare the effect with a map of a cerebral cortex (Figure 10.40). What conclusions can you draw from this exercise?

12. Advanced exercise: Write a program simulating the behavior of the robot described in Section 10.9. Attempt to simulate the skills of associating the sensory stimuli describing the environment with behaviors favorable to the robot by causing changes in the environment. Determine the type of representation of knowledge of the robot's simulated environment to be used and processed by a self-organizing neural network acting as its "brain." By changing the environmental conditions, determine which conditions the robot can discover in its self-organizing network and which ones are too difficult.

Chapter 11

Recurrent Networks

11.1 Description of Recurrent Neural Network

Based on examples described in earlier chapters, you know that a neural network is explained as a single-layer or multilayer, linear or nonlinear system taught by an algorithm or discovering knowledge on its own. The neural networks discussed to this point are *almost* free to choose their learning parameters. We say *almost* because we have not covered recurrent networks yet. These networks include feedback mechanisms that recycle signals from neurons in the input layer to neurons of previously hidden layers (Figure 11.1). Feedback is a relevant and significant innovation. As you will see, a network with feedback has more upgradable possibilities and computing capabilities than a classical network restricted to one-way signals from input to output.

Networks with feedbacks show phenomena and processes not revealed by one-way networks. After stimulation, a network with feedback can generate thorough sequences of signals and phenomena as outputs (results of signal processing in n iteration) and return to the inputs of neurons to produce new signals, usually in n + 1 iteration. Specific phenomena and processes of recurrent networks arise from complicated signal circulations (e.g., vibrations varying between the rapid rise of alternate extremes), equally rapid suppressions, or chaotic roaming (that looks like undetermined progress).

Recurrent networks with feedbacks are less popular because they are difficult to analyze. Their ability to circulate signals through a network from input to output, then from output to input, and then back to output requires a more complex structure than a simple one-way system. The recurrent neural network responds to every input signal, even short-term types. It proceeds through long sequences of intermediate states before all essential signals are established.

We will use a simple example to illustrate how a recurrent device works. Imagine a linear network consisting of only one neuron. It has two signals: the first is an input signal and the second is an output signal that becomes the second input. Thus we created feedback (Figure 11.2). It was easy, wasn't it?

We now check how this network works. We can use Example 12a in Figure 11.3 to determine its parameters. Weight factor (feedback weight) determined by a feedback signal will enter the neuron along with the input signal (input signal strength) that runs the network. You can decide

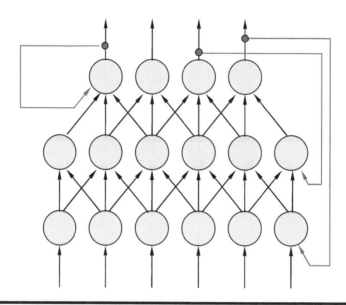

Figure 11.1 Example of recurrent network structure. Feedback connections are distinguished by exterior arrows in red color.

(by activating or not activating `single _ input _ impuls`) whether the input signal will enter continuously or temporarily (only once at the beginning of simulation). This program will compute signals going around a network, step by step, demonstrating network behavior. You will quickly notice a few characteristics:

- The described network displays combined dynamic forms: after entering a single (pulse) signal at the input, the output sustains a long-lasting process, during which the output signal changes many times before it can reach the state of equilibrium (Figure 11.3).
- Equilibrium in this simple network may be achieved (without output signal that continues throughout the simulation) only if a constant product of a certain output after multiplying by weight of a proper input yields an output signal precisely equal to the feedback signal needed to create an output signal; signals at both neuron inputs will balance themselves out.
- An output signal that complies with this condition is called an attractor. We will soon explain this term.

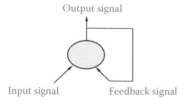

Figure 11.2 Simplest network structure with feedback.

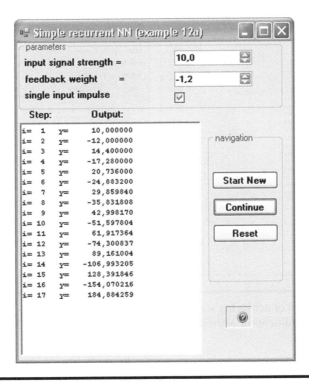

Figure 11.3 **Complicated operation despite simple input situation in system with feedback.**

■ Attractor location depends on network parameters. For a network with a weight factor of feedback value of 1, every point is an attractor. For any other network, we can achieve equilibrium only when the value of the output signal is 0 (Figure 11.4). This feature is distinctive for this simple linear network. Nonlinear networks obviously involve more attractors and we will make use of them.

■ If the value of a synaptic weight factor in a feedback circuit is positive (positive feedback), the system displays an aperiodic (non-oscillating) characteristic (Figure 11.5). It is worth noting that this process may proceed through positive values (left side) of signals or negative (right side) values. As time passes, positive values become more positive and negative values become more negative. No processes allow signals to change from positive to negative or vice versa.

■ If the value of a synaptic weight factor in a feedback circuit is negative (negative feedback), the system displays a periodic (oscillating) characteristic (Figure 11.6).

■ In systems with negative feedback, oscillating character depends on network parameters. If vibrations increase rapidly, a network may toggle between large negative values and even larger positive values, followed by larger negative values and so on. This is catastrophic. The network behavior closely resembles that of human brain suffering from epilepsy or a space rocket that loses stability during take-off and crashes. However, vibrations sometimes lead to zero values, the network is stabilized, and work is handled correctly.

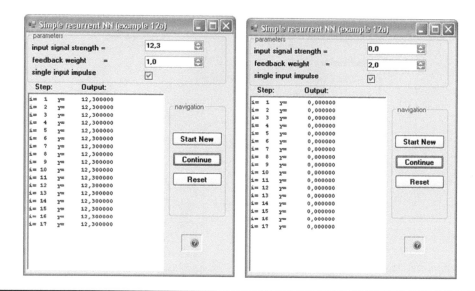

Figure 11.4 Two ways of achieving state of equilibrium in a linear network: zero signals (left) or single feedback amplification without simultaneous input signal (right).

■ While observing behavior of systems with feedbacks, you will see that even small differences in parameters values will cause effects that may be extreme. Systems without feedback do not produce such differences. This somewhat extreme reaction is a distinctive feature of recurrent systems.

■ We now analyze the above phenomena quantitatively. After few simulations, if the absolute value of a weight factor in feedback exceeds a certain established value (stabilization point), absolute values of signals continuously increase in both systems with negative feedback, and

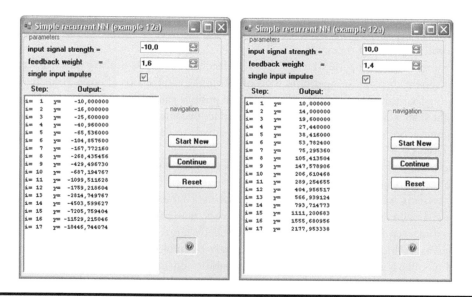

Figure 11.5 Typical progress of system with positive feedback.

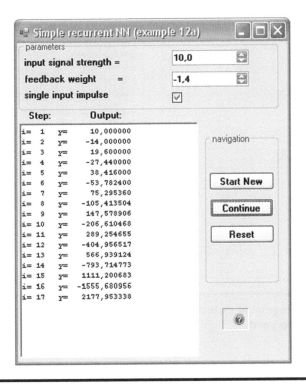

Figure 11.6   Typical progress of system with negative feedback.

systems with positive feedback (Figure 11.5 and Figure 11.6). This phenomenon is known as unstable behavior.

■ However, if the absolute value of weight factor in feedback is smaller than the established value, a circuit with either positive or negative feedback will attempt to reach equilibrium (Figure 11.7).

An input signal could be also given for the duration of simulation by unmarking the `single _ input _ impulse` checkbox (Figure 11.8). The state of equilibrium may be achieved, but the value of the output signal (the network is stabilizing for this signal) is different and depends on the input signal value.

11.2 Features of Networks with Feedback

Let us summarize and draw conclusions of some researchers that will be useful when we follow the next steps. Processing of input signals in a network with feedback can display two different variabilities. First, if the value of a weight factor in feedback is positive, the signal changes aperiodically (in one way). Second, when value of a weight factor in the feedback is negative (regulation), oscillations occur in a network by which the output signal alternates between lower and higher values.

If a neuron is nonlinear, the system may behave in a third way involving roaming chaotic signals ("butterfly effect," strange attractors, fractals, Mandelbrot's sets, etc.). We will not cover this type of operation in this chapter but much information is available on the web.

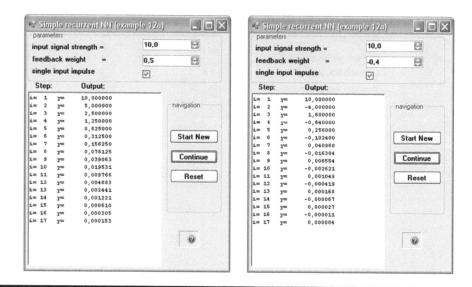

Figure 11.7 Stable progress of system with feedback after decreasing value of weight factor well below stabilization point.

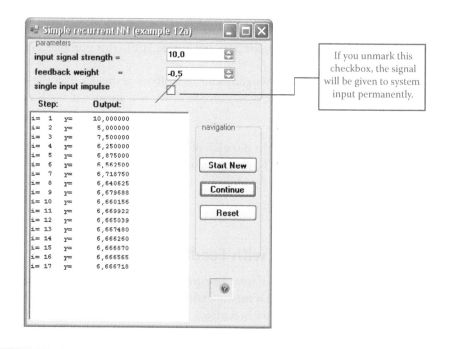

Figure 11.8 Behavior of system with feedback when established value of input signal is permanent.

Along with dividing network behavior into aperiodic and periodic sections, networks with feedback display stable behaviors (signals with value restraints that usually converge into a certain final value after a few iterations) and unstable behaviors in which absolute values of successive output signals increase in size and finally exceed acceptable values. During simulation, these behaviors give rise to mathematical errors like floating point overflow. In electronic or mechanical systems, components may burn or explode. All these behaviors also occur in real neural networks.

Positive feedback creates a progressive effect. It is an amplification of positive values of signals in a system as shown on the left side of Figure 11.5. An inverse effect is similar to a human's negative attitude toward some experience and is depicted on the right side of Figure 11.5. If a closed circuit of positive feedback is not disconnected, it can produce disturbances. The condition is dangerous in humans. Negative amplification leads to a condition called manic psychosis; excessive amplification of positive values can create an unrealistic state of euphoria. Non-stability phenomena also occur in human nervous systems. One result is a grave illness called epilepsy. It is characterized by brief disturbances of electrical activity in the brain that cause rapid involuntary muscular contractions and convulsions. It is easy to see how incorrect functioning of artificial neurons and the consequences resemble nervous system malfunctions in humans.

We suggest you use your computer to detect the stabilization limits for a simple system with feedback. Try to discover which factors cause stable or unstable behavior. You can then use the Example 12a program to compare your findings. As you work with Example 12a, you will notice that output signal alterations depend on factor values whereas input signals exert weaker influence both at the start of a program and during operation.

When examining network behavior and considering algorithms, it is important to know whether the absolute value of weight factor for a feedback signal is more or less than 1. For factors less than 1, you have a stable process—aperiodic for positive values and oscillating for negative values. The process is always unstable for factors greater than 1. When a value of factor is exactly 1 and feedback is positive, all input signals will be network attractors. Negative feedback produces continuous (not fluctuating) oscillations. We call this state the stabilization limit.

In more complex networks, stabilization conditions are more complicated and calculation of stabilization limits requires advanced mathematical methods such as Hurwitz's determinants, Nyquist's diagram, Lyapunow's theorem, and others. The theory of neural networks with feedback in complex dynamic systems has been an active research area for all kind of theorists for many years.

11.3 Benefits of Associative Memory

The operation of a network consisting of a single neuron is simple and easy to predict, so the opportunities to observe interesting practical applications are limited. That is why the Example 12a program does not yield practical results. Large networks of dozens of nonlinear neurons and feedback capability display complex and interesting behaviors that serve as bases for practical applications. However, large networks with many neurons that transfer output signals to each other via feedback are also open to more operational issues and unstable behaviors than single neuron systems. In a complex network, states of equilibrium may be achieved by different values of output signals, but it is possible to select certain joint structures and certain network parameters to ensure that the states of equilibrium will be equal to the solutions to certain problems.

This is a requirement for most nontrivial network applications. For instance, in some networks, the state of equilibrium is the solution of an optimization problem after a search for the most beneficial decision that will ensure the highest gain or smallest loss by taking restraints into account. These networks are capable of solving the well-known traveling salesman problem used as a training example. They have been used to research optimal distribution of finite resources such as water and select investment portfolios.

That is why in this chapter, we are going to present you another example in which solution of a certain important and useful computer problem could be interpreted as achieving one among many states of equilibrium by network: so-called associative memory. This type of memory the goal of many computer scientists who are tired of current methods that require searching for information in primitive data bases. We will discuss this kind of memory and how it works.

We all know that storing millions of records that include vital information can be accomplished effortlessly with few delays. The task is simple if you understand key words, code words, specific values, and other items that differentiate one record from others. A computer will find any record and allow access. The process is quick and efficient if the base is indexed and constructed appropriately. A Google search is a good example of this process.

Retrieval of data does not look so simple when you do not have key words or other identifying information to focus your search. If you do not know how the desired information is described by the search system, you may receive outputs that are unresponsive or unreliable. You may receive plenty of unnecessary information if you cannot provide specific search data. Excessive information is the lesser of the two evils of retrieval; the other is inadequate information. Narrowing a search to dig out essential data may be described as drudgery.

Usually you need just a scrap of information to find what you want effortlessly. Sometimes a single word, image, picture, conception, idea, or formula will deliver instantly a complete collection of data, references, suggestions, and conclusions. This is similar to the way a fragrance, melody, or sunset can trigger the human brain to deliver memories, feelings, and senses. Based on a bit of information, your brain can respond to a request. Computers do not know how to respond to such triggers yet, but what about neural networks?

Associative memory represents a small segment of a discipline called cognitive science that has attracted increased attention recently, especially among philosophers, pedagogues, and psychologists. Many specialists are passionately fond of this subject, especially physicists, who normally work with theoretical descriptions of simple physical systems of elementary particle or specialize in describing systems composed of many interacting particles (statistical thermodynamics). If you search a library or the Internet, you will see that a huge number of physicists are conducting research in this area.

Their research focuses on the behaviors of networks when exposed to feedback and other processes that may lead to practical applications. This is how the so-called Boltzmann machines were developed. They utilize thermodynamic phenomena based on algorithms of simulated annealing and Boltzmann's distribution analogous to the operations of neural networks. Professor Jacek Zurada at the University of Louisville in the U.S. and Professor Leszek Rutkowski of Czestochowa University in Poland specialize in cognitive studies, specifically simulation of neural networks. They have made significant contributions to the field, but the greatest contribution was made by John Hopfield, a US scientist who studied network feedback.

11.4 Construction of Hopfield Network

Hopfield's networks constitute the most important and most often adapted subclass of recurrent neural networks used in practice and that is why readers should understand them. If we had to classify them, they act as exact opposites of feed-forward networks described in earlier chapters.

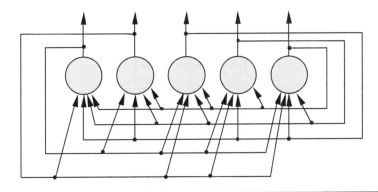

Figure 11.9   Structure of a simple Hopfield network.

Networks in which feedbacks are allowed (so-called recurrent networks) can contain a certain number of feedbacks, whereas feedbacks in Hopfield networks are not real (Figure 11.9).

All joints in non-Hopfield networks are feedbacks, all output signals are employed as inputs, and all inputs transport feedback signals to all neurons. In Hopfield's network, each neuron is connected to all other neurons within entire network, The connections are based on the two-sided feedback rule so a Hopfield network looks and acts like a single-feedback network. Hopfield's system is an exact opposite of earlier networks that without exception were feed-forward networks—feedback was impossible.

Hopfield networks are important because their processes are always stable. Thus these networks work effectively and users need have no anxiety about failure. The stability of processes in a Hopfield network was achieved by the application of a few simple concepts.

They are easy to design and use as computer programs and also in certain specialized electronic and optoelectronic circuits. The internal structure of the network is based on connecting all the neurons in an everyone-with-everyone fashion. This simple (and costly) principle was used in networks described earlier (e.g., networks taught by the backpropagation method; see Chapter 7) in which connections of neurons from hidden layers and neurons from the output layer were organized this way. Hopfield's network uses tested models but involves one significant difference. Connected neurons work as both information transmitters and also as information transceivers. They constitute one collective system (Figure 11.10), not separate layers.

Another important characteristic of the Hopfield network is that feedbacks involving one neuron are impossible. An output signal cannot be given directly to its input neuron. This principle is obeyed in Figure 11.9. Notice that it does not rule out a situation in which an output signal from certain neuron influences its own value in the future because it can achieve feedback via other (intercalary) neurons that provide stability (Figure 11.10).

The entered weight factors must be symmetrical. If a connection from neuron X to neuron Y is defined by a certain weight factor W, the weight factor defining the connection from neuron Y to neuron X has the same W value (Figure 11.11). We can fulfill these conditions effortlessly. The first two describe a simple scheme of connections. If you choose Hebb's method (described in Chapter 9) to teach your network, the final one condition is met automatically.

The simple structure and easy application of Hopfield networks made them highly popular. They are widely employed in various optimization tasks and to generate certain sequences of signals that follow each other in a specific (and modifiable) rotation. These networks made it

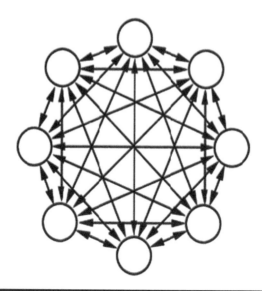

Figure 11.10 Scheme of Hopfield network emphasizing equality of rights of all neurons and symmetry of connections.

possible to generate and forward control signals to many types of objects, for example, walking machines that stand on two, four, or six legs (Figure 11.12).

The "brains" that control movements of these machines always includes feedback components that allow the machines to generate their own control signals periodically. Treading machines, regardless of the number of legs, follow a consistent process by which each leg in a specific order is lifted, moved forward, lowered until it contacts a stable surface, and moved back to transport its "body" forward. Each leg also provides support when the driving force is provided by other limbs.

Treading on a rough surface requires all these movements and an additional mechanism that will adjust the machine to accommodate a changing situation such as an uneven surface. Thus, such machines must be able to generate consistent behaviors and adapt to changing situations. A Hopfield network meets these challenges. Intelligent learning and treading robots have been developed for exploring remote planets, cave interiors, and ocean floors, but for now we will use a Hopfield network to construct associative memory.

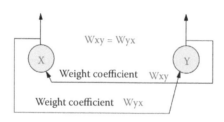

Figure 11.11 Symmetry rule of Hopfield network.

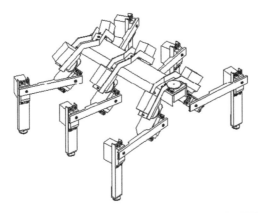

Figure 11.12   Treading robot. Legs are controlled by periodic signals generated by its "brain" (Hopfield network).

11.5 Functioning of Neural Network as Associative Memory

The Example12b program contains a Hopfield network model designed to store and reproduce simple images. The whole "flavor" of this memory lies in its ability to reproduce a message (image) on the basis of a strongly distorted or disturbed input signal. The phenomenon is called auto-association* and it allows a Hopfield network to seek incomplete information. Figure 11.13 has been reprinted and reproduced on the Internet (www.cs.pomona.edu and eduai.hacker.lt) many times. It illustrates the efficiency of a Hopfield network in removing interference from input signals and completely recovering data in cases where the inputs consisted only of fragments.

The next three lines of this figure show each input. The middle column shows the transition state when the network searches its memory for the proper pattern. The right section shows the result—reproduction of a complete pattern. Of course, before the network could "remember" the relevant images, they had to be fixed in the learning process. During learning, the network was shown images of a spider, two bottles, and a dog's head. The network memorized the patterns and prepared to reproduce them. When the network was shown a "noisy" picture of a spider (top row of Figure 11.13), it reconstructed the image of the spider without noise. When shown a picture of one bottle, it remembered the two bottles presented during learning. Finally, showing the dog's ear to the network was sufficient for it to reconstitute the whole picture.

Figure 11.13 is interesting but does not relate to practical tasks. Despite the whimsical example, auto-associative memory can serve many practical purposes, for example, reproducing a complete silhouette of an aircraft from an incomplete camera image obscured by clouds. This ability is critical for military defense systems that must quickly differentiate friend from enemy. A network employed as an auto-associative memory can provide complete answers based on incomplete

---

* Auto-association is a network working mode that associates a specific message with itself. The application of auto-association to even small fragments of stored information (e.g., images) reproduces the information in the memory completely and includes all the details. An alternative is hetero-association that allows one message (e.g., a photograph of a grandmother) to trigger memories of other information (the taste of a jam she prepared). A Hopfield network can operate with auto-associative or hetero-associative memory. The auto-associative method is simpler and we will focus on it.

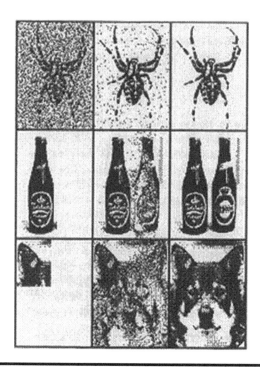

Figure 11.13   Hopfield network working as associative memory.

information in a database if the user asks questions correctly. If a question posed to such a network does not correspond to preconceived models, the database will not know how to respond.

Auto-associative memory can work effectively with database management programs to ensure that searches will be performed correctly even if a user inputs an imprecise query. The network will be able to provide the missing details. An auto-associative Hopfield network mediates between a user and a database like a wise librarian who knows what book a student wants even if the student has forgotten the author, title, and other details.

Auto-associative networks are useful in other ways, for example, removing noises and distortions from signals when noise levels preclude the use of common methods of signal filtration. The extraordinary effectiveness of Hopfield networks results from their ability to utilize a distorted or incomplete image as a starting point and reproduce the complete image based on stored information.

We can now proceed to practical exercises using the Example12b program. For demonstration purposes, we will illustrate Hopfield network performance using pictures, but remember that such networks can memorize and reproduce any other type of information based on how it is mapped and represented.

You should understand the relationship between the modeled Hopfield network and the pictures presented by a program. Each neuron of the network is connected with a single point (pixel) of an image. If the output signal of the neuron is +1, the corresponding pixel is black. If the output neuron signal is −1, the corresponding pixel is white. We will not consider other color possibilities because the neurons used to build a Hopfield network are highly nonlinear and can be distinguished only as +1 or −1 and cannot handle other values. The considered network contains 96 neurons that for presentation purposes are arranged as a matrix of 12 rows of 8 items each. Therefore, each specific network state (set of output signals produced by the network) can be seen as a monochrome image of 12 × 8 pixels as shown in Figure 11.14.

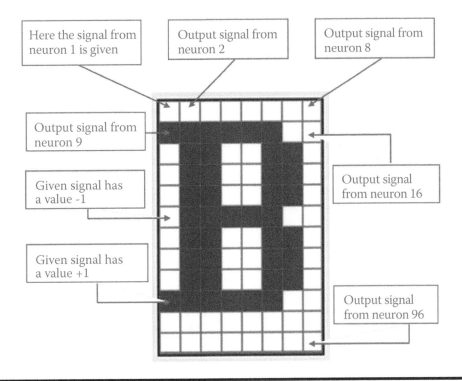

Figure 11.14   Distribution of output signals of neural networks.

Illustrations for presentation may be chosen arbitrarily, but we limited our choices for creating a set of tasks for the network. We chose images of letters (because they are easy to input via a keyboard) or abstract images produced by the program based on certain mathematical criteria.

The program will remember a number of images provided by a user or generated automatically and then list them (without user participation) as patterns for later reproduction. Figure 11.15 depicts a set of patterns to be remembered. Of course, a set of patterns memorized by the network may include any other letters or numbers that you can generate on a keyboard, so Figure 11.15 should be considered one of many possible examples.

The process of introducing more patterns to the program will be explained shortly. Initially, we want to focus on what this program does and what the results are. The technical details will follow shortly.

After the introduction of all the patterns, Example12b sets the parameters (weight factors) of all neurons in the network, so that these images become points of equilibrium (attractors) for the network. We will not go into an explanation of the theory of Hopfield network learning because it

Figure 11.15   Set of patterns prepared to memorize in a Hopfield network.

involves difficult mathematical equations and calculations. After the example program introduces new patterns into the network memory, you simply click the Hebbian learning button.

This automatically launches the learning process, after which the network will be able to recall its stored patterns. The learning of the network is realized by Hebb's method that was explained earlier. Keep in mind that the values of weights produced by this learning process will reach equilibrium state when its output images appear to match a stored pattern.

After learning is complete, the network is ready for testing. First point at the pattern for the level of control you want to check. Patterns and their numbers are visible as inputs in the teaching or recalling window and you can choose the one you want the network to remember. Selection of any pattern will cause its enlarged image to appear in the window titled Enlarge selected input. The chosen measure of its similarity to all other models will be visible directly under the miniature images of all the patterns in the Input pattern(s) window (Figure 11.16).

The level of similarity between images can be measured in two ways. The Input pattern(s) window contains two choices: DP (dot product) and H (Hamming distance). DP measures the level of similarity between two pictures. A high DP value for any pattern indicates that it can be confused easily with the currently selected pattern. Hamming distance, as the name indicates, measures the differences between two images. If a pattern produces a high H value, it is not similar to the one selected. A low H value indicates a pattern similar enough to be confused with the current image of choice.

After you select the image to be memorized by the network you want to examine, you can manipulate the pattern. It is easy for a network to recall an image based on an idea but not so easy for it to handle a randomly distorted image. In that situation, a network can demonstrate its associative skills.

Simply indicate in the box on the right marked with the percent symbol (%) the percentage of points of the pattern you want the program to change before it is shown to the network. You can specify any number from 0 to 99 but you must also press the Noise button to specify noise or distortion. You can also challenge the network further by choosing a reversed (negative) image by pressing the Inverse button. The distorted pattern selected will appear in the enlarged selected input window. Can you guess what pattern generated the picture? You can also assess whether your modified pattern has or has not become more similar to one of the competitive images after

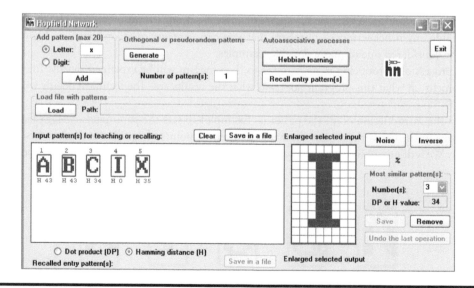

Figure 11.16 Patterns to be memorized are entered into Add pattern feature.

the changes. You will note the affinity of the distorted pattern with other patterns presented as numbers located below the thumbnail images of all the patterns in the Input pattern(s) window for teaching or recalling.

We suggest you do not set large deformations of the image at the start of teaching because the result will be difficult for the network—and you—to recognize and compare with the original. From our experience, we suggest that distortion not exceed 10%.

Good results are achieved with large numbers of changed points. Although this seems paradoxical, large numbers allow the image to retain its shape; the distinguishing feature is a color change (white on black and vice versa). For example, if you choose 99 as a percentage of the points to change, the image produced is a perfectly accurate negative that contains the same information and can be traced easily in the modeled network.

When changing fewer than 99% of the points, the resulting image will contain minor changes and be recognized by the network without difficulty. However, poor results are achieved when attempting to reproduce the original pattern with distortions ranging from 30 to 70%. The network recalls some information and needs many iterations to reproduce the image. As a result, the process takes a long time and the reconstructed pattern is deficient because it will still show distortions. Figure 11.17 shows a slightly distorted starting image on the left and a strongly distorted starting pattern on the right based on the user's choice of the percentage of distortion.

A network remembers a memorized pattern based on signals specified at entry. The neurons transform the signals into new outputs that again by feedback inputs are processed. This process stops automatically when no changes occur in the output signals of an iteration. The stop indicates the network "remembered" the image. Usually the result is the distorted version of the image you applied the network.

If the image that triggers the remembering process is only slightly different from the standard, the result may appear almost immediately, as shown in Figure 11.18. Note how the network recalled the correct shape of the letter B, starting from the distorted pattern in Figure 11.17 (left).

Figure 11.18 and the following figures in this chapter show sequential (from left to right) sets of the output signals from the tested network. Figure 11.18 shows that the output of the network reached the desired state by generating an ideal reproduction of the pattern after only one iteration. Slightly more complex processes were introduced. In this case, the network needed two iterations to achieve success (Figure 11.19).

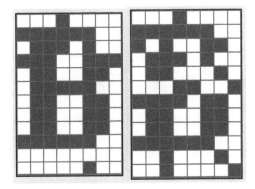

Figure 11.17   Patterns from which the process of recalling messages stored on the network begins. Left: Less distorted pattern of letter B. Right: Strongly distorted pattern of letter B.

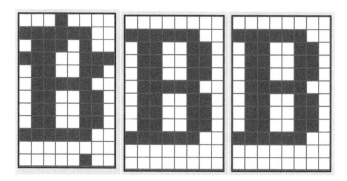

Figure 11.18 **Fast reproduction of a distorted pattern in a Hopfield network working as an associative memory.**

One of the interesting characteristics of a Hopfield network will become clear after you experiment with the program: the network's ability to store both the original pattern signals and the signals that are negatives of stored patterns. This can be proven mathematically. Each state of network learning that leads to memorizing a pattern automatically creates an attractor corresponding to a negative of the pattern. Therefore, the network can recover a pattern by either finding the original or its negative.

Both images contain exactly the same information (the only difference is that +1 values are converted to –1 values and vice versa). As a result the network's finding of a negative of distorted pattern is considered a success. For example, Figure 11.20 depicts the reproduction of a heavily distorted pattern of the letter B because the network found that negative.

11.6 Program for Examining Hopfield Network Operations

These results and many more can be observed and analyzed with the Example12b program. The program begins by accepting automatically generated patterns or those a user provides. These patterns that are meant to be remembered by the network are images of digits or letters input via a keyboard or abstract images generated by the system. To maintain the quality of the thumbnails, the associative memory has a limited capacity. Example12b limits the maximum number of input patterns to 20. You can utilize as many patterns as you wish, but in reality constraint works

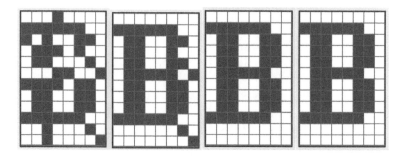

Figure 11.19 **Reproduction of a highly distorted pattern in a Hopfield network.**

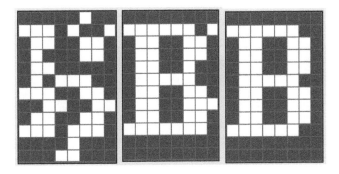

Figure 11.20   Associative memory reproducing a negative of a remembered pattern.

better here. The fewer the patterns, the shorter the learning time. This means the network will work faster after learning and make fewer mistakes.

If more than 16 patterns are set, the network starts to combine and over-impose the data because of the limited number of neurons for remembering the patterns provided. The significant errors that result can be observed as crosstalk that appears as artifacts from other patterns in the images generated. This crosstalk effect can be seen in Figure 11.21. Note that in this figure and the following ones, we used a slightly different form of network presentation for Example 12b. From left to right, we show:

- Reproduced pattern without distortion
- Intentionally distorted pattern
- Consecutive steps of reconstruction of pattern by network

This kind of layout will be useful when we start to work with patterns of different shapes. We can compare original patterns on the left with the final outputs of the network on the right.

Figure 11.21 indicates that overloading a network with excessive remembered patterns causes an uncorrectable disturbance of its operation. The disturbance appears as the system attempts to reconstruct a pattern that appears distorted and distinctively different from the original used during learning. This phenomenon can be observed even if the reconstruction process begins with a virtually undisturbed signal (Figure 11.22) because the structure of the character remembered by the network includes permanent memory imprints from other patterns.

One other interesting phenomenon is illustrated in Figure 11.21. During the first iteration, just after a strongly distorted pattern of letter X was added to the network, the program reconstructed

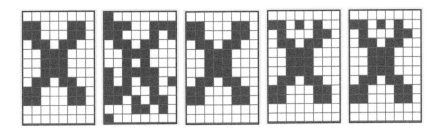

Figure 11.21   Sample patterns distorted by crosstalk.

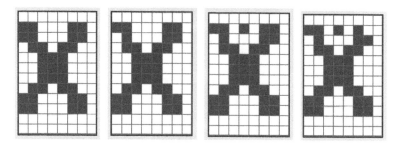

Figure 11.22 Pattern distorted by crosstalk cannot be correctly recalled even if an undamaged version is supplied at input.

a perfect image of the pattern. However, further processing resulted in distortion of the reconstructed pattern with "echoes" of other pattern memories. This can be related to the real-life experience when you learn (sometimes too late) that the first idea that came to mind was in fact the best. Considering the result from different perspectives led you to realize that your conscious choice was inferior to the initial impulse provided by your intuition.

We should discuss some details of the Example12b algorithm. When executed, the program collects the information to be remembered by the network in the form of patterns and requests a pattern (Figure 11.23) that can (but does not have to) be remembered by the network. The patterns to be remembered may be input in the Add pattern group field. You can add a letter or digit in the proper field, then confirm your choice of letter or digit by clicking the Add button. The selected letter or digit will appear in the Input pattern(s) window for teaching or recalling. Remember that the maximum number of patterns you can add is 20. The program will give you full control over the input patterns. After each digit or character key is pressed, the system will illustrate a precise structure of the image in the Enlarged selected input field.

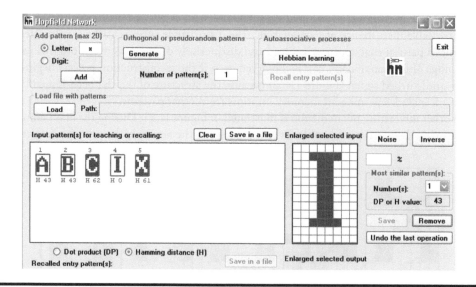

Figure 11.23 Inputting data for associative memory with the ability to modify or reject each supplied character.

After the patterns to be memorized are input (they will appear in the teaching or recalling dialog window), you can select any of them with a mouse, invert them by clicking Inverse and Save, or remove them from the learning sequence with the Remove button. Removal may be the only option if you find that a pattern is too similar to another input already presented. It is also possible to generate the patterns automatically (discussed later), but the automatic ones tend to have shapes that are difficult to understand. It is advisable to use few of them when you start working with the program. It is best to start with a few letters (e.g., A, B, C, I, X). After entering each letter in the Letter input field, press the Add button.

After you finish inputting and perhaps modifying the pattern sequence to be memorized (presented in the Input pattern(s) window for teaching or recalling), press the Hebbian learning button. You can use this button often, especially when you want to teach a different set of patterns. After the Hebbian learning button is pressed, the Recall entry pattern(s) button will become active almost immediately. It indicates that the learning process has been completed and the network is ready for examination.

You can now verify how the network recalls each memorized pattern. Pressing the Recall entry pattern(s) button when no pattern is selected in the Input pattern(s) for teaching or recalling dialog box will recall each input pattern visible in Input pattern(s); recalled patterns will appear in the Recalled entry pattern(s) window. It is interesting to see how the network memorizes and recalls letter patterns. The example network recalled B very well; performed less well with C, I, and X; and regularly generated crosstalk when recalling A (Figure 11.24).

When you click any pattern visible in the Input pattern(s) window, the Noise and Inverse buttons displayed on the right side of the enlarged selected input become active. You can use the input field below the Noise button (labeled with a percent sign) to set the percentage of points in the input pattern to be changed. You can enter any number from 0 to 99. After the Noise button is pressed,

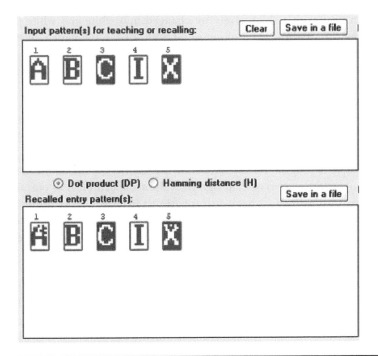

Figure 11.24 Recalling all patterns provided to the network.

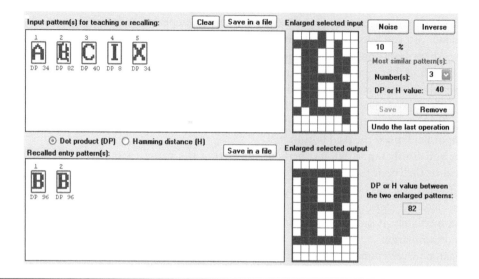

Figure 11.25 Images available in enlarged selected input and enlarged selected output, and their likelihood metrics (DP or H values between enlarged patterns).

the program will randomly change the number of pixels as you requested and insert an enlarged thumbnail of the pattern in the Enlarged selected input window (Figure 11.25). If you then click the Save button under the Enlarged selected input window, this noise-distorted pattern will be inserted into the sequence, which is visible in the Input pattern(s) for teaching or recalling window.

The Inverse button near the Noise button displays a similar behavior. The Inverse button will invert the pattern selected (i.e., blue pixels are changed into white and white pixels into blue). The changes made with the Inverse button must be confirmed in the same way as with the Noise button—by clicking the Save button. The results of saving are identical in both cases. If you want to discard the last change, you can use the Undo button that cancels the last Save operation. It will also cancel the last removal of a pattern via the Remove button. The button titled Undo last operation cancels the previous save or remove action.

The question of similarity (or lack of it) of the memorized patterns is crucial and we will therefore give it more focus. As noted in our discussion of Figures 11.21 and 11.22, signal patterns sometimes overlap and produce crosstalk. This phenomenon is amplified if the memorized patterns are similar. This is a logical result. With similar patterns, the memory imprints (all located within the same network) tend to overlap tightly. If the same neuron is to output +1 as part of a remembered letter A, sometimes −1 because it is part of a letter B, and +1 for recalling a letter C, the resolution becomes difficult. If the memorized patterns differ greatly, the issue is less serious because fewer conflicting pixels are involved. If the patterns are very much alike, their representations by interconnection weights become so mixed in the neural memory that recalling of any single pattern becomes problematic (Figure 11.26).

If you want to observe the performance of a network under reasonably favorable circumstances, you must invest some effort, at least in the beginning, into providing clearly distinctive patterns. As a result, the program will support you in two ways. First, while inputting new patterns, the program will immediately calculate and provide you with a similarity factor between the new and already memorized patterns. You can then control in real time the effects of pattern overlaps while inputting the characters with a keyboard.

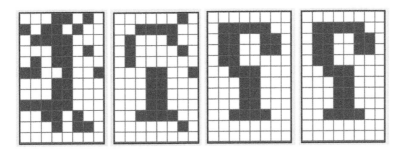

Figure 11.26 **Effects of mixed memory imprints resulting from strongly mixed input signals.**

This step is simple because clicking one of the thumbnails of the previously input patterns (visible in the Input pattern(s) for teaching or recalling window) will display the numbers under each of the thumbnails representing similarities between the previously provided patterns and the new one. This similarity can be displayed as dot product (DP), in which case the higher the number, the higher the level of similarity to the already provided pattern. The result can be displayed as Hamming (H) distance, in which case the higher the value, the better because it indicates more distance between the new and previously provided patterns.

Second, the enlarged selected input window will display any pattern you select. On the right side, just under the Noise and Inverse buttons, there is a Most similar pattern(s) field that will display a pattern that most closely resembles the selected one. This field allows you to analyze potential risks because you can see related patterns that may be mistaken for the selected the current one. This number of potentially conflicting patterns will appear in the Numbers field. The input DP (maximum value of scalar product) or H (minimal Hamming distance) value will show the chosen similarity value.

11.7 Interesting Examples

We realize that the description of the handling and functioning of the Example 12b program is complex but the work is worth the effort. Our experiments with this program will demonstrate the interesting tasks it can handle and allow you to carry out further studies in areas that interest you.

We can analyze the situation presented in Figure 11.27. As seen in the upper section, we already entered patterns A, B, C, and D. The E entry is weakly differentiated in relation to the others. The measure of the similarity of E to the letter A pattern is 22 (a decent result). The strength of the similarity to the letter B is 74 units; strength scores for C and D equal 56 units. At the right side of the window you will see in the Most similar pattern(s) group box how the program warns the user that the entered E pattern will be mistaken for the B pattern. You can then reject the B pattern if you so choose. Using the inversion (negative of the pattern) does not change the similarity values (Figure 11.28).

The basic measure of the similarity of a new image to patterns defined earlier is calculated in the program as the dot product (DP) of the vectors describing these signals in the input signal space. More precisely, the absolute value of the scalar product is taken into consideration but you really need not reflect on what it means. The DP is displayed in the appropriate radio at the center of the screen. If you click the Hamming distance (H) button, the program will utilize another way

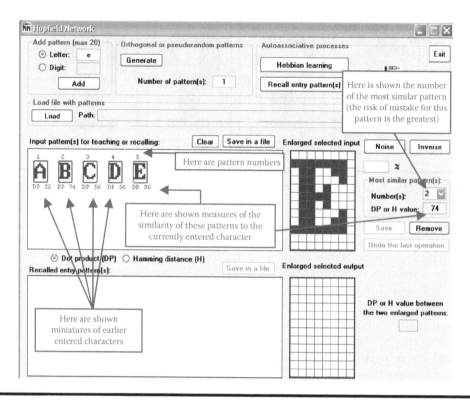

Figure 11.27   Demonstrating degree of similarity of a new image to an already remembered pattern.

to calculate pattern similarity (Figure 11.29). The chosen measure will be displayed under each pattern miniature.

Figure 11.29 shows different values under individual patterns. The pattern that is the most similar shows the least distance. You should know how to interpret this because the Hamming distance (H) measure was selected. You may wonder why the program allows two similarity measurement possibilities. Depending on the result desired, the two measures provide different information and apply to different objectives.

During the generation of new images, it is better to rely on the observation and maximization of the scalar product. The Hamming distance may be misleading because it is sensitive to pattern

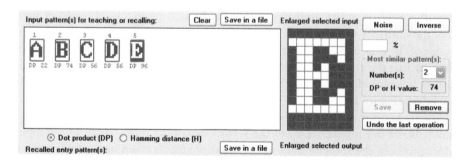

Figure 11.28   Inversion shows the exact same degree of similarity to earlier patterns.

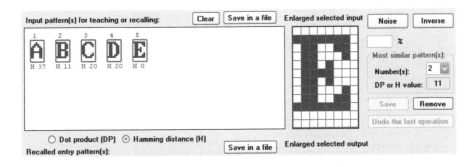

Figure 11.29   Signal similarity measures expressed by Hamming distance.

inversion. Compare Figure 11.30 with Figures 11.27 through 11.29 to see what should and should not happen when new patterns are entered.

As you observe a network and track its analysis of patterns, Hamming distance will be a more useful measure. It will allow you to evaluate whether the search is proceeding correctly or the network is moving away from the correct pattern. You may also observe a very interesting phenomenon: the network's rejection of the correct pattern and acceptance of completely different information (Figure 11.31).

This example corresponds to the situation of entering a disturbed stimulus into the network. For the original signal (1), 20 random changes were performed and the 1 became less similar to its own pattern and also to all the other patterns. This is confirmed by both the signal appearance and Hamming distance values shown. At this moment, the dynamic process of network feedback starts. At first, the network generates an image that dangerously resembles a 3. The network continues to work and generates a 9 pattern.

Note the numbers appearing under the pattern sets in both the Input pattern(s) for teaching or recalling box and the Recalled entry pattern(s) box. They indicate Hamming distances between the signals currently in the network input and all the considered patterns. Hamming distance helps you see which signals correspond to which distance sets. Figure 11.32 shows scalar product values.

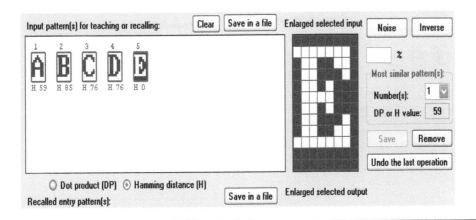

Figure 11.30   Value change of Hamming distance with character inversion.

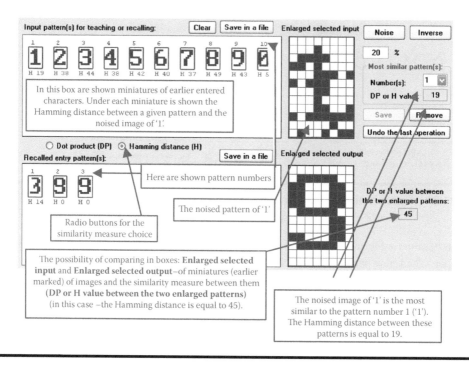

Figure 11.31 Pattern search finished in failure observed with Hamming distance choice.

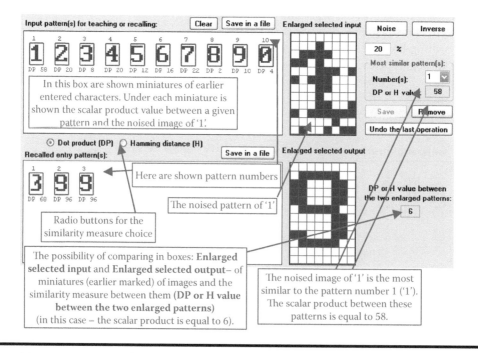

Figure 11.32 Pattern search with scalar product measure resulting in failure.

Compare the Hamming distance values between the noised 1 pattern and all the patterns in both the input and recalled entry patterns boxes. At the start, the Hamming distance between the correct version of the 1 and the signal shown in the network input is 19. Other patterns are safely distant (37 to 50 units). The program increases distance units if the signal and stimulus are dissimilar (0 and 1) and decreases the units as similarity increases.

You can repeat this experiment easily on your computer. You can generate hundreds of similar results with other patterns and signals. The exercise is worthwhile because you will learn how various combinations produce expected and unexpected results. Experiments performed with a Hopfield network will show you that some patterns can be reconstructed easily and others produce unpredictable or unwanted results (Figure 11.33). In the next section, we will discuss such patterns.

11.8 Automatic Pattern Generation for Hopfield Network

While creating patterns to be memorized by a network, you should observe the value of the scalar product to achieve a set of patterns with minimized crosstalk. You already know that a reasonable set of patterns has DP values as low as possible based on comparison. The ideal solution is to have both patterns display zero scalar product values and is known as orthogonal design. Getting closer to an ideal solution will optimize both learning and network performance.

Creating an orthogonal set of patterns manually is virtually impossible. You can try to get close to the ideal, but you will find out that the images of characters input with a keyboard will always be somehow correlated and their scalar products will not be zeroes. You can, however, delegate this task to the Example12b program that can support you by creating orthogonal patterns without help.

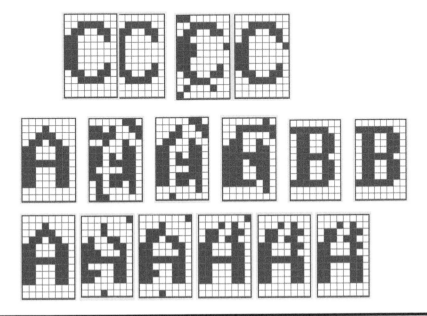

Figure 11.33 Successful reconstruction of letter C pattern and two reconstruction failures of letter A pattern.

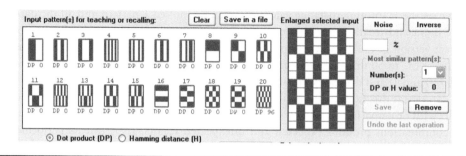

Figure 11.34 Automatically generated orthogonal patterns.

A grouping field for choosing orthogonal and pseudo-random patterns appears in the top part of the screen along with a field that allows you to enter the number of patterns you want the program to generate. Remember to confirm your decision by pressing the Generate button. Also, make sure that the number of patterns you request in the Number of pattern(s) field when added to the number input earlier does not exceed the 20-pattern program limit. Pressing Generate will also produce additional thumbnails of orthogonal patterns (as many as you requested) appearing in the Input pattern(s) window. You can start generating and adding automatically generated patterns from the beginning (Figure 11.34) or try a combined approach by adding one or a few patterns.

If you select all generation of all the patterns at the beginning, the program will create a set of pairwise orthogonal patterns that will improve memory performance greatly. The patterns generated automatically will be simpler and more consistent than patterns entered manually. This is because the patterns generated by a user are pseudo-random, not pairwise orthogonal (Figure 11.35 and Figure 11.36).

When you enter a character with a keyboard before requesting automated pattern generation, the program will create a number of pseudo-random patterns. You may notice the low values of the scalar products. Orthogonal patterns are very useful when a network works as an associative memory, because orthogonal and also pseudo-random patterns allow reconstruction of the original input image, even if it was severely distorted (Figure 11.37 and Figure 11.38). This, of course, applies to each memorized pattern. However, it is difficult to verify whether a pseudo-random pattern has been correctly reconstructed because these patterns generally appear somewhat exotic.

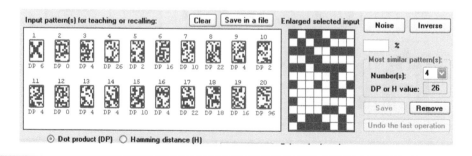

Figure 11.35 Pseudo-random patterns generated based on initially supplied character X.

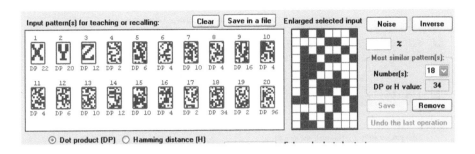

Figure 11.36 Pseudo-random patterns based on initial X, Y, and Z characters.

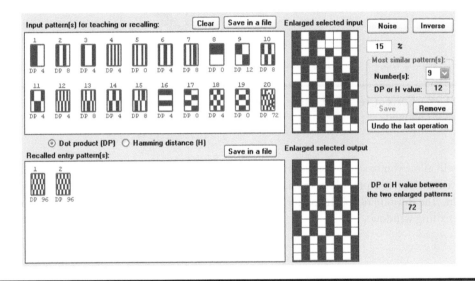

Figure 11.37 Correct recall of distorted pattern using set of orthogonal patterns.

Reconstruction of correct images with memorized orthogonal or pseudo-random symbols by a Hopfield network, even for severely distorted patterns, has limitations (Figure 11.39 and Figure 11.40). If you distort a pattern too much, the ability to reconstruct it will be lost irretrievably. For example, in Figures 11.38 and 11.40 you can see that a network with pseudo-random patterns can quickly and effectively recall a pattern of a letter Z even 26 and 24 pixels, respectively, were changed.

You can repeat these experiments and a different result will be generated with each attempt, because the distorted patterns will be different and the pixels to be changed will be selected randomly. Quite often, a single pixel difference (e.g., damaging 25 instead of 24 pixels in the original image) will cause inability to reconstruct the image because of the persistent small artifacts that appear in the result (Figure 11.41).

With increased damage to the input pattern, the reconstruction process becomes longer and the final result decreases in quality, until at some point it disintegrates and the network outputs "garbage" only. Even then, it is possible that pure luck may produce heavily distorted patterns that are brilliantly reconstructed (Figure 11.42).

To experiment with a set of patterns that you created and stored on your hard drive, you can use the Load file with patterns grouping field. When the Load button is pressed, a new window

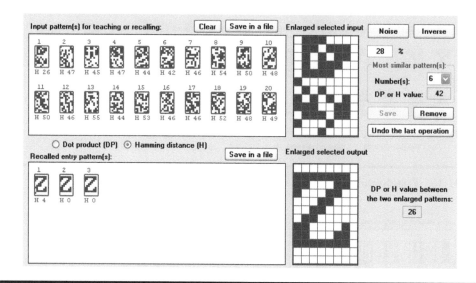

Figure 11.38 Correct recall of letter Z pattern in which 26 randomly selected pixels (28% noise) were changed.

display will allow you to select the file with patterns to be loaded into the program. If the file (with a .PTN extension) you provide exists and can be loaded, the program will list it in the editable Path field. The thumbnails of the patterns in the file will appear in the Input pattern(s) for teaching or recalling window.

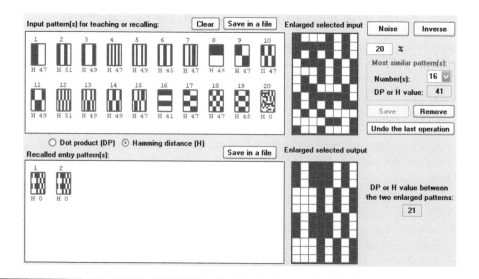

Figure 11.39 Imperfect recall of orthogonal pattern in which 19 randomly selected pixels (20% noise) were changed.

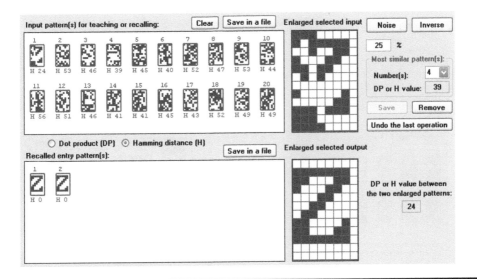

Figure 11.40   Correct recall of letter Z pattern in which 24 randomly selected pixels (25% noise) were changed.

11.9 Studies of Associative Memory

The Example12b program will enable you to conduct a series of studies that will help you understand the nature of associative memory constructed with a Hopfield network. We have shown you how to inscribe information into the memory and how the information reproduced. Now we will try to describe the capacity of the associative memory constructed with use of the neural networks.

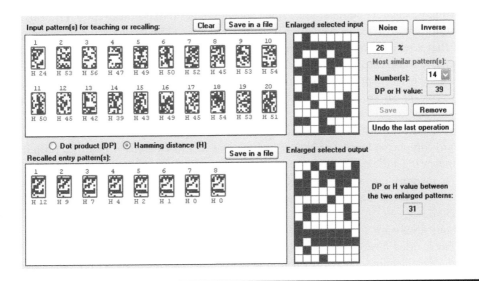

Figure 11.41   Incorrect recall of letter Z pattern for which 25 randomly selected pixels (26% noise) were changed.

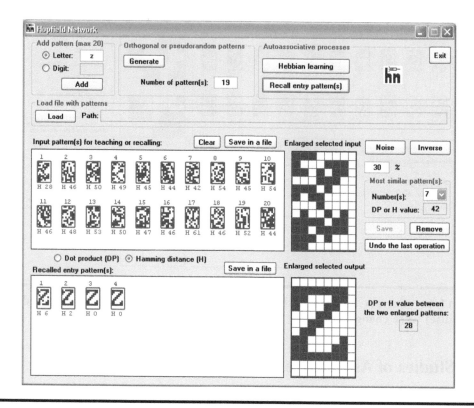

Figure 11.42 Accidentally correct recall of letter Z pattern.

The capacity of a standard RAM or ROM computer memory is limited because all information in the memory is assigned to different locations. You acquire access to certain information by inputting its memory address. The same concept applies to hard disks and CDs. This implies that the information saved in every type of memory is defined precisely by addresses designed for storage. That is why a computer user can determine immediately how much memory is available.

A memory constructed in a Hopfield network follows a different system. It has no specific locations designed to store specific information for memorization or recall. All neurons are engaged in learning a certain pattern. This implies that the patterns must overlap in specific neurons and can cause a problem known as overhearing.

A method of information recall (reading) from a neural memory differs from the method used in standard computers. Instead of indicating the name of a variable that contains certain information or indicating a file name (both methods refer to addresses) to access data, a user can give an associative memory incomplete or distorted information and still receive a suitable answer. For this reason it is almost impossible to determine an upper limit of messages that may be introduced into a neural network.

Obviously, we want a precise theory that explains all these issues in detail. One of the authors wrote a book titled *Neural Networks* that you may find helpful. The aim of the present book is to introduce elementary concepts of neural networks by experimenting with them. Conducting experiments will help you understand the capacities of neural networks. We can attempt to give you the most practical information on the subject but your experimentation will be the best path to thorough understanding of neural networks.

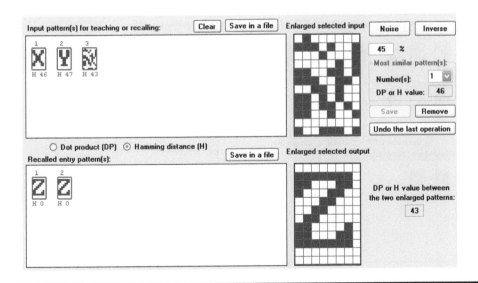

Figure 11.43 **Reliable recall of information for a small number of patterns.**

The first and primary factor determining the simplicity and reliability of recalling memorized signals is the amount of data recorded in the network in the form of memory traces. After memorizing relatively small numbers of patterns (e.g., three), recall of information is reliable even in the presence of significant distortions (Figure 11.43). However, the results of recall depend also on differences in memorized information. Figure 11.44 depicts an experiment conducted on a network with a small number of patterns with high degrees of similarity that led to improper recalls.

If you intend to examine maximum network capacity, you should operate with highly differentiated signals. The most desirable are orthogonal or pseudo-random signals. Only then you

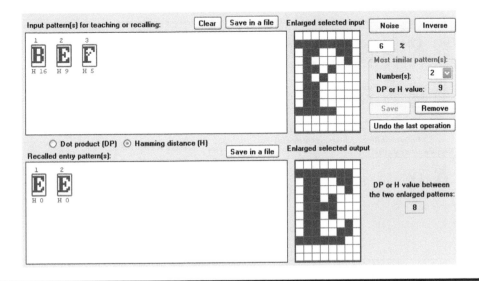

Figure 11.44 **Failure observed when the number of patterns is small and patterns are very similar.**

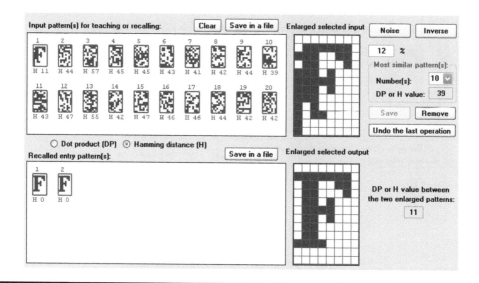

Figure 11.45 **Proper reconstruction of destroyed input signal when maximum pseudo-random patterns are used.**

can achieve good results even with maximum number of patterns (20 in the example program; see Figure 11.45).

With non-perfect orthogonal patterns (e.g., pseudo-random patterns that emerge if you choose automatic generation after selecting two signals), the results may be acceptable. This will happen only if you select very different initial signals with relatively small distortions (Figure 11.46). Application of more distorted entries will reveal strong overhearing (Figure 11.47).

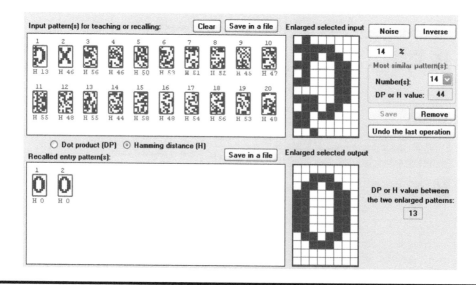

Figure 11.46 **Success achieved when the network remembers large numbers of non-exact orthogonal patterns.**

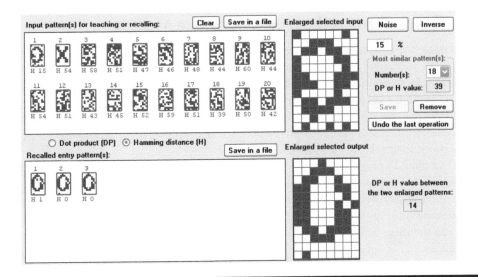

Figure 11.47   Overhearing resulting from destruction of input signals by noise.

Proper recall of patterns in a system utilizing orthogonal or nearly orthogonal signals may be affected by large numbers of memorized signals (e.g., entrance images are far more numerous than memorized signals). Even though most patterns in Figure 11.48 are non-orthogonal (and the remainder are orthogonal), the network produced undesirable overhearing; it happens even in cases of insignificant deformations of entrance signals.

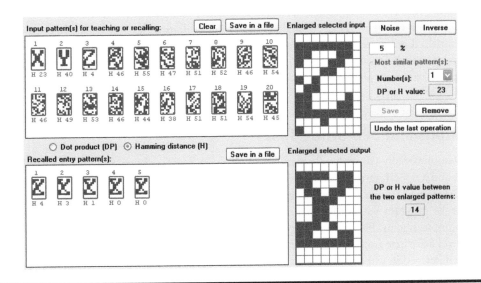

Figure 11.48   Overhearing observed for a minimally destroyed input signal if remembered patterns are not orthogonal.

11.10 Other Observations of Associative Memory

Remembering the correct form of a network model based on a deformed structure introduced as an input is a dynamic process, resembling that in a single-element network and presented in the Example12a program. The next steps in this process are displayed on the screen in the form of images. You can view how the distorted image in the Recalled entry pattern(s) window slowly emerges from the chaos. You can click on any image and track the number that indicates degree of similarity between images produced by the network and individual patterns to view the progress as the network selects the correct images.

The Example12b program allows you to study the use of scalar products and Hamming distance. Both data entry and image reconstruction operations can be performed by pressing proper buttons (without modifying parameters) to switch from a display of scalar products (dot product or DP) to the Hamming distance (H) display and vice versa.

You can use these tools to observe qualitatively and quantitatively how the network-generated approximations of images change their distances from stored patterns and how the values of scalar products change. Some interpretations of results require mathematical knowledge. However, even without it, we can understand the dynamics of the knowledge recovery process in associative memories and the change processes and neuron outputs in Hopfield networks.

The Example12b program also gives you tools for tracking pattern recovery and differentiating steps of the processes. The various choices allow a user to monitor the measures of similarities of patterns expressed as scalar product or Hamming distance. As we follow the network processes of extracting images, we can see what the network does and why. Complete understanding, however, requires considerable patience and work. The memory trace ends only when the next iteration reaches a steady state (i.e., introduces no more amendments to the image). The process can be stopped when oscillations appear.

The "jumping" of a network is interesting. Instead of improving the correct pattern reconstruction, the network suddenly associates a deformed image with a completely different pattern and starts to clean and polish its result (Figure 11.32). A network may create an entirely new idea (non-existent pattern) that represents a hybrid of existing elements combined in an extraordinary and unrealistic way (Figure 11.27)—snakes with wings or dogs with three heads. In our network, we have utilized only pieces of letter images, but they were sufficient to demonstrate how neural networks operate differently and more imaginatively than regular (and dull) algorithms. You can discover other network phenomena by working with the program. Good luck!

Questions and Self-Study Tasks

1. Describe briefly (10 sentences maximum) all the differences between a feed-forward neural network and a neural network having feedback.

2. Develop a formula for predicting the stable output value of the network simulated by the Example 12 program with different parameters (coefficients of synaptic weights), and different values of input signals. How do your results compare with the results obtained with simulations?

3. Read an article from a website or a book on *chaos theory*. How are this theory and the phenomena described in it related to the issues of recursive neural networks?

4. Research publications and/or the Internet for information about time-varying electrical potentials (electroencephalograms or EEGs) of the human brain. Do you think that these signals indicate the lack of feedback in the human brain or the opposite?

5. Consider whether the human memory (surely an associative memory) is analogous to the crosstalk phenomenon appearing in a Hopfield network? If so, how are they perceived and evaluated subjectively?

6. Based on experiments, determine which similarity measures (dot product or Hamming) can better predict which patterns will be reproduced well by a network and which will pose problems?

7. A relationship that may be derived mathematically exists between the number of neurons in a Hopfield network and the number of patterns that can be efficiently stored with a minimum probability of cross-talk. We know that the more neurons a neural network has, the more patterns it can remember even though each individual pattern involves all neurons across the network. Relate this to the human brain memory that contains about 100 billion neurons. How can you explain the fact that some people have better memories than others?

8. The Hopfield networks discussed in this book were all auto-associative. They formed associative memories that were used to play back memorized patterns. Hetero-associative memory is capable of memorizing associations of different patterns. What scheme must a network have to utilize hetero-associative memory (e.g., the images of objects and first letters of the names of objects)?

9. In this chapter, we used Hopfield networks for very primitive patterns that involved only simplified outlines of letters and numbers. Undoubtedly, it would be far more interesting to work with a network that could operate with images similar to those in Figure 11.13. Why has this not been done?

10. When building a large Hopfield network consisting of many neurons, computer resources are being consumed very quickly. Why does this occur and which resources are affected?

11. Advanced exercise: Build a version of the Example12 program in which the output values produced at the output after the consecutive steps of the simulation are shown in the form of a figure instead of a table. This program should show the time course of the network output values in graphical form (as a chart). What was the main difficulty that had to be overcome?

12. Advanced exercise: Build a version of Example12b in which arrays of neurons representing various stored images will be significantly larger (e.g., increased three times in each direction). Using this improved tool, perform similar experiments as described in this chapter. Compare the observations from such experiments with the statement in Question 7.

Index

.NET Framework, installation, 75–76

A

Acceptance thresholds, 47–48
Accuracy, 48–50
Adaptive linear (ADALINE) networks, 32
Additivity, 115–116
Advanced teaching, single neuron, 97–100
Aggregation of signals, 31–32
Algorithmic forecasting, 22
Aperiodic network behavior, 245–247
Artificial neural networks. *See also* Neural networks
　building, 27–28
　choosing design structure, 41–43
　comparison with biological networks, 20–21
　development of from brain research, 1
　impact of structure on capabilities, 39–41
　layered structure of, 11–12
　learning failures, 67–69
　limitations of, 23
　linear, 87–91
　network tutoring, 59–60
　observation of recognition learning process, 159–170
　operations of, 34–39
　self-learning, 61–62
　use of biological information to design, 5–9
Artificial neurons, 5
　characteristics of, 32
　constructing, 28–33
　structure and elements of teaching, 95–97
Associative memory, 35
　benefits of, 247–248
　functioning of neural networks, 251–256
　observations of, 274
　program for examining operations of Hopfield networks, 256–265
　studies of, 269–273
Attractors, 242–243
Auto-association, 251–256

Automatic pattern generation, 265–269
Automatic recognition and classification systems, 22–23
Axons, 6–7, 28–29

B

Backpropagation of errors, 72
　definition of, 133–134
　teaching multilayer networks, 141, 146–148
BIAS, 135
Biological information, use of to design neural networks, 5–9
Biological networks, comparison with artificial neural networks, 20–21
Biological neurons, 28–30
　coding of signals in, 135
　modeling, 33–34
　unipolar characteristics of, 117
Bipolar input signals, 89
　nonlinear neurons, 116–117
Boltzmann machines, 248
Brain cortex, 4
　layered structure of, 10
Brain functions, 2–3
Brain research
　Brodmann's areas, 11–12
　current methods, 13–19
　development of artificial neural networks from, 1
BRAINInitiative, 14
Brodmann's areas of the brain, 11–12

C

Cajal, Ramón y, 4
Calm networks, 184–185
Cerebellar cortex, 28
Cerebral cortex, 4
　layered structure of, 10
Chaotic learning, 197–199
Classification model, 48–50

Competition
  benefits from in self-learning networks, 199–202
  results of self-learning with, 203–206
Computer modeling, 19–20
Continuity characteristics, 136
Continuously changing operations, 136
Convex combination, 74

D

Data
  clustering of, 212–214, 219–222
  coding, 45–46
  self-organization of by Kohonen networks, 225–228
Data pairs, use of for network tutoring, 59–60
Data processing, 36
de Schutter, Erik, 34–35
Decomposition, 19–20
Dendrites, 6–7, 28–29
Design of networks
  random, 40–41
  selecting, 41–43
Differential characteristics, 136
Diffusion MRI, use of to map brain connectivity, 14
Digital signal processing, use of simple linear networks for, 105–111
Divergence, 64
Duration of learning, 71–72
Dynamic teaching process, single neuron, 99–100

E

Eccles, John, 7
Enthusiastic networks, 184–185
Equilibrium, 242–243
Error surface formation, 64–65
Errors
  backpropagation of, 72
  influence of on teaching process, 97–100
Everything-or-nothing rule, 118
Excitatory inputs, 31

F

Fanatic networks, 184–185
Feed-forward neural networks, 41, 43
Feedback networks, 241–245. *See also* Recurrent neural networks
  features of, 245–247
Filtration of signals, use of simple linear networks for, 105–111
fMRI
  use of to map brain activity, 18
  use of to map brain connectivity, 14–15
Forecasting, 22–23
Forgetting processes, 195–196
Friston, Karl, 15

Function ϕ(), 32
Functional magnetic resonance imaging. *See* fMRI

G

Gauss function, 32
General regression neural network. *See* GRNNs
Gierymski, Aleksander, 129–130
Gnostic units, 231–234
Golden mean, 162–163
Grandiosity, 192–194
Grandmother cells, 231
GRNNs, 27–29
Grouping effects, 212–214
Gyrus postcentralis, 232–233

H

Hamming distance, 254, 261–265
Hard competition, 203–205
Hardware-based neural networks, 21
Hebb rule, 64
Hebb, Donald, 73
Hebb's method, 254
Hidden layers, 35–39, 52–54
  backpropagation of errors in, 133–134, 146–148
  determining number of neurons for, 54–57
  teaching, 72
Hodgkin, Alan, 4
Homogeneity, 115
Hopfield networks, 42–43
  automatic pattern generation for, 265–269
  construction of, 248–251
  functioning of as associative memory, 251–256
  program for examining operations of, 256–265
Hopfield, John, 42, 248
Human brain
  Brodmann's map of, 11–12
  coding of signals in, 135
  feedback effects in, 247
  functions of, 2–3
  gnostic units, 231–232
  use of imaging techniques to map connectivity in, 13–19
Human cognitive processes, memories in, 9
Human Connectome Project, 13–16
Human mind, use of neural networks to study, 19–20
Huxley, Andrew, 4
Hyperbolic tangent function, 137

I

Image recognition, 52–54
  associative memory, 251–256
  implementing a simple neural network for, 152–155
  use of multilayer neural networks for, 151–152
Imagination and improvisation, 190–194

Inborn preferences, 100–101, 160
Information gathering, methods of, 62–63
Inhibitory inputs, 31
Input layers, 44–45
Input scaling, 44
Input signal space, 120–121
Input signals, 29–30
    aggregation of, 31–32
    assignment of for multilayer networks, 138
    behavior of a single neuron, 81–85
    bipolar, 89
    scaling of, 44–45
    self-learning networks, 176–177
Input space dimensions, tools for transformation of, 233–238

K

Kidnapping effect, 204
Knowledge generalization, 119–120
Kohonen neural networks, 215–217
    changes in via self-learning, 228–230
    handling of difficult data, 225–228
    network learning in, 221–222
    tools for transformation of input space dimensions, 233–238
    uses of, 222–225, 230–234
Kohonen, Teuvo, 24, 215
Kolmogorov, Andrei, 116
Konorski, Jerzy, 231

L

Layer-structured networks, 39–41, 43
Lazy rule, 89
Learning coefficients, 184–186
Learning processes, 7–9
    artificial neurons, 31
    chaotic, 197–199
    duration of, 71–72
    failures, 67–69
    information gathering methods, 62–63
    network tutoring, 59–60
    number of neurons and, 55–57
    observation of for recognition tasks, 159–170
    organizing network learning, 64–67
    self-learning, 61–62, 72–73, 176–186
    self-learning cautions, 73–74
    sequence of for nonlinear neurons, 126–129
    single neuron, 97–100
    teaching hidden layers, 72
    use of momentum, 69–71
Learning rate coefficient, 140, 168
Learning sets, 59–60
Linear neural networks
    applications of, 92–93
    building a teaching file for, 95–97
    construction and use of, 87–91
    recurrent, 241–245
Logistic curves, 136–137

M

Machine learning processes, 180–186. *See also*
    Learning processes
Magnetic resonance imaging (MRI), use of to map brain connectivity, 14
Mapping
    self-organizing neural networks, 209–212
    tools for transformation of input space dimensions, 233–238
    use of in presenting activity of Kohonen networks, 221–222
Maps
    creation of for training multilayer neural networks, 157–159
    creation of for training simple neural networks, 153–155
Marcus, Dan, 15
Massive parallel processing (MPP), 35
Memory processes, 7–9, 35
Momentum, 168
    use of in the learning process, 69–71
    use of in the teaching process, 140
Multilayer nonlinear neural networks
    capabilities of, 124–126
    functioning of, 137–140
    hidden layers in, 133–134
    observation of learning process, 153–170
    teaching, 140–148
    training for recognition, 156–159
    use of for recognition, 151–152
Multilayer perceptron (MLP), 32–33
Multiple-output networks, 50–51
Multiplicative scaling behavior, 115

N

Negative feedback, 243–245, 247
Neighbor neurons, 217–222
Neighborhoods, implementing in self-organizing neural networks, 215–217
NetTALK products, 24
Network assignment, 29–30
Network behavior, teaching process and, 101–105
Network learning
    capability, 22
    failures, 67–69
    organizing, 64–67
    use of momentum, 69–71
Network structure
    choosing, 41–43
    dependence of behavior on, 168–170
    impact of on capabilities, 39–41

selecting for recognition experimentation, 155–156
self-organizing neural networks, 209–212
Network tutoring, 59–60
Neural cells, 5
Neural networks. *See also* Artificial neural networks
advantages of, 21–23
artificial, 1–5
associative memory, 251–256
benefits from competition, 199–202
bipolar, 89
building, 27–28
capabilities of multilayer nonlinear, 124–126
classification model, 48–50
comparison with biological networks, 20–21
effect of failure of elements, 38
implementing neighborhoods in, 215–217
knowledge generalization, 119–120
layered construction of, 10–12
learning failures, 67–69
limitations of, 23
linear, 87–91
mappings resulting from self-organizing, 209–212
observation of recognition learning process, 159–170
operations of, 34–39
regressive model, 48–49
rivalry in, 92–93
self-learning, 61–62
single-output *vs.* multiple output, 50–52
teaching process for one-layer networks, 101–105
use of biological information to design, 5–9
use of to study the human mind, 19–20
Neuroinformatic systems, structural complexity of, 21
Neuromediators, 7
Neurons, 27–28
amplification of connections, 73
capacity of, 77–81
characteristics of, 32
construction of, 4–6
determining number of, 54–57
imagination and improvisation, 190–194
inborn abilities of, 100–101
information gathering methods, 62–63
neighborhoods of, 215–217
nonlinear, 116–118
responses of to self-teaching, 188–190
Nominal data, coding, 45–46
Nominal variables, 46–48
Non-oscillating character, 243–244
Nondeterministic polynomial time computational problems. *See* NP-complete problems
Nonlinear networks, teaching, 118–120
Nonlinear neurons
capabilities of multilayer networks of, 124–126
demonstrating actions of, 120–124
learning sequence, 126–129
shapes of characteristics of, 135–137
Nonlinearity, advantages of, 115–116

Normalization of input signals, 44–45
NP-complete problems, use of Hopfield networks for, 43

O

One from N method, 45–48
One-jump neural networks, 53
One-layer neural networks
applications of, 92–93
building a teaching file, 95–97
functioning of, 87
uses for, 105–106
Orthogonal patterns, generation of, 271–273
Oscillating character, 243–244
Output layers, 46–48
multiple *vs.* single outputs, 50–52
network models, 48–50
Output signals, 29–30
distribution of in Hopfield networks, 252–253
distribution of in self-organizing neural networks, 211
interpretation of, 46–48
neuron response, 81–85

P

Paradigms of networks, 64
Pattern recognition, 22, 52–54
associative memory, 251–256
Perceptron, 5, 22
use of for image recognition, 151–152
Periodic network behavior, 245–247
PET imaging, use of to map brain activity, 15–18
Positive feedback, 243–245, 247
Positron emission tomography. *See* PET imaging
Prediction, 22–23
Procedural memory, 7–9
Pulse code modulation (PCM), 135
Punishments, 63
Purkinje cell, 34

Q

Quadrants, 175
Quickest fall rule, 64–67
duration of learning, 71–72

R

Radial basis functions (RBFs), 33
Radial neurons, 33–34
Random inputs, self-learning networks, 196–199
Random network design, 40–41
Recognition. *See also* Image recognition; Pattern recognition
associative memory, 251–256
learning processes of self-learning networks, 176–186

observation of learning process, 159–170
teaching multilayer networks, 156–159
use of multilayer neural networks for, 151–152
use of simple linear neural networks for, 152–155
Recurrent neural networks, 41–42. *See also*
Hopfield networks
associative memory, 247–248
description of, 241–245
features of, 245–247
Regressive model, 48–49
Rejection thresholds, 47–48
nonlinear neurons, 117
Retina of the eye, layered structured of, 10
Rewards, 63
Rivalry, 92–93
benefits of competition, 199–202
results of self-learning with competition, 203–206
Roaming chaotic signals, 245
Robotics, use of Kohonen networks in, 230–234
Rosenblatt, Frank, 22, 38, 40–41, 151
Rule of the quickest fall, 64–67
duration of learning, 71–72
Rumelhart, David, 72
Rutkowski, Leszek, 248

S

Scaling behavior, 115
Scaling inputs, 44
Sejnowski, Terrence, 24
Self-learning networks, 61–62
basic concepts, 173
benefits from competition in, 199–202
cautions, 73–74
evaluating the process of self-teaching, 186–188
forgetting processes, 195–196
Hebb rule, 72–73
imagination and improvisation of, 190–194
learning processes, 176–180
neighborhoods in, 217–222
observation of learning processes, 176–180
responses of neurons to self-teaching, 188–190
results of competition, 203–206
triggers for, 196–199
Self-organization
changing via self-learning, 228–230
handling of difficult data by Kohonen networks,
225–228
uses of, 212–215
Self-organizing neural networks
implementing neighborhood in, 215–217
mapping by, 209–212
uses of Kohonen networks, 222–225
Sigmoid curves, 136–137
Signal processing, use of simple linear networks for,
105–111
Signal scaling, 29–30

Signal transformation, 93
Simple learning coefficient, 140
Simple linear neural networks
building a teaching file for, 95–97
construction and use of, 87–91
observation of learning process, 159–163
recognition using, 152–155
teaching, 101–105
uses for, 105–106
Simplex phenomenon, 124–125
Single neurons
building a teaching program, 95–97
examination of multiple inputs, 85–86
examination of single input, 77–81
nonlinear, 116–118
teaching process, 97–100
Single-layer neural networks
applications of, 92–93
bipolar neurons, 118–120
building a teaching file, 95–97
functioning of, 87
Single-output networks, 50–52
use of for pattern recognition, 152–155
Soft competition, 203–206
Speed of functioning, neural networks, 21
Stabilization point, 244–247
Structure
choosing, 41–43
impact of on capabilities, 39–41
Sum of squares errors, 64
Supervised learning, 184–186
Synapses, 6–7
Synaptic weights, 31
effects of in feedback networks, 245
recurrent networks, 243

T

Teachers, 59
Teaching process, 35–36
building a program for a single neuron, 95–97
evaluating for self-learning networks, 186–188
multilayer networks, 140–148
nonlinear networks, 118–120
recognition, 159–170
single neuron, 97–100
Teaching ratio value, effect of on outcome, 101
Threshold values, 47–48
modification of, 66
nonlinear neurons, 134–135
Transfer function, 32
nonlinear neurons, 136–137
Traveling salesman problem, 42–43
Tutors, 59
Twisted network learning, 228–230
Two-dimensional input space, mapping into one-
dimensional neural topology, 235–237

U

Unipolar characteristics, use of with nonlinear
    neurons, 116–117

V

Van Essen, David, 13
Visual Studio.NET, installation, 76

W

Weight coefficients, 31
    assignment of for multilayer networks, 138
    behavior of a single neuron, 81–85

    information gathering and, 62–63
    learning failures, 68–69
    paradigms of networks, 64
    self-learning networks, 176–177
    use of momentum, 69–71
    wide ranges of, 228
Werbos, Paul, 72
Widrow–Hoff technique, 129
Winner-takes-all (WTA) rule, 92, 199

Z

Zurada, Jacek, 248